LONDON TEMPS HANDBOOK

Pitman

PITMAN PUBLISHING
128 Long Acre, London WC2E 9AN
A division of Longman Group UK Limited

First published in Great Britain 1989

© Longman Group UK Limited

British Library Cataloguing in Publication Data

The London temp's handbook.

1. London. Secretaries. Employment
331.7′61613741′09421

ISBN 0-273-03116-3

All rights reserved; no part of this publication may be reproduced stored in a retrieval system, or transmitted in any form or by any means, electronic, mechanical, photocopying, recording, or otherwise without either the prior written permission of the Publishers or a licence permitting restricted copying in the United Kingdom issued by the Copyright Licensing Agency Ltd, 33-34 Alfred Place, London WC1E 7DP. This book may not be lent, resold, hired out or otherwise disposed of by way of trade in any form of binding or cover other than that in which it is published without the prior consent of the Publishers.

Typeset in Great Britain by P4 Graphics Limited

Printed and bound in Great Britain at Richard Clay, Bungay

Contents

Acknowledgements vi

Introduction vii

1 Starting Out 1

    Tempting prospects 2

    A variety of jobs 4

    What it takes to temp 7

    The Successful Temp's Checklist 15

2 The Agency 17

    Great expectations 17

    Prime locations 25

    First steps 26

    Take the market by storm 34

    Temporary perks 36

    The Agency Checklist 43

3 Survival Tips 47

    Negative vibes 47

    Get up and go 50

    First impressions 51

    The first day 55

    In sickness and in health 59

    Home sweet home 64

    The Survivor's Checklist 71

4 Money Matters 73

    Bank on it 73

The budget action plan 75
Convenience cash 77
Borrowing money 78
The Money Matters Checklist 84

5 **Business Organisation** 87
The business spectrum 87
Categories of organisation 91
Around the company 96
Checklist of equipment 105
Checklist of experiences 105

6 **Taking Off** 107
Where to now? 107
On the wanted list 108
Taking off with training 109

7 **The London Temp's Directory** 113
Alphabetical listing of recruitment agencies 114
Geographical listing of recruitment agencies 154
   North London 154
   East London 155
   South London 160
   Central London 164
   West London 174
   Bedfordshire 176
   Berkshire 177
   Buckinghamshire 180
   Cambridgeshire 181
   Essex 182
   Hampshire 184
   Hertfordshire 186
   Kent 190

Middlesex 192

Norfolk 196

Oxfordshire 197

Suffolk 198

Surrey 198

Sussex 202

East Sussex 203

West Sussex 203

Private Secretarial Colleges 205

Glossary of terms 217

Abbreviations and acronyms 224

FRES Code of Good Recruitment Practice 227

London Underground Map 230

Acknowledgements

We are grateful to the following people for their commitment to the production of this book: Caroline Dudley, freelance journalist who has written on a wide range of issues; Sally Goldsby, Public Relations Manager, Color Me Beautiful; Helen Harding, Principal Lecturer, Lancashire Polytechnic; Stephen Humphries, Corporate Affairs Department, Abbey National and John Wilson, Senior Product Manager, Current Accounts and Savings, Personal Banking Services, National Westminster Bank PLC.

Our thanks also to the many recruitment agencies and London based temps who gave us the benefit of their knowledge and experience. Finally, we are indebted to Lauren Plaskow for her tireless efforts in compiling the directory and inputting the entire manuscript on disc.

Photography by J. Sierra (pages 16, 46, 72, 86, 106, 112); Michael Rogers and Barrie Carr (page viii).

Introduction

Temporary work is gaining popularity and prestige and the average temp now commands more respect and more money than ever before.

The image of a career in temping has been evolving and now from a thousand advertising hoardings and tube displays smile a range of glamorous faces, both male and female, which flaunt the new status of the temp.

This book is part of that sensible, but sophisticated move to top billing. Temping is about success, style, money and freedom.

Today's temp is the go ahead type, with ambitions and a range of skills to match; a person who enjoys the flexibility of a temping timetable and the varied work. She or he has also weighed up the negative aspects and worked out how to combat them and ensure success and enjoyment.

Temping is for everyone and anyone can make it pay. That's what *The London Temp's Handbook* is all about – success. At a time when more and more talented people are turning to temping as a career or a stop gap, the need for a succinct guide on do's and don'ts is more than obvious.

The London Temp's Handbook is your guide through the exciting world of temping work: how to get started, how to choose an agency, how to budget, how to survive. It's all here. You're already tempted by the prospects of such a career. *The London Temp's Handbook* makes that career possible.

Chapter 1

Starting Out

You've picked up this book because you want to be a successful temporary worker and with the help of *The London Temp's Handbook*, and your own determination and talent, you are going to make it to the top.

You may be a shorthand genius or a brilliant word processor, but there are other skills and tips that you are going to need to make it big. This text is designed to map out your journey to the top.

Choosing a career in temping could be the best decision you ever made. You not only have an exciting career, but the challenge of a range of jobs and the flexibility to pursue other interests and even other careers. If you are starting out, there are a number of things you should do.

For one thing, you've chosen a great place to temp. The streets of the metropolis may not be paved with gold but there's no doubt that business of all kinds is booming. While the slimming down of industry in the North of England has led to an increase in unemployment, the story in London and the South East is very different. Computer based industries in the Thames Valley, light industry on the increase, a huge expansion of service industries such as hotel and catering have combined to ensure prosperity for this corner of the UK — a 'corner' which is spreading westwards as far as Bristol.

Within this expanding economy, the market place for temporary workers offers richer pickings than ever before.

Tempting prospects

In years gone by, the vast majority of temporary assignments came up during the summer as cover for staff on their annual holidays. But come September, the wise temp was well advised to get out of the cold into a permanent job.

Summer is still the busiest time but the climate has changed and there is less fluctuation: one London agency which places senior secretarial staff reported as much as 48 per cent of business done between September and April and 52 per cent between April and September, a balance which would have been unthinkable five years ago. There are many reasons, cultural, political and demographic, for the upsurge in opportunities for temps.

The annual fortnight's holiday for permanent staff has been overtaken by four or even six weeks' leave a year: not just to the Costa Brava but the ski slopes of St Anton as well, so almost as much holiday cover is needed from January to March as in July.

January to February is traditionally the time for job changes: 'New Year-New Job', cry the adverts, so again the temp can carve a niche during personnel changes and maybe get a re-booking at this time of year to cover for staff with colds and snuffles.

Sickness cover has always been a good, if erratic, source of temp work and maternity/paternity leave cover can offer a very congenial, longer-term assignment.

Business needs

Business, whether small or large, established or expanding, cannot afford 'floating' staff — permanent workers on a fixed salary whose services can be called for within any department. These days, businesses tend to operate at realistic staff levels and use temporary staff to fulfil their extra needs, wisely increasing their permanent staff in response to increased business, not in anticipation of it. Temps can be called on to fill a variety of positions:

- Basic clerical positions
- Computer operators
- Accountancy placements
- Word processor operators

Starting Out 3

- Catering and hotel staff.

Skills and tasks include:

- Basic clerical work: opening, checking and sorting paperwork
- Inputting data
- Acting as 'query clerks', sorting out anomalies
- Updating records
- Handling accounts and cheque requisitions
- Keying-in reports, letters and agendas.

Some businesses are subject to seasonal fluctuations and these are reflected in job opportunities for temps with different skills. Accounts clerks and book-keepers, for example, can find themselves inundated with offers of work as the end of the financial year approaches: hotel staff, both catering and clerical/secretarial will be in particular demand during the summer. Temps conversant with the publishing world can be rushed off their feet during the autumn season of book fairs and Christmas time ensures that shop and store staff are in demand.

Hand in hand with the increased demand for temps comes the fact that the number of school leavers is decreasing and industry is looking for sources of untapped talent. One of the most important of these is women returning to work after a career break to raise families.

Temping for everyone

To those with a flexible approach, temping has a lot to offer. It gives an unique opportunity to work on your own terms. Temping offers something for everyone:

- The graduate, filling in time before beginning full-time employment.
- School and college leavers looking for a taster of various office environments.
- Returners to work, keen to begin a new career once the children are older.
- All those with family commitments who need the flexibility temping offers.

- Those with other, intermittent careers, like writers and actors who need to finance their way to success.

The pay-off

Pay scales for temps are, on average, at the upper end of the rate for a job. Certainly students with keyboard skills can use the summer vacation to pay off the overdraft that inevitably accumulates during the university year.

The top rate package for a permanent secretary in the City could be as much as £25,000 per annum: £12,500 as salary and the rest in health insurance and other perks. But this type of package is unusually generous and a secretary could also earn as little as £8,000, without any perks.

Compared with this, temping is an attractive proposition, offering an hourly rate of £7.00 for a secretary with word processing skills working in London's West End. An audio secretary could expect to earn around £12,000, and a top level secretary in the City could realistically aim at £14,000, including overtime, and that's another advantage of temping. Unlike permanent staff, who have to accept overtime working as one of life's hazards, the temp is paid for the hours worked, so more overtime means more money, with higher hourly rates for late night, Bank holiday or weekend working. (Salaries and hourly rates quoted here were correct at the time of going to press).

Some agencies offer holiday and sickness pay to temps, while others claim to offer a higher hourly rate on the basis that some money should be put by in the event of sickness.

A variety of jobs

Temping provides a 'fly on the wall' view of different types of operation, allowing you a glimpse of the way the business operates — and the personalities involved. You might work in advertising one week, accountancy the next, followed perhaps by a month in an engineering firm and a couple of weeks at the BBC.

Some agencies specialise in certain areas of work: publishing and the media; legal work or banking, for example, but the larger agencies have clients covering the whole spectrum, as the Directory at the end of the book shows. If you don't have any definite preferences you can find yourself working for an infinite variety of businesses, learning a lot about them and, more importantly, finding out a lot about yourself and your abilities.

Rich pickings

A wide range of temporary work is available in the South East, from unskilled jobs in catering, through packing, warehousing, driving, drawing office, accounts, to every conceivable type of office work up to part-qualified accountant and office manager level. The main scope of this book is to offer guidance to office staff, who want or need a spell of temping.

Opportunities range from, at the lower level, junior clerical assignments, where the temp could be expected to do the filing, make the coffee, run errands, learn to use a small switchboard, greet clients, take completed typing for signature and then collect and mail it. Duties could also include faxing, photocopying and use of the telex. The chance to learn new skills would depend on the office itself. Small offices where the staff work as a team can offer good opportunities in this area.

At reception

If you have switchboard skills, either as a result of British Telecom or in-house training, then telephonist or reception work may be for you. Sometimes reception work is combined with clerical tasks or may offer the chance to brush up on some rusty typing.

It is rare, however, for accounts clerks to double as receptionists. Accounts work, by nature, tends to be a backroom occupation, seldom combined with other duties.

Technology at your fingertips

If you wake up in a cold sweat at the thought of telex machines, Rapid File, word processing packages and the latest typewriter gadget — you've got the hi-tech blues. But don't panic. Technology is easy and it's designed to make your job manageable and more effective.

As a temp, the more technology you can manage the better equipped you are to cope with the well paid assignments. Technology comes in all forms and sizes and companies do expect temps to be even better at using it than the permanent staff they are replacing! This needn't be a problem. If you have mastered your basic keyboard skills you'll find that most agencies will help you develop a knowledge of other specific types of technology. Chapter 2 on The Agency, details some of the training packages you can expect to get from certain agencies. These will develop the skills you need for the more lucrative job placements.

The key is confidence. If you can type you can use the word processor, operate a computer and learn to use a range of software packages. Never be afraid to say you don't know how to use a particular piece of equipment. Even if the office you've been sent to expected a technology whizz-kid, they'll respect your honesty and help you. If you're attentive, you'll pick up the process easily. Technology is easy and you can master it in no time. For information on the training offered by agencies, see page .

Keyboard skills — the keys to success

There are many colleges where you can learn keyboard skills (see Directory) and a course, day or evening, at a college offers good value for money and will give you highly marketable skills.

The course should include tuition in the layout and presentation of documents and often the rudiments of office practice too, rather than simply teaching you to find your way round a keyboard with no tuition in how to apply what you have learnt.

If your skills are rusty you can take advantage of the Skillware centres run by Manpower. Here temps, known as 'field staff' can brush up on typing or do a two-day course in word processing by means of interactive video, a user-friendly software package, which you use at your own pace during office hours so you can ask the supervisor for help if you need it.

Having learnt to use one make of word processor, it is relatively easy to adapt that skill to other makes or software packages. If you are familiar with, say, IBM, you can take a one-day Skillware course to cross-train to another type, such as Wang, thus continually increasing your marketability. If you can't afford a day off, you can even do the course on a weekend.

This training is completely free and there is no commitment to work for Manpower afterwards, although they would, obviously, make strenuous efforts to find a placement for you.

Alfred Marks, also has word processor training facilities, which are available to temps after they have worked for that agency for some time. Smaller agencies, will often help new temps come to terms with electronic typewriters and some also offer career counselling.

The demarcation between jobs is anything but rigid as each job is different and requires a different type of person to do it. You might find a clerical job where the client would be only too grateful for your laborious typing and this might give you the practice and confidence necessary to market yourself as a typist on the next assignment.

What it takes to temp

Whatever your reasons for wanting short-term assignments, now's the time to consider whether you have the necessary attributes to operate successfully as a London Temp.

Qualifications

Don't worry if you lack formal qualifications. While GCSEs and RSA, PEI or LCC shorthand and typing certificates are very useful, particularly for school and college leavers with no previous work experience, they are by no means essential.

The agency will give you a test relating to the type of work you are applying for, be it shorthand, audio typing, word processing or clerical. This is less fearsome than it sounds. There are 11,000 agency branches in the UK and they all need staff to place so it is in their interests to put you at your ease. Also, if you don't do very well at one agency, you can always try another. Alternatively, try for a lower grade of job and ask to be retested later when you have gained experience.

Remember:
- Top jobs call for 60 wpm typing and 100 wpm shorthand.
- 45 wpm typing and 80 wpm shorthand is adequate.
- Accuracy is essential.
- Any type of shorthand is acceptable, be it Pitman New Era, Pitman 2000, PitmanScript or Speedwriting.
- Word processing requires accuracy, speed and the ability to edit and move text. Ideally, aim for advanced level.

Experience

Previous experience can dictate the type of assignment you will be offered when you start temping. If you are familiar with the terminology and office automation in say, banking, it makes sense to build on this and go for banking placements when they are available.

On the other hand, owing to the unpredictable nature of client requests, it is just as likely that you would be placed in a totally different field of business.

If you have a confident and mature approach and possess good skills, there's no reason why you should not walk into a responsible job straight away.

When you enter an office as a temp, nobody knows you and you don't know them, so if you can do the work competently, the details of your past career are irrelevant. As a rough guide however, it is unlikely that a person under the age of 22 would have the experience to take on a placement as a managing director's secretary.

As a temp, you are employed primarily for your skills and these will dictate the level of responsibility — and rate of pay — that you get. Certainly, your track record of assignments with a particular agency will influence your future bookings: if you are reliable and competent, with a pleasant personality and make it clear to the agency what sort of bookings you want, you will stand a better chance of getting your choice.

Most agencies, except those which specialise in senior staff placements, welcome those who are new to work. An enthusiastic approach and willingness to learn will more than offset lack of work experience.

Special requirements

If you are interested in medical or legal work bear in mind that you will need certain skills.

Speed, accuracy and attention to detail are vital in the legal and medical professions and they tend to attract more mature people. No special qualifications are needed for temps but if you want to make a career as a medical or legal secretary, one or two year courses are available at many technical colleges. For shorthand writers, a copy of Pitman's Medical Shorthand, which gives outlines for medical terms can be a good investment.

The courses leading to the Certificate of the Association of Legal Secretaries include audio or shorthand, typing, office practice, law, a choice of accounts or economics and additional options of word processor training or shorthand speed tests. Plans are also afoot to offer this training as a correspondence course.

The Association of Medical Secretaries is an educational and professional body and sets exams leading to the Certificate of Medical Secretarial Studies. Courses leading to this qualification last two years for GCSE entrants and one year for A level students and are run by technical colleges. They cover shorthand, typing, practice administration and legal aspects of medical secretarial work.

Personal attributes

Top of the list for any kind of temp work is flexibility. This will determine, to a large extent, how much work the agency can get for you.

Clearly, if you can only work in one area, or only between certain hours, or only in one field of business, you will be harder to place than the temp who is prepared to travel further and work longer hours.

You will be working for a variety of businesses and you should be able, chameleon-like, to fit in with the image of all of them. In this respect, how you present yourself is very important.

Reliability

As temp bookings are a quick-turnover business, reliability is vital. Always tell your agency if you are going to be late for work, or are unable to get there, or have to leave early so that they can arrange cover in your absence, thus keeping the client, ie., a source of temp work, happy.

This also applies to overtime working. The agency should tell you if extensive overtime is likely and it is a good idea to state at once what your availability will be. If you have a theatre date on Wednesday and a yoga class on Thursday, say so but be prepared to do overtime the other evenings if you can.

Assertiveness

To temp successfully, you must be assertive at times. Although you need the agency, the agency also needs you and if you particularly dislike a certain type of business or really don't want to travel too far to work, you must stand up for yourself and say so.

After you have proved yourself, you might decide not to take bookings shorter than a week as it can put you out of the market for longer assignments.

From the agency's viewpoint, the ideal temp is one who has a good range of office skills, is reliable, flexible, dresses fashionably without looking outrageous and can adapt swiftly to new situations with a ready smile.

Short and long term jobs

The work pattern varies from temp to temp depending on your skills and the assignments you choose to take. The present climate is very much a seller's market and if you have good skills, you can follow your own inclination.

Bookings can last from half a day to two years or more but, the average is three weeks. Some people like constant variety: a series of short assignments, each lasting no more than a fortnight, while others prefer 'permanent temporary' assignments, which can last for months or even years.

These long-term assignments are often found in local authority or other public sector offices and come about because of budgetary requirements: the department is allowed to pay out for a temp but not to increase establishment by taking on more permanent staff.

Chances are, if you start out with marketable skills, that you will have two or three assignments making up to a full month's work. As to how much variety to expect, this depends both on your preference, your skills and on your agency's list of clients.

If you are interested in a particular type of work, either register with a small agency which specialises in it or go to a large agency whose list of clients includes your chosen field — or register with several.

But when it comes to starting out as a temp, the following tips from people who have done it will help.

Temp talk

Waiting for the big break

Angela, an actress, temped for several years in between theatre jobs, before changing tack entirely and making a career in publishing, which began with a job where secretarial and editorial skills were combined.

'I hated learning to type but once I could do it, I realised what a good meal ticket it was. Actress friends of mine who lacked keyboard skills had to wait till shop jobs came up, or take clerical work, which was less well paid, but I was always solvent.'

'To start with, I registered with five different agencies. Two were useless, but three got me various assignments and eventually one job carried on so long that the other agencies lost interest and the remaining one kept me in work.

'However, I did have one or two grotty bookings. One office was just like a sweatshop. You couldn't stop for coffee and the clients weren't that keen if you even took a lunch break,' she says.

'On the Friday, I asked my temp controller if I could go somewhere different the following week and she said she'd been wondering how long I would stand it as none of the other temps had lasted more than three days.

'From then on, the agency felt I'd proved myself and they tried really hard to give me decent assignments.

'I also discovered that some of the most unlikely jobs turned out to be the best. I had always thought I'd fancy a job in the media, but processing invoices for an advertising agency was mind-bendingly boring.

'Doing this tedious job, surrounded by terribly flamboyant people was hideous but, oddly enough, one of my favourite jobs was for a firm of actuaries and another was with an engineering firm, where the people were delightful.

'Often, if you get on well with a client, they will ask you back, which is great as you get greeted like an old friend and you don't have to keep breaking in afresh. I lost count of the number of permanent jobs I was offered.'

Returning to work

Rene, who is 46, had different reasons for temping. She brought up her family and then spent some years helping her husband to establish a business, returning to the job market with very rusty typing skills and a great lack of confidence.

'I do enjoy meeting people, but on my first assignment, I was absolutely petrified. It was a job as assistant to a company director's secretary and while there, my confidence grew so that I felt able to tackle a wide range of assignments. However, I am finding it hard to adapt my typing skills to word processing, but I'm determined to master it sooner or later,' she says.

Rene's outgoing personality ensured that she was readily accepted in most of her assignments and she has won the Manpower Silver Award for 400 hours' work, on the recommendation of the clients for whom she has worked. But like most temps, she encountered the occasional problem. 'Usually I found the permanent staff very welcoming and they would include me if going out for a drink, or ask if I wanted a coffee, but there were one or two offices with a very young staff, who ostracised me as though I were senile. Fortunately, I told the agency and they moved me to a more congenial job.'

Rene lives near Enfield, North London, but travels to work in the City.

'I tried working in Enfield, but the rush hour traffic is so bad, that it took me ages to get there and the money was not nearly so good. Now I jump on the train to the City and although the fares cost more, they are more than made up for by the higher City pay rates.'

Job seeking in comfort

Earning a good salary while looking for a career job was Sarah's reason for temping.

'After 'A' levels, I took a secretarial course and then worked for two years before going to University to read Spanish and Latin American Studies. Now I want a job which uses my degree but as it's a very specialised field, it might take me a while to find what I'm looking for.'

Sarah is registered with several agencies. 'They vary enormously in quality,' she says.'Some are very arrogant and always on the client's side, so I work for them once and never again, whereas others seem genuinely concerned about you as a person.

'I have word processing skills and have never been out of work. At first, I would go wherever the agency sent me, but now I can pick and choose where I go and what firms I work for.

'I'm always straight with the agency, too, and I think that pays dividends. All of them know that I am on the books of others and that seems to keep them on their toes.

'Being a graduate has given me a lot of confidence, but when I go to a new assignment, I always play it down. I am very careful not to put on airs and graces with the other secretaries, and feel it is important to be aware of other people's sensitivity.

'Another thing is, I always pretend to know less than I do. When asked if I know how to use a certain word processor, it's better to say you are a bit rusty, even if you used one last week, because every company's software is slightly different and if you pretend to know it all and then get stuck, you look foolish and people are less inclined to help you.

'Bearing in mind the high hourly rates that clients pay for temps, it is only fair that they expect you always to look busy. If you finish your work early, it is better to find something constructive to do, even if it's just tidying the desk, rather than get out your library book and I find that clients appreciate that bit of extra effort.'

A temporary way of life

For Brenda, in her early 20's, temping on a variety of word processors is a way of life. 'I thoroughly enjoy it and I'd recommend it to anyone. I prefer to work locally, in Fulham, although the pay is less than I'd get in the West End, but I don't like a long journey to work. I have been fortunate in that my agency has always kept me in work, but lack of work might be a worry if you have sole responsibility for a mortgage.

'I have found a great difference in how firms treat me and one thing I find hard to take is the automatic assumption that temps will be useless. You have to prove yourself all the time and it's insulting to know you are expected to mess up everything except the simplest functions.

'To be a temp, you must go to an assignment, with a completely open mind and without any fixed expectations. Also, whatever kind of reception you get, don't take it personally.

'Sometimes, if the agency wants to fill a job, they'll hype it up and tell you it's the most marvellous office in the world and the reality can come as a shock.

'On one assignment with a big construction company, I arrived on the Monday in high heels and business suit, only to find my 'office' was a mobile cabin on the other side of a quagmire. When I got there, I was greeted warmly and the working atmosphere was great, but from then on jeans and wellies were the order of the day.'

The Successful Temp's Checklist

All kinds of people temp successfully for all kinds of reasons, but there are some attributes which are common to them all. In no particular order, but in large measure, helping of the following are needed:

- Good skills
- Flexibility
- Robust health — you may not be paid for sickness
- Outgoing personality
- Willingness to help
- Adaptability to different environments
- Good presentation — observe client's dress code
- Reliability — be honest with your agency
- Assertiveness
- A keen sense of humour

Chapter 2

The Agency

Finding an agency is easy — names and telephone numbers will jump at you from adverts on the tube, in papers and in magazines. The Directory section at the end of this book offers a variety of agencies, in London and the South East, including brief details of the industries they cover and the type of skills required. Many agencies advertise in a range of newspapers and magazines: *Girl About Town*, *Ms London* (distributed free at Underground stations), the *London Evening Standard*, *Yellow Pages* and local newspapers are just some of the places to look.

Great expectations

Choosing the right agency requires a little more effort on your part. Before you begin the quest, it's worth knowing what to expect.

- Each agency or group of agencies has a client base of businesses which requires temps.
- Each agency has a register of temps and one or more temp controllers or supervisors. It is their job to match the temps' skills to the jobs available.

- The client pays a fee to the agency which covers the temp's hourly rate plus the agency's commission.

In the money

Pay is obviously of great interest to you — and up until December 1 1988 agencies didn't advertise rates of pay if they were members of the Federation of Recruitment and Employment Services Limited (FRES). FRES lays down a code of good recruitment practice binding on all members and their staff — details appear on page 21. An agency carrying the FRES logo can be identified as a safe bet, but many reputable agencies are not FRES members, often because they wanted to advertise their rates of pay.

So what can you expect in the way of hard cash? The lists below compare four agencies, the figures for Atlas contrasting West End/City rates with local rates.

London pay scales

The following provides a guide to the hourly rates for various grades of temporary worker in the London region. The rates should go up every six months but this gives an indication of the differentials. Bear in mind that FRES member agencies may not advertise their pay rates but will offer rates comparable with those of other agencies.

Remember, when you increase your range of skills, by typing or taking dictation faster, learning a new WP system or switchboard, always ask if your agency will re-grade you at a higher rate.

Atlas Employment Agency Ltd

West End/City rates		Local rates
£6.50 per hour	Shorthand secretary: 50 wpm typing, 100 wpm shorthand	£5.00 per hour
£4.00 per hour	Figure clerk	£3.30 per hour
£3.50 per hour	Clerk	£3.00 per hour

Keystone

£9.00 per hour	WP operator with shorthand
£8.80 per hour	WP operator

£7.50 per hour	Shorthand secretary
£6.70 per hour	Audio secretary
£6.00 per hour	Copy typist/VDU
£5.50 per hour	Telephonist (all boards)

L A Consultancy Services Ltd

| £8.40 per hour | WP operator with legal experience |
| £7.40 per hour | Audio secretary with legal experience |

Mistprestige
up to:

£8.00 per hour	WP operator
£8.00 per hour	Secretary with legal experience
£7.00 per hour	Shorthand secretary
£7.00 per hour	Audio secretary
£6.00 per hour	VDU operator
£5.80 per hour	Copy typist
£5.50 per hour	Switchboard operator
£4.25 per hour	Clerk

Cash in hand

Most agencies offer a choice of payment methods. You can elect to have your money paid directly into your bank account, or arrange for it to be sent to you at home, although this method carries the risk of postal delays.

Or, you can call into the agency to collect your cheque on Friday lunchtime. Many agencies lay on wine and a snack lunch, turning the occasion into a social event, where you can meet and chat informally with your temp controller, find out details of next week's booking and get to know your colleagues on the temping scene.

A well-established agency should also have made arrangements with a nearby bank so that you can cash your cheque at once. Ask if the agency offers you the opportunity to open a 'charge-free' account.

Very few agencies these days pay their temps at the end of the first week's work, OV Selection pays for the full week on Friday lunchtime but this is rare.

Usual practice is for temps to fill in their worksheets on Friday afternoon, get them signed by the client and send them to the agency to arrive the following Monday. Cheques are drawn and are available for collection on the Wednesday. Some do not release the cheques to temps until the Friday, ie. you work for two weeks before receiving your first week's money. Ask which system the agency uses.

A fair rate

As to rates of pay, aim to get a fair rate for the job but don't be completely bowled over by an agency which is offering a lot more than the rest of the market. It could be that it has just landed a big contract to supply temps, is desperate to attract more to its books but after that assignment is over, it may lack the breadth of client base to keep those temps in work.

Remember that even if you are getting a high hourly rate, a gap between bookings will erode the financial advantage at a stroke. Ask how often temp rates are reviewed - they should go up every six months.

Continuity of work is very important. Make a point of asking whether or not your details will be transferred to other branches if the one you have registered with does not have a booking for you. Groups of smaller agencies have formed themselves into commission-splitting networks, giving the temps the benefits of a small agency allied to the work-seeking benefits of a chain.

Some agencies give holiday pay after a qualifying period, others claim that temps prefer a higher hourly rate. As for Bank Holidays, some stick rigidly to the 'payment for hours worked' criterion, whereas others take a more relaxed view, offering Bank Holiday pay where the temp works the days either side.

Owing to the competition between agencies to attract and keep staff, some, such as Kelly and Manpower offer rewards to those who spread the word and get their friends to temp for them.

Loyalty bonuses, too, can form a useful part of the package. Word Factory Word Processing offers a loyalty bonus of £175 to temps who have worked 750 hours (around six months) for them.

FRES

The Federation of Recruitment and Employment Services Limited

(FRES) lays down a code which ensures that all its members conduct their business ethically to promote good recruitment practice. From the code printed in full on page 227, you can see how the deal offered to you by your agency compares. But here are the main points that affect you:

- The agency shouldn't persuade you to leave one assignment to take up another. Once placed it's up to you or the client to terminate the contract.
- You should be made aware of the provisions of the Employment Act, 1980, which states your rights as an employee concerning maternity, redundancy, health and safety, equal opportunities and sick pay.
- Equal opportunities must be promoted by the agency.
- FRES will act as an arbitrator between you and your agency.
- The agency must ensure you are suitable for the assignments you are sent on.

Safeguards

As a temp, you will find that choosing a FRES member agency will give you certain safeguards, including the provision which requires members to ensure temporary workers are suitable for the assignments for which they are supplied. This could save you being thrown too far in at the deep end.

Also, if things do go wrong, FRES offers an arbitration service between the agency and the temp.

Watch out

As with any prospective career or job environment, there are negative aspects you should be wary of. But bear in mind that most agencies are out to help you and to run a sound and efficient business, ensuring that the client companies are well satisfied.

If problems do occur, they will more likely stem from your dislike of a particular job placement or from a poor temp controller. Be wary of the temp controllers who send you for a job you are not qualified to do; take to task those who say you will have work next week and then let you down. Never be pushed into an assignment you know you won't like and will fail to complete.

Pressure

Some temp controllers may try to pressurise you into taking a job using less than your full qualifications, with a pay rate to match, saying that they cannot get you a higher-paid assignment that week, while keeping the better assignment for another temp. And then there are those who may fail to support you in any dispute between you and the client, even if the client is being unreasonable.

Another problem, which can arise with high branches of an agency is having to deal with several temp controllers. None of them can really get to know you, your needs and abilities and you will not benefit from being passed from hand to hand. Usually you can expect to be interviewed by the person who will be your temp controller and it is worth insisting on this.

Cut your losses

If you don't like the way your temp controller treats you, the best thing to do is to say so and leave. Cut your losses and register with another agency, where you and your temp controller understand each other better.

Agencies spend a lot of money advertising for temps so it is galling for them to lose one who is skilled and experienced or willing to learn. In any case, the market is much in your favour as there is a great demand for temps in London and the South East, a factor which itself helps to regulate the conduct of agencies.

Little and large

Agencies vary enormously in size and scope: some, such as Word Factory Word Processing and OV Selection are small concerns with just one office, others such as Manpower and Alfred Marks are massive chains, each with around 150 branches nationwide.

Others again like Acme Appointments, a family-run business, are of medium size with a dozen or so branches in London only. Director Nicholas Holmstock sees the strength of his agency as a broad client base, able to provide work to suit the skills and aptitudes of a wide range of temps, while avoiding the impersonality of a large agency, where a temp may feel like 'just a number'.

Pick and choose

Every agency claims to take a personal interest in the welfare of it's temps and indeed, if you deal with one branch of a big chain you can build up just as friendly a rapport with your temp controller as you can with a small agency.

One graduate, Deidre, seeking temp work in the publishing industry registered with a small agency specialising in this field and advertising a friendly service. Nothing could have been further from the truth.

'My temp controller was so arrogant and off-hand, treating me simply as office fodder, that I completed my week and never went back again. I registered with Grosvenor Bureau, again a small agency specialising in publishing and the contrast could not have been greater. Everyone at Grosvenor was genuinely helpful and I have been in continuous work for six months,' she says.

The best deal

As you will be the employee of the agency, not the client, it will pay you to choose your agency with as much care as you would choose any other employer to ensure you get the best possible deal for yourself.

What the deal is will depend on your own requirements and what you want out of temping. In general, the larger agencies offer more tangible perks such as holiday pay, sick pay and sophisticated training facilities, but you may find a small agency which pays a higher hourly rate, or whose client base is focused on the area of work you prefer. Details of packages and perks offered by some major agencies are given at the end of this chapter.

In training

The Grosvenor Bureau takes a high proportion of graduates on its books and specialises in publishing and media assignments, offering, in addition, an informal career counselling service so it may suit you to work for such an agency, even though it does not offer WP training facilities.

On the other hand, if you want to train on as many systems and software packages as you can lay your hands on, a stint at one of Manpower's Skillware centres could pay you well. You are not formally obliged to work for them afterwards, although they will, obviously, make strenuous efforts to place you in an assignment which uses your new skill.

If you are a competent typist, you might like to start temping with Kelly and, if suitable, they will train you to operate a variety of WPs and software packages, doing their utmost to find assignments for you, which use those skills.

Yet another training plan is used by Atlas, a large chain with 58 branches, all within the orbit of the M25. If a client needs a WP temp and none is available for that system, Atlas will pay a day's salary while she/he cross-trains in the client's office at no cost to the client. This has the advantage that the temp learns not only the system but that particular client's software package too.

Sticking to just two systems, the one-office agency, Word Factory Word Processing, based near London Bridge, takes great pride in keeping its 200 temps in constant work and specialises in Digital and Wang, widely used by the blue-chip client companies.

Word Factory also provides free cross-training for suitable applicants in summer when demand is at its peak, after which the temps are expected to work a minimum of six weeks for the agency. This, of course, means the temp has a good run of work, so cross- training, may not be offered in the autumn and winter months.

By keeping to two systems in which operators are thoroughly trained, Word Factory ensures its temps are completely confident of tackling any assignment, increasing temp and client satisfaction.

Some agencies cater solely for people with a limited range of skills: others for specialist clients. Each has its merits and demerits. It's up to you to find the agency which suits you best.

No age limits

College leavers and mature workers alike are welcomed by most agencies, although Manpower does not accept applicants under 18 years. Amanda Barrington, Managing Director of Amanda Barrington Appointments is most enthusiastic about employing young people.

'College leavers are marvellous,' she says. 'We are always looking for more as our client firms like to train young people into their ways of doing things. Older staff, too, are welcomed, especially by commodity and fund managers, who are happy to pay top rates for mature, well-trained people,' she adds.

Alison Crowe, temp controller at Mistprestige goes further. 'I always state the age of the temp we are sending, so that the client knows what level of experience to expect. There has never been a problem and if a client discriminated on the grounds of age or race we would simply refuse to supply them with any more staff — and we'd tell them why,' she says.

Prime locations

If you want to work in Surrey or Hampshire, use agencies in those areas or chain agencies with branches in the town you want to work in (see the Directory or use the local Yellow Pages).

Perhaps you are planning a move to London or are moving house within the South East. If so, consider registering and working for a branch of the same agency so that your previous work experience can stand you in good stead.

Even if you do this, you will be interviewed and tested at the new branch. This is to your advantage because your new temp controller must meet you in order to assess which bookings would suit you best. It also gives you a chance to strike up a rapport with him/her and lets you see whether your skills measure up to the standards required in the new area.

London

The City of London and West End offer by far the most opportunities for temps and if you are prepared to work in either of these areas, you have a good chance of remaining in continuous work. However if, you are limited to working in one or two London suburbs, you will need a wider range of skills in order to work all the time. Be aware, too, that pay rates in the suburbs are dramatically lower than in the City and West End, both of which command the same high rates from most agencies.

But out of town pay rates are not to be despised. In the Thames Valley they are creeping up towards those of inner London in a bid to attract temps to towns such as Slough, Reading and Bracknell, which indicates that there are plenty of work opportunities in those towns. Again, if you are outside London, you might have to be prepared to work in several neighbouring locations.

Busy times

Agencies really don't mind at what time of year you register but from the temp's viewpoint regular work prospects are brighter in the spring and summer. Should business decrease after the summer holiday season, the agencies will do their best to keep their regulars in work and you, as a newcomer, may have to wait longer for your first assignment. This, however, is very much the luck of the draw and depends on whether your skills are in demand.

If top secretaries are having to take clerical assignments just to keep in work, you may find that if your skills are limited to clerical only, you are not easy to place.

The best times of the week to get assignments are Monday mornings, when permanent staff have taken a long weekend, for whatever reason or booked temps have failed to turn up, and Friday mornings, when clients are phoning in their requirements for the following week.

First steps

Having found the names of some likely agencies you will need to register and have an interview. The best approach is to phone for an appointment so that the temp controller can allocate some time to you without being interrupted. It is possible to deduce a lot about the agency's professionalism, or otherwise, just from the way the interview is set up and conducted.

You can, of course, drop in if you happen to be passing and have an interview there and then, but it may be rather rushed and disorganised if the temp controller has other commitments.

As temp bookings are very much a minute by minute business, there is little point in writing for an interview. Most agencies are not geared up for this approach.

Many temps can vouch for the fact that the interview and skill test is the most daunting part of temping but temp controllers are well aware of this, all of them have been through the same experience themselves and, don't forget, part of their job is to attract temps to the agency. They want you to do well and it is in their interests to put you at your ease.

As with any interview, arrive on time, looking smart, clean and tidy. The details of the procedure vary from one agency to the next but most will follow a general pattern.

You will be asked to complete a form showing details address, age, education, qualifications and experience and whether you are a smoker or non-smoker. Many client firms now have smokefree offices, so temps who smoke have to curb their habit or forgo the booking.

Curriculum Vitae

If you have prepared a Curriculum Vitae (CV) you may be able to attach it to the form, which could save you writing out all the details again, but a prepared CV is by no means essential for temps, except, occasionally when a client wants a temp for a long-term booking, such as covering for maternity leave.

In this case, if you have already worked for an agency, a good temp controller, who knows the client's requirements will be only too pleased to help you prepare a CV if you do not already have one.

Amanda Barrington Appointments, for example, insist on preparing their own CVs for temps so even if you had prepared one, it would be re-written to fit that agency's format. An example is shown on page 28.

CURRICULUM VITAE

NAME Sarah Williams

ADDRESS 42 Medford Road
East Dulwich
SE22 0AQ

TEL 01-693 7663

DATE OF BIRTH 17.10.67

EDUCATION & QUALIFICATIONS

1978 - 1983	*Hazel Grove High School for Girls*
	8 'O' Levels English Language, English Literature, Maths, French, Biology, Chemistry, History, Geography
September 1983 - July 1984	*Pitmans Secretarial College*
	Pitmans Typing Beginners, Intermediate, Advanced 60 wpm, Pitmans Word Processing 60 wpm, Audio, Pitmans Shorthand 80/90, Office Practice, Business English

EMPLOYMENT

1986 - Present	*McCormick Publicis*
	Secretary to an Account Handling Team of Four
	Duties included: Typing reports, presentations, letters, etc. on a Word Processor. Answering the phones, taking messages. Arranging lunches, meetings and travel arrangements. Keeping diaries up to date. General administration and secretarial duties.
August 1984 - December 1985	*Collett Dickenson and Pearce* Junior Secretary to an Account Handling Team.
	The team consisted of Account Director and his team; one Account Manager and two Account Executives.
	Duties included: General secretarial duties, keeping diaries for all ten, arranging meetings, in-house lunches.

WORD PROCESSING PACKAGES USED: Wordperfect, Wordstar and Multimate

Relevant detail

The amount of detail your CV should contain will vary according to the stage you have reached in your career. If you are a college leaver, then details of your schooling, GCSE's, A levels, college course and qualifications obtained, together with any work experience, be it holiday jobs or delivering newspapers must be set out in full. These facts will illustrate your ability to take responsibility and honour your commitments. If you have other credits, such as editing the school magazine or leading the debating society, these can provide proof of initiative and an outgoing attitude.

But if you have already been working for some years, give the educational credits that relate to the type of work you want, followed by brief details of your career to date. In this case a long list of hobbies would be not only irrelevant but irritating to a busy agency.

Be realistic

Although the purpose of a CV is to show your suitability for an assignment in the best light, do not exaggerate your abilities. There's no point in saying you can type at 60 wpm when you know you can only do 45 wpm accurately. In any case, you will be tested, so it is better to be realistic about your abilities. As soon as your speeds have increased, the agency will be pleased to re-test you.

Another point relates to word processors. Some systems are similar to each other, others are very different: all have their own peculiarities. Do not, on any account, pretend that because you can work one system, you will necessarily be able to work another. Outline your experience and say that you are keen to cross-train but do not try to bluff as you could end up in deep water, letting down the client, the agency and yourself.

References and certificates

You will be asked to supply the names of at least two referees and the agency will take up references themselves.

If you are to be sent out on an assignment immediately after registering, the agency will usually accept a telephone reference but this will be followed by a written application for a reference.

An exception to this may be made in the case of people from overseas applying for work here. Many temps from Australia, New Zealand and Zimbabwe bring written references with them and these may be accepted, given the difficulty of taking up references from overseas.

As a school or college leaver, you will probably have your new certificate to hand, in which case by all means take them to show at the interview. But perhaps your formal education ended some years ago and your skills have developed through practical experience, without the need to take exams. No matter, every agency sets more store by its own testing than by previous qualifications, so don't worry if you don't have any 'bits of paper'.

The interview

Always approach an interview with confidence. Remember they want to find someone for the job, so they're not out to get you! If you appear calm and confident, then everything from your dress to your ability to communicate will come together as a brilliant package. Before the interview:

- Mentally run over all your good points — don't just visualise your own self-image but recall the positive comments of friends and past employers.
- Acknowledge your weaknesses, but counter them with the good points you've already assessed.
- Try the morale boosting mirror game: take a good long look at yourself and say 'I'm looking good and I'm going to be great.'

It sounds trite, but it works, if only because it makes you laugh and helps you believe in yourself.

- Practice thinking before speaking — nobody minds a momentary pause or even the comment, 'I hadn't thought about that, let me see...'
- Dress immaculately and you will feel great. Always remember, as a temp, good grooming should be an everyday occurrence not just for the interview.

During the interview:

- Take stock of the person or people interviewing you and assess what concerns them and what they are looking for. You're

> probably right for the agency — so convince the interviewer of this.
> - Be cheerful and never morose or moody. We often fail to project the right image in a short space of time.
> - Be an attentive listener and speak fully and articulately. Avoid yes and no answers.
> - Be conscious of body language. Don't smoke or fiddle with jewellery, cuffs or handbags. The aim is to appear calm and confident.

If you come from overseas, your temp controller will ask to see your work permit before sending you out on an assignment and may also help you obtain one.

Two-way traffic

The interview is very much two-way traffic. Obviously, it gives the temp controller a chance to meet you and find out where your aptitudes lie but just as important it enables you to find out if the right agency for you.

If you are nervous, the old advice about taking a couple of deep breaths before entering the room may help. Smile and look the interviewer right in the eye. What's so interesting that you have to gaze at the floor? Show a receptive attitude during the interview. Don't be afraid to ask questions but do take in what the interviewer is saying in reply.

Make yourself comfortable and sit well back in the chair, rather than perching on the edge of it, but avoid the temptation to indulge in nervous habits, such as picking your nails, fiddling with your handbag, swinging your legs or smoking.

The springboard for the conversation will most likely be your registration form, which the temp controller will talk through with you, asking you to expand on the details and discuss the reasons for your wanting to temp, your projected timescale, the types of work you have done in the past and what you want to do now.

Here you can interpose some leading questions to evaluate the service offered by the agency.

It is important is to find out the hourly rates, although you may not be told until after you have tested as the temp controller will not know yet which grade to put you on. The next two sections address the areas you should cover in an interview.

What type of client?

Ask about the types of businesses that make up the agency's client portfolio. Do they interest you and do you feel you have aptitudes to offer them? What types of work do they offer?

If you are seeking WP or data input work and the agency doesn't have training facilities, ask what arrangements they have with clients for cross-training staff and which temps are eligible to apply for training.

What's the support like?

You can find out a lot about an agency by enquiring about the level of support offered to temps. Ideally, the temp should be well-matched to the job and the agency should check twice on the first day that an untried temp takes on a new assignment and once on the day that any temp, however experienced, goes to a new job.

Potted versions of operating instructions for the most popular WPs and software packages and even switchboards can be a great confidence booster now that office automation is becoming increasingly diverse. Many agencies keep stocks to lend to temps for the duration of an assignment and in addition, Kelly has its own helpline, a service which temps can ring if they have problems with any of the 15 most widely-used systems installed by client firms.

Branches of the major chains usually give their new temps a wealth of literature to welcome them to the fold. This will include some background on the agency, client base and categories of work offered, plus do's and don'ts of dress code and procedures.

Essential details

Almost all will issue an introduction card, which tells you the date and time that the booking starts, who to report to at what address, your job title, hourly rate, plus any other details, maybe that you will be expected not to smoke or any other stipulations made by the client firm. Ask how much information you will be given on the client firm. This kind of support from the agency can be valuable to you and will make you more confident when reporting for the assignment.

Following on from this, ask whether the temp controller visits all clients before booking in temps. This is important as, again, the temp controller will be better able to match temp to booking if she has visited the client's premises and checked that a bona fide business is being carried on there.

No guarantee of work

Beware of the agency that guarantees to keep you in work. It is not ethical to give such a guarantee as the agency may not be able to fulfil it. The most that a responsible temp controller can say is that all the temps are currently working: that she believes that you can be placed; that she will try hard to place you, and the like.

One of the provisions in the FRES Model Conditions of Work (Temporary Workers) states specifically that the Employment Business (agency) and the Temporary Worker agree that the nature of temporary work is such that there may be periods between assignments when no work is available.

However, you should not have to wait more than a couple of days for your first booking, so if you are told that you will have to wait a week or so, it may indicate that the agency is not selling its temps aggressively enough.

Several on the boil

Because no agency can give you a guarantee of work, there is nothing to stop you registering with several agencies at once. Temp controllers are only human and if they know there's another agency competing for your services they may try harder to place you first.

If you register with half a dozen agencies you will usually find that the first one or two to book you out will keep you going. To prevent others losing interest keep phoning to say you particularly want to work for them.

Amanda Barrington makes the point that a temp registering with several agencies will not get the best service because he/she cannot build up a sufficiently good rapport with the temp controller and will have a lot of pressure coming from different directions.

Since agencies know that they cannot have an exclusive claim on your time, there is little point in being secretive with them. If you work one week for a certain agency and are offered a booking the following week by another, do be honest with the first one and tell them what you are doing. The one cardinal sin is to agree to both bookings and then let one agency down.

Skill testing

After the interview, you will be asked to do a test relating to the skills you claim to possess. This might consist of a copytyping test or a passage taken down in shorthand at 80/100 wpm and then transcribed, or audio-typing. A minimum of 50 wpm for typists is required by the majority of agencies, with slower speeds being acceptable for clerk-typist bookings.

WP operators may also be asked to take a practical test. At Manpower, for example, the skill assessment, called Ultraskill, is in two parts. The basic WP operator is asked to set up the machine and follow instructions supplied on a piece of paper for the keying in of a one-page document. The advanced operator is asked to return to the document, lengthen it, correct it and insert further pieces of text, ending up with a two-page document.

Manpower also has a range of skill assessment packages designed to measure candidates' ability to think in a realistic work situation. These are less fearsome than they sound and have no pass or fail element. They are simply designed to assess degrees of skill so as to discover how many jobs you will fit.

Where the agency does not have WP facilities, be prepared to answer oral questions about the WP and software packages with which you say you are familiar.

If you do not have a maths qualification and you are going for a job which deals with figures you might be asked to do a number aptitude test. Unless you are very experienced, you might also be asked to do a grammar, spelling and/or punctuation test if you are aiming for secretarial or clerical work.

The test results will be given to you at once and the temp controller will most likely discuss them with you. Again, the objective is merely to assess your abilities, so temp controllers are usually willing to give extra help with areas of weakness or let you come in to practice on the office typewriter if speed or accuracy need brushing up. If nervousness has got the better of you and caused you to do a very sub-standard test, ask to go back another day and re-take it.

Take the market by storm

Nicholas Holmstock, Director of Acme Appointments, outlines his agency's requirements for a marketable temp.

'The term temp used to be a dirty word,' he says. 'It gives the impression that people were temping because they couldn't hold down a permanent job. Now all that has changed.

'Quality is the most important attribute. If a temp has good skills and a pleasant personality, able to settle in fast and adapt to constantly changing situations, a good consultant should always be able to find them a booking.

'Good quality temps are always in demand,' he explains. 'They generate their own work by being asked back to the same firm time and again. Word processing skills are becoming more and more marketable so the temp who is au fait with more than one system has a headstart on the rest.'

This is echoed by Anona O'Sullivan, Managing Director of Atlas Employment Agency Ltd.

'A good temp is one who has wide experience of office practice, a smart appearance and pleasant personality,' she says. 'Minimum skills of 50 wpm typing, 80 wpm shorthand for a shorthand-typist and 100 wpm for a shorthand secretary are prerequisites and the more WP packages she is familiar with the better.

'A good temp with such attributes will keep getting repeat bookings and if they were out of work, we would canvass her round to our clients while she sat in the office until we found something for her.'

Be reliable

A temp has the right to turn down any booking and temp controllers tend to take a philosophical view of this. However, if you are offered several suitable bookings which you refuse without a good reason, you must realise the agency is not going to waste an infinite amount of time trying to place you again. Be reliable, temp controllers dread unreliability.

- It detracts from the agency's image.
- It can lose the agency a client.
- It does your employment prospects no good.

The first assignment

Once registered, all you have to do is get your first assignment. If you are lucky, a phone call may come in during your interview and you could be booked out right away.

Unless your marketability is very limited you should get a booking within 48 hours but if not, go to the agency and sit there while your temp controller rings round the clients.

If you leave the agency without a booking and, for some reason you cannot be contacted by phone, arrange when you will phone in and be sure to keep to the arrangement as your temp controller may be taking a risk by keeping an assignment especially for you.

Good relations

Once you have found an agency which appears to offer what you want, the development of the relationship between you and your temp controller will begin.

Ideally, this will be founded on a high degree of honesty and trust. As Alison Crowe, of Mistprestige observes, 'The temps are our bread and butter. We regard them as our friends and without them we are nothing.'

Equally, without the temp controller, life will be a lot harder for you, so mutual co-operation is the name of the game.

Each time you accept an assignment, you should be given a contract for services (not a contract of service, which permanent employees get), which sets out your rights and responsibilities and those of the agency. It should include the job title under which you are booked for that assignment: clerk-typist, WP operator, for example and your hourly rate of pay for that job.

Temporary perks

Many of the larger agencies offer special 'temp' packages which are designed to attract and keep the prospective temporary worker. However, it's wiser not to join an agency just for the perks - they are only a small part of any job. It's a case of look before you leap, so assess how important perks are to you personally and consider whether they are essential to your needs or not.

If you feel financially secure, the perks that an agency offers may be a temping extra, worth working for, but bear in mind that sometimes 'perks' mean less take home pay. If you're looking for the highest take home salary, you might be advised to join an agency that offers a straight rate of pay with no trimmings to detract. But then perks do come in all shapes and sizes; so it might be helpful to give you a taster here.

The nature and number of perks available from different agencies, whether large or small, will always vary. The large agency chains, competing for a broad range of workers with no final idea of which agency to join, have created a special temp package partly in an attempt to persuade them to join one agency rather than another.

Training

Training is one of the most useful perks offered by most agencies. The better trained you are the more successful you will be in both a temporary and permanent work situation.

Most agencies don't offer training until you've been with them for a period time — this can be anything from 3 months to a year. Alfred Marks has a 3 month period after which the temp is eligible for:

- Free word processor training
- Personal computer training

Both Alfred Marks and Kelly Girl are flexible with regard to the 3 month no-training zone. If the market demands certain skills at certain times, temps will be trained accordingly.

The larger agencies tend to offer more opportunities for in-house training than the smaller agencies who may have to rely on outside facilities. Small agencies may or may not pay for this external training, so it is worth checking up on this.

Alfred Marks offers a very up-to-date training package and they are able to train and cross-train on a broad basis. Their training takes the form either of instructor led study groups or a more flexible self-teaching method using interactive video.

Kelly Girl, who also offer free word processor and personal computer training, use a micro-computer which is able to simulate the functions of six major wordprocessing systems and elect PC/WP packages currently in business use.

Both Kelly Girl and Alfred Marks have a telephone hot line which will deal with queries about a word processor or personal computer system.

Another year, another package

Each year brings a new package with new perks and benefits so it is difficult to lay down a hard and fast list of what you can expect. The sort of perks you can expect, though no one agency would offer all of them together, are as follows:

- Training
- Holiday pay
- Sickness benefit
- Free gifts for hours worked
- Parties - to ensure temps meet each other
- 'Awards' for merit - such as the Manpower Silver Award.

Holiday pay

Various agencies offer differing deals. At Kelly Girl, you are entitled to one week's holiday pay when you have completed 750 hours on assignments. After that you receive one week's holiday pay for every subsequent 500 hours. You also get paid for public and Bank holidays after 750 hours, but you do have to work either side of these holidays.

- You do not lose the hours you've accumulated if you have a break for any reason — they will be kept on reserve until you return.
- You can take holiday pay as an extra bonus.

Alfred Marks covers you for holiday pay in the weekly wage packet — it's up to you to put that money aside for your breaks.

Sickness benefit

For most agencies, sickness benefit is covered by statutory sick pay (SSP). This is a scheme administered by the employer on behalf of the DHSS. There are 2 rates of payment:

- £49.20 a week if your weekly, average gross earning is more than £79.50.
- £34.25 if your weekly, average gross earning is between £41.00 and £79.49.

Where agencies do offer sick pay, it is often after a qualifying period of three months and is added to SSP.

In order to draw SSP you must be paying National Insurance and be below pensionable age. You don't qualify for SSP on a short contract, so you need to be with the agency for some time.

Your responsibilities

When signing the contract you will also be agreeing amongst other things, not to engage in any conduct detrimental to the interests of the agency, to be present during the agreed hours each day or week, to take reasonable steps to safeguard your own safety or anyone else's who may be affected by your actions at work and to comply with all reasonable disciplinary rules or obligations in force at the client's premises.

The agency's responsibilities

For the period of the assignment, you are the employee of the agency, which is obliged to deduct income tax, National Insurance and pension contributions together with any other deductions which may be required by law.

However, when the assignment ends, the agency is under no obligation to find you further work, nor are you under any obligation to take any assignments that may be offered.

If you have a P45 form from your previous employer, you must hand it to your temp controller, so that the correct amount of Pay As You Earn (PAYE) tax can be deducted from your salary. But if you do not have a P45, the temp controller will help you fill in the necessary forms to obtain one and tax at emergency rate will be deducted until your correct coding is obtained. You can then reclaim the overpaid tax.

If you are ill and need to claim State statutory sickness benefit, your temp controller, again, should help you obtain and fill in the forms.

The agency's commission is derived from supplying staff to client companies. It is illegal for office recruitment agencies to charge commission or registration fees to temps. In this respect they differ from theatrical and modelling agencies, where the worker pays commission.

Give and take

A temp has fewer obligations and also fewer rights than a permanent employee. For instance, you are not obliged to give notice to an agency if you wish to cease working for them. But obviously it makes life easier if you do as the temp controller will not then waste time in trying to find you a booking which you do not want.

However, if you have a friendly relationship with your agency, you will have told her anyway that you plan to: return to Australia, spend the summer with your children; move to another city; go to university, or whatever your plans happen to be.

A situation may arise where it seems sensible to change the hours of work from those contracted, by agreement with the client. This is fine but you must tell your temp controller at once what the new arrangement is. Variation of hours can often occur where a temp with family commitments begins working, say 9 am to 5 pm. It may then become more convenient to start at 8 am, take only half an hour for lunch and finish at 3.30, in time to meet the children from school and this pattern of work is often perfectly acceptable to clients.

It is unlikely that, having registered with an agency, they will actually go so far as to remove you from their books. But if you breach the terms of your contract by doing something which will bring the agency or the client firm into disrepute, you must expect them to take a dim view.

Fair deals

In the event that your work is not up to scratch and the client complains to the agency, the temp controller should take a share of the blame for sending you to an assignment beyond your capabilities.

The client should, if possible, produce evidence, such as copies of work containing keyboard errors or other proof that you have failed to follow instructions and the temp controller should go through these with you to establish why the work was sub-standard.

This should not reach the proportions of a major problem as the client is at liberty to ask you to leave after the first two hours of an assignment if it is clear that you are unsuited to it. As the agency is responsible for choosing suitable jobs for you it is very unlikely that they would fail to pay you for the hours worked.

You might meet situation where the agency places you in a temp assignment which ends and subsequently the client contacts you at home, offering to pay you a higher hourly rate in return for sidestepping the agency's commission.

This is cheating and if the agency is a FRES member and finds out what is going on, it can complain to FRES, which, in turn will write to the client and put a stop to the practice. Also, you will put yourself in a very bad light with your temp controller. Sometimes clients will contact you and apply considerable pressure to get you to work in this way. Simply refuse to be a party to it and refer the booking to your agency in the normal way.

Trust breeds support

The degree of support you can expect from your temp controller in the event of a dispute over you between agency and client, will depend largely on the degree of trust between you and your controller.

Anne, a tried and tested audio secretary went on an assignment to a small legal practice. On arrival she was given coffee-making duties and errands to run, which she carried out cheerfully but when presenting her timesheet for signature at the end of the week, she was very upset to receive a complaint from the client because she had failed to finish the typing.

She tore up her timeseheet, saying that she did not wish the client to be invoiced if he had not had value for money. Her temp controller was horrified that a loyal, competent worker had been treated like this. Anne was paid in full and the agency refused to supply any more temps to the client.

Supportive agencies

With the advent of office automation and businesses' dependence on computers, the potential of a moment's carelessness to cause untold damage is very great so do take care of clients' equipment.

One unfortunate WP operator managed to spill a drink on to a disc, which subsequently corrupted the entire system. Needless to say, the client was not very happy but as the temp had a good track record with the agency, the situation was smoothed over.

On another occasion a temp working for a small agency suffered a bereavement. Her bank turned down her request for a loan to fly to Barbados for the funeral but the agency helped her out. Not only did she repay the loan on time but she is unlikely to seek work from another agency! These are just examples to illustrate the value of maintaining a good relationship with your temp controller.

Why push your luck?

Conversely, if you repeatedly turn down suitable assignment or fail to turn up after agreeing to do so, the agency might keep you on their books to call on if they are desperate, but they will certainly put your card to the bottom of the heap and avoid calling you if they can. Such is the demand for temps that this should not happen until you have had at least three chances, or warnings, usually verbal but sometimes written. Why push your luck?

Keep in touch

The key to a successful relationship is to keep in close touch with your temp controller. If you need to take time off or want to take a permanent job: tell her. If you are working for another agency or are unhappy in a particular assignment let her know. Your temp controller should be made aware of a domestic problem causing you to be absent from work. You must also tell her if you start working different hours from those contracted. And, if you think she's doing a good job for you, it doesn't hurt to mention that as well!

The Agency Checklist

When choosing your agency, always consider how many of the following factors it offers:
- Friendly temp controller
- Competitive hourly rates
- Six-monthly pay rises
- Free banking/cheque encashment facilities
- Sick pay over and above State statutory sick pay — what qualifying period?
- Bank holiday pay
- Holiday pay — what qualifying period?
- Loyalty bonus
- Recruitment bonus
- Life/accident insurance
- Discount on holidays
- Discount on medical health insurance
- Maternity/paternity leave
- A good chance of regular work
- Choice of assignments
- Interesting clients to work for
- Opportunities for you to be re-graded at a higher level
- Support from your agency when on assignment
- Work in your preferred area
- Work for the hours you choose
- Training facilities to improve skills
- Informed career counselling
- Social contact with other temps
- FRES membership

AT LAST...

...a chance to break out of that hum drum job and into something more exciting.

How about advertising? Or media? Or the professional sector?

If you've been waiting and hoping for a better job, talk to Amanda Barrington.

She always has great clients who are crying out for enthusiastic temporary and permanent secretaries. At all levels.

So whether you're looking for your first job or you're a PA wanting a good career move, here's your chance. So take it!

Amanda

She's fussy, because you are. Call 379 7007

AMANDA BARRINGTON SECRETARIAL RECRUITMENT

· RECRUITMENT SERVICES ·

Ludgate House, 107-111 Fleet Street, London EC4A 2AB 01-583 5441

TEMPING AS A CAREER?

We at Mison value our temporaries, we CARE.

This means long or short term bookings when you want them, time off when you really need it. A holiday pay scheme, regular contact with your Temporary Manager — who cares and will endeavour to meet your requirements.

Learn new skills — we will cross train secretarial staff free of charge on a variety of WORD PROCESSORS — this will increase your earning power.

Work for the most prestigious clients in the CITY & WEST END, our client portfolio is second to none.

Please telephone Ann Stone, she will be delighted to help.

ESTABLISHED 1960

a good variety of assignments always in:
Arts . . . Design . . Sport . . PR
Medicine & Science . . Banking . . Broking etc.
SMALL & FRIENDLY – PROFESSIONAL & RELIABLE
WE PAY YOU IN FULL EVERY FRIDAY
We need Typists, Audio & Shorthand Secretaries
with Wordprocessing experience –
BUT
if your skills need nursing, we'll do our best
to get you started. Give us a ring!

Temp Controller: **Sian Thomas**
01 370 5066
118 Cromwell Rd
London SW7 4EG

Chapter 3

Survival Tips

Temping, we've established can be fun: meeting new people, getting an insight into different types of company, not having to put up for long with work or personalities that irritate you. Yet like any career, there are drawbacks and obstacles to be acknowledged and overcome. You must be aware of the stresses of the lifestyle you have chosen and be prepared in order to survive it. Forewarned is forearmed and if you spend a little time on preparation, you can ride smoothly over the worst of the bumps.

Negative vibes

It has to be faced — there are a number of negative sides to temping and you've got to overcome those. Although the positive aspects of temping are very alluring: good money, flexible hours and freedom to work as and when you will, temping isn't the proverbial bed of roses. There are a few thorny snags to manoeuvre.

The freedom not to work is fine, but what if the agency has no work to offer you? If you have a mortgage and other commitments, an irregular income can be a serious worry.

If you have a range of marketable skills and register with more than one agency, you should be able to keep in work but when bookings are thin on the ground, you may have to take assignments which do not use all your abilities.

Hard times

You may be an accomplished word processor operator, but if the agency can only offer you switchboard work one week you will have to decide whether to take the lower rate or be out of work altogether. Similarly, if your skills are limited to clerical functions only and the agency hits a slack time, you could face a patch of unemployment.

Periods of sickness, too, can mean that your income takes a nosedive. True, some agencies offer sick pay for temps who have worked for them for a certain length of time; others pay a higher hourly rate instead, but a few temps put that money by for times of sickness, so be aware that a bout of flu could leave you very much out of pocket.

On your own

There is also the problem of isolation, particularly for those new to London, who have no established social life to fall back on. If your personal and social life is just building up following a move from your home town to London, you may find that the rootlessness of being a temp and having neither permanent colleagues nor family and friends can make you feel insecure and depressed.

It is possible to make lifelong friends during a short assignment, but many people take longer to form relationships and need the predictability of a permanent workplace.

Despite the constant change of environment and colleagues, you may feel at times that you are in a rut and that you can never really progress.

Superficial relations

However much you improve and expand your skills, your relationship with client firms will be superficial. It can never be 'your' firm, promotion is unlikely and you may feel there is no point in getting involved and taking on extra responsibility as you will soon be moving on.

Graduates seeking a career job in management should be cautious about temping for too long as it does not look good on a CV, and especially for women, it is not always wise to say you can type as you may be pigeon-holed into a secretarial position from which it is difficult to break free.

On a strictly practical level, you may find that you are temping so hard, that you don't have time to ferret out and apply for career jobs. With the happy thought that 'this job won't last forever', you may wake up to realise that six months have passed and you haven't sent out a single job application.

Game for a laugh

A degree of self-awareness, as well as a sense of humour can be a great help, and will tide you over the occasional feeling of isolation. Some agencies organise get-togethers for their field staff. Manpower holds Christmas functions and Valentine's Day get-togethers, while others offer pate and wine on Friday lunchtimes, so that temps calling in for their pay cheque, can meet each other and have a chat.

Knowing that other temps in their offices are probably feeling just the same way, can allay that feeling of Monday morning loneliness when you arrive in an office and don't even know where to find a cup of coffee.

Ways and means

It is only realistic to accept the fact that there may be lean times. Maybe a job fixed up for you on a Friday, to cover for staff sickness will be cancelled on Monday morning owing to the incumbent's miraculous recovery. These things happen and there is no point in being phased out when they do.

Although you need to have a responsible attitude to money in order to budget effectively, you will need to develop the ability to live well within your means when times are good, so that you can enjoy, without worrying, some unexpected time off when the demand for temps is less intense.

Again, this may not always work out according to plan. You might have accepted, quite happily, the fact that you would have a week's unofficial holiday, only to receive a call on Monday morning, just when you had turned over for another hour's sleep, asking you to be in the City, ready for work in an hour's time.

In at the deep end

Temps are thrown in at the deep end so, you owe it to yourself to make life easier for yourself whenever you can.

The agency earns its commission from placing temps and the client needs a job done. You are the link and that makes you piggy in the middle.

But remember that your skills are needed. There are more jobs than there are competent temps in the London area and you must keep this clearly in mind when under pressure from your agency, maybe to take a job you don't feel qualified to do or to work in an area you do not care for.

One of your most important assets will be a good relationship with the temp controller/supervisor at your chosen agency (see Chapter 2 The Agency).

The other single most effective thing you can do in the office situation is to nip misunderstandings in the bud.

Iron out these teething troubles and temping can be plain sailing, even if everyday is a potential Monday morning!

Get up and go

Travel to each new assignment is a problem every temp faces. But you can save yourself a lot of hassle by planning your route the day before. If your temp controller visits all her clients she will be able to give you exact directions, including which door to use. This can be helpful in the case of very large companies.

In many City streets, buildings are named but not numbered and it can be frustrating to arrive at the correct street in time, but be unable to find the right building. Call up to get a description of the building the day before.

For London jobs, consult the London Underground map, which you will find at the end of this book. Buy, from any newsagent, a copy of the Geographers A - Z Atlas of London, or the Nicholson London Streetfinder, for around £2.50p and carry it with you always.

If working out of London, obtain maps of the areas in which your assignments are likely to be located and keep them handy, along with up to date train and bus timetables, available from bus garages, Underground and railway stations.

Because your assignments will vary in length it may not be wise to buy a long-term season ticket. London Underground Travelcards, which cover Underground travel in various zones plus bus travel and London Underground Capitalcards, which cover the above plus British Rail travel can save money and are worth investigation. Both can be obtained from Underground stations and are valid for seven days or longer.

Ticket to ride

Both Travelcards and Capitalcards require you to have a Photocard, so take a passport photo with you when you apply. Also, try to give 12 hours' notice when you purchase a Travelcard or Capitalcard and avoid busy times at the point of purchase.

Perhaps it is more convenient to drive to work, but don't assume that the client company will have parking space for you. Try to find out in advance what the parking facilities are like and bear in mind that a relatively short journey during off peak hours can take an inordinate length of time during the rush hour.

If, despite your best efforts, you do get hopelessly lost and it becomes clear that you are going to be very late, always phone the agency so that your temp controller can placate the client and, if necessary, send in a replacement temp until you turn up. Even if the other temp stays in the job and you lose out on that occasion, it is still better to be reliable than not to turn up and you might get the chance to fill in for another 'lost soul' next time.

First impressions

When embarking on a spell of temping, you are representing the agency and also the client if your work involves contact with the client's customers. Research shows that 58 per cent of the impression we make depends on how we look. First impressions count.

It will make life easier, and increase your marketability if you adapt your style of dress and make-up to fit in with the client company's standards. Some agencies have a dress code which says for example, that women must wear skirts or dresses: men must wear a collar and tie.

Client firms, too, may have their own dress code. Everyone, whether male or female, working in a City stockbroker's office, is expected to wear a dark suit and women should wear low-heeled shoes, white blouses and never, ever trousers.

Occasionally, you will find an office which bans jeans, but accepts women in tailored trousers: others discourage women from wearing trousers other than as part of a trouser suit.

In the City, women have to wear tights even in the height of summer, whereas outside the Square Mile, suntanned legs are quite acceptable.

The best thing is to play safe the first day and dress in a fairly conventional style. When you get to the office you can see what others are wearing and you can ask if a more casual style of dress is acceptable.

Firms which have a creative bias, such as advertising agencies and television companies, along with some departments of the civil services tend to have a more laidback approach and allow staff to dress according to their own preferences.

If you see way-out clothes and make-up as an essential part of your identity you will severely limit the type of companies which you can work for. Even if you feel dress codes are stuffy and old-fashioned, it is true to say that the company has to earn a living and in order to do so, it must put the right image across to its customers. If you form part of the public face of the company, it is only fair to be bound by the rules.

But making a good impression is not just about rules — it's also about being aware of your own image.

Image conscious

Have you taken a look at your image recently to see if it is pushing you forward or holding you back?

The first step in getting your look together is to look more closely at your wardrobe and the image your clothes are projecting for you. You don't need a great deal of money to put together a wardrobe suitable for both business and pleasure. You may, however, need some advice on what's unique about you and how to dress appropriately for your colouring, build, personality and lifestyle.

Are you well dressed?

Why not answer our questionnaire to see if you care enough about your image.

DO YOU CARE ABOUT YOUR IMAGE?

		YES	NO
1	Do you buy a new coat only when your old one wears out?	☐	☐
2	Do you take more than 3 minutes on your make-up and hair in the morning?	☐	☐
3	Does it boost your morale if someone compliments you on your appearance?	☐	☐
4	A relative/friend gives you a present of a blouse which you don't like. Do you wear it?	☐	☐
5	Do you care about the colour/style of your hosiery so long as they are clean and free of ladders?	☐	☐
6	Would you consider buying a new suit if you had a 3 month assignment with a City stockbrokers?	☐	☐
7	Do you enjoy choosing accessories, ie. jewellery, belts, hosiery, etc?	☐	☐
8	Do you always wear the same suit and blouse combination?	☐	☐

These answers can be found on page 69.

To be well dressed you must develop your own style. Fashions may come and go but your style will never change. Being well dressed means wearing clothes that compliment you physically, are an extension of your personality and are suitable for your lifestyle.

Choosing clothes to suit all these requirements can be difficult. Begin by throwing away all the items in your wardrobe you have not worn for six months or those that are out of date. For women, do the same with your make-up and accessories. Looking at the remaining clothes, think through their suitability for your work and social environment. Do you have lots of clothes that do not work together? Do you have any gaps in the wardrobe? If this is the case you need to decide which clothing items you should buy next.

If you know the colours and styles of clothes that suit you, you will always have a wardrobe of clothes to wear for any occasion. The items will all work together and you will save time and money when shopping.

The professional look

Clothes for the office do not necessarily have to be plain and ordinary. There is a great deal of choice with extensive ranges of suits and separates available on the market. You should invest in at least two suits (for women), three suits (for men) and rotate the use of them so they are given a chance to 'recover' from each wearing. Suits may not be appropriate for every profession but you never know when you might be asked to attend a meeting unexpectedly.

Hair

You should look after your hair on a regular basis. On average, you need to have it cut every 4 — 6 weeks. If your hair is long, tie it back when you are at work otherwise it can be a distraction. For men, your hair should not be longer than collar length.

Make-up

Wearing make-up enhances a woman's looks, improves her credibility and, most importantly, her self esteem. According to research, women who wear make-up earn 20 per cent more than those who don't, however, some women are reluctant to wear make-up or they only go half way. Don't cheat on yourself, you are your best investment.

Jewellery

For women, keep your jewellery to a minimum and keep it on the conservative side. For men, a wrist watch is the only item acceptable. Remember, jewellery can be a big distraction so save it for social occasions.

Develop your style

It is very difficult to judge yourself objectively. If you are having trouble determining the colours and styles that suit you or you want some advice in developing your style, Image Consultants can be of great help.

Why not contact Color Me Beautiful at 66 Abbey Business Centre, Ingate Place, London SW8 3NS, tel: 01-627 5211.

The first day

Every day can be a first day for a temp, so when you start work with a new client organisation, there are some things which must be established right away.

You should arrive in good time on the first day: you will gain a psychological advantage by arriving first and if the preliminaries can be sorted out in the ten minutes before work officially begins, you will be able to start on time.

Some of the following information may be given to you on the introduction card supplied to you by your agency, in which case you can check it through with the person you have been asked to report to but if you have received a last-minute booking by phone, you may not have been given full and accurate details.

If possible, see that you are qualified for the job which you have been sent. This is not as daft as it sounds. Some agencies will do almost anything to fill a booking and may, on occasion, send someone along for a job to which they are totally unsuited.

The plus point of this is that if the card says 'Receptionist/some typing' the job may give you the chance to improve your typing, or if you have no typing skills, the client may be happy that you can at least look after the switchboard and greet customers. All this will help to boost your confidence and increase your marketability.

But if, after having the job explained to you, you can tell that it is way beyond you, have the courage to say so, phone your agency and leave. If you battle on in misery, you will not be happy, the client will feel he/she has not had good value for money and the agency will feel that you have let them down even if it was not your fault.

This, again, is a good argument for being on the books of more than one agency, so that if you fall out with one, you can still work for the other.

Top cat

Having arrived at the client's office, establish who your 'boss' is for the period of the assignment. This may not be as easy to discover as it is seems.

In a small firm the chances are that the name on your introduction card is that of the person whose work you will be handling but in a larger organisation it may be the name of the personnel officer or staff supervisor. Always:

- Find out the name of the person or people, from whom you can accept work.
- Establish the client company's style of letter and memo layout.
- Keep the company's telex and fax numbers to hand.
- Ensure you have access to the typewriter/WP manual.
- Know what happens to work once you've finished it.
- If your boss is absent do you pp or 'sign in her absence'? The latter absolves you of any responsibility for the letter's contents.
- Familiarise yourself with equipment and ask for help.
- Check the location of fire exits.
- Check your first few pieces of work with your supervisor to ensure you are on the right lines.

Lunchtime, hometime, overtime

Offices vary in their lunch hour arrangements: some having a fixed break; others allow staff to take an hour at any time between say, 11.45 am and 2.30 pm. Check this together with the finishing time and also ask when to report for work next day as the first day's starting time is often different from subsequent days.

If a considerable amount of overtime is required, the agency should tell you at the outset. If you cannot work overtime at all, make sure the agency knows this. But if you are happy to earn the extra money that overtime offers, you can help to offset some of the leaner weeks.

When the subject of overtime comes up, be as flexible as possible and help out if you can. Even if you can't work late that evening, suggest another time when you can. Overtime may arise when you are given a long report to do ten minutes before the normal finishing time. If such a situation occurs, always tell your agency so as to be sure you are paid for it.

It could be that you work extra hours, then the boss is away on holiday when your timesheet is made up and the personnel officer disputes that the overtime was worked, so always have a witness to the fact and extent of your overtime working.

From the viewpoint of your own safety, estimate how long the job will take you and ask who else will be in the building till that time. When does the doorman clock off and how can you ensure that you won't get locked in?

You and the agency

Central to successful temping is forming a good relationship with your agency, or agencies, if you are registered with more than one.

The details of the temp/agency relationship are covered fully in Chapter 2 but below are a few points which will aid your survival:

- Be honest
- Be reliable
- If personality clashes occur at the agency or on an assignment, talk about it
- Never walk out of an assignment, discuss the problems with your temp controller
- Be friendly and flexible.

Look after the pennies

Money is dealt with more fully in chapter 4, Money Matters but your financial status will play a major part in your survival, or lack of it, as an office temp.

You will need to budget carefully because your income as a temp may be irregular. How you do this up to you, but as a guide, you might like to assume you will work only three weeks in a month so that you have a little bit stashed away against the lean times or a period of sickness.

When paying for major items you may find that credit cards, although carrying a high rate of interest, are more suited to your needs than direct debit or standing order arrangements, as you have a month to pay. This can be less frightening than having a fixed amount automatically taken from your bank account on a set date each month.

For people with an irregular income, irregular dates for paying things can be a great relief.

Few people would choose to take their vacation during school holiday periods, so if you are free of these constraints, why not consider taking your holiday either in the spring, when resorts are at their newly-painted, sparkling best, or in the autumn when the Mediterranean heat has mellowed a little?

In both seasons you can enjoy fewer crowds and lower prices with the added advantage of working for high summer pay rates when temp work is plentiful.

Commuting to work can be a burdensome expense as short assignments mean you cannot take advantage of long-term season tickets, but see above for Travelcard and Capitalcard arrangements.

As a very rough guide to budgeting, you can reckon on being paid for a seven-hour day, no payment for the lunch hour, at the following hourly rates in London: Secretary/WP operator £7.50; audio/secretary £6.50; switchboard operator £5.00 and junior clerk £4.00. Rates in some suburbs and outside London may be lower, but even outside London, where there is a demand for skills, pay rates can rival those in the metropolis.

Agencies usually increase their rates every six months, but there are other ways of swelling your pay packet. If you extend your range of skills or experience, you may be able to obtain a payrise by asking your agency to re-grade you, for example, from shorthand-typist, to shorthand-secretary.

Some agencies, especially the larger chains have a very wide range of job classifications, so use them to your advantage.

Sick pay

As temping is by its nature a nomadic occupation and in general you are paid only for the hours you work, do not expect to be paid while absent from your desk for dental or hospital appointments, or even ante-natal appointments. Temps work under a contract For Services (as distinct from permanent staff, who work under a contract Of Services) so payment for those attending ante-natal appointments is very much at the discretion of the employer.

'A healthy constitution is a particular advantage to a temp, but we are all human and may need to take sick leave from time to time. The sickness benefits offered by agencies vary widely (see Chapter 2).

Other agencies have found that temps prefer a higher hourly rate, part of which is intended to be saved to cover periods of sickness. If you need to claim statutory sick pay, your temp controller should help you obtain and fill in the necessary forms. But, if you do fall ill how can you get back on your feet quickly and stay well?

In sickness and in health

One of the major causes of illness amongst office workers is stress. As office automation eliminates much of the routine drudgery of yesterday's office practice, it also erodes the need to perform calculations, to move about the office and talk to colleagues, and can diminish job satisfaction to the point where staff become demoralised and feel they only exist to serve the machines.

As a temp, you will experience the added stresses of constantly meeting new people and adapting to new routines but there is much you can do to make it easier on yourself.

First of all, you need to be in good condition physically, which means ensuring that you get sufficient sleep and nutritious, regular meals.

If you have a very active social life it will be tempting to burn the candle at both ends but you will enjoy all aspects of your life much more if you make it a rule to be in bed by 10 pm at least one night a week.

Try also to have one proper meal a day, either at lunchtime or in the evening. If your client firm has a staff dining room offering subsided meals, use it and make do with a snack in the evening, or, alternatively, find a health food shop which sells wholefood goodies at lunchtime and enjoy a full meal in the evening.

Either way, it will pay you to keep the energy level up so you might also consider taking a multivitamin tablet each day.

Causes of stress

The modern office environment, dominated as it is by machines, can be a source of stress.

The heat generated by lighting and automated office equipment, especially in rooms not designed for VDU use can cause workers to suffer drowsiness, dry, itchy eyes and throats and even in some cases, dizziness and skin rashes. These symptoms are often caused by inadequate ventilation/air conditioning and insufficient humidity.

Ergonomic problems: desks and chairs which are not of the right height in relation to each other; lighting, too much, too little, or glaring on the screen, can all contribute to stress, especially where a repetitive task like word processing is performed for many hours a day with little respite.

Noise, too, can be a major cause of stress, particularly in offices where printers are located next to the work station or where audio typists have to soldier on with poor quality tapes, turning up the volume to an uncomfortable level in order to obtain clarity of speech. For those engaged in telephone work, faulty headsets coupled with high frequency noises on the telephone lines can turn a working day into a misery.

A further cause of stress is the feeling that one's work is of no value and forms no part of a worthwhile end product. This can apply very much to temp work as, although the pay rates may be high, the concept of 'another day, another dollar' is not always totally satisfying.

How to cope with stress

- Take a break — but avoid caffeine based drinks. Switch to a herbal tea or a fresh fruit juice.
- Always try and have a lunch break.
- Don't go out every night of the week. Sleep is a great cure for stress and tiredness.
- Control the pace of a difficult situation.
- Set yourself realistic objectives.
- Acknowledge when you are stressed and try to counter it.
- Develop an efficient way of working.
- Learn to communicate with work colleagues and clients.
- Know what you are doing — this will give you a sense of purpose and make sure you have got the skills to carry it out. If you can't cope, ring the agency. There's no point in killing yourself tackling a job that isn't for you.

Working conditions

As a temp you will rapidly become a connoisseur of working conditions. Don't be afraid to ask for new tapes or a headset that functions properly and take a little time to adjust your chair to the correct height.

Environmental conditions, of course, are not so easy to remedy and as a temp there is a limit to what you can do about them. If conditions are very uncomfortable, tell your temp controller the reasons and ask for a transfer. If several temps make the same complaints and the temp controller tells the client firm, there's a chance that improvements might be made.

The good news is that as you will not be in one place using one type of equipment for too long, the risk of sustaining Repetitive Strain Injury, sometimes found in keyboard operators, may be less than for permanent staff.

If you use a VDU, make sure you do not have to view it at an uncomfortable angle or with an unacceptable degree of glare.

Small risks?

The risk of miscarriage resulting from exposure to the radiation from VDUs is still being hotly disputed by trade unions and employers. It would seem that the risk is very small but it almost certainly does exist so you will have to make your own decision on whether to continue with that type of work while you are pregnant.

If you do want to make a stand to improve office working conditions, the most effective course of action is to join the white-collar union APEX (the Association of Professional, Executive, Clerical and Computer Staff). This will certainly make you feel less isolated. The union, which combined with the GMB (General Municipal Boilermakers and Allied Trade Unions)in March 1989, has around 150,000 members. It has produced several health and safety reports including one on New Technology, which gives recommendations for an improvement in working conditions.

To increase your own feeling of self-esteem at work, you may find satisfaction in mapping out your temping career to include improving your skills, learning new switchboards, new WP systems, new software packages to ensure that you always feel you are making progress.

Smoking — the burning issue

If you smoke, tell the agency that you prefer an environment where smoking is allowed and on arrival, ask what the rules are regarding this.

Some offices allow smoking anywhere, others only in certain designated areas. If you are sharing an office, it is only fair to ask the other staff if they object to your lighting up, but be aware that even if they do not object, they may still find it offensive, so keep your habit to a minimum.

If you do not smoke, you should tell your agency if you want to work only in a smokefree environment, which, of course, may diminish your chances at work.

Take a break

Even if the workload at your client firm is very heavy, do make sure you take a lunch break. It can be tempting to plod on and discover halfway through the afternoon that you feel very stale and fed up. If you can, leave the building and go for a walk or jog even if only for ten minutes and you will return refreshed, able to tackle the afternoon's work with renewed effectiveness.

If you are fortunate enough to be near a pool, a lunch hour swim can help ease aching muscles after a morning at the VDU screen. It is worth making time for a yoga session one evening a week, too. This will gently stretch and mobilise all the muscle groups, enhancing a sense of energy, well-being and help you to relax.

The demands of word processing and data inputting are such that it is possible to sit for several hours without moving from the work station so make a point of getting up, stretching and walking about every half hour or so. Take a few deep breaths at an open window if you can and give your eyes a rest from the screen by focusing on a distant object, a picture or the office plants at least every quarter of an hour.

You don't have to stand on your head in the office but there are yoga exercises which can be done unobtrusively in a small space during the day.

Personal safety

London is undoubtedly a lot safer than many big cities, but the sad fact is that street crime is on the increase and attacks on women, and men, are not uncommon. Your safety is your responsibility and there are a few basic rules which will help:

- Never, never, go into unlit alleyways or take deserted shortcuts, especially in the dark.

- If the street lights happen to be out on your normal route home, keep away from clumps of bushes and places where attackers can take cover.
- Try to get to know people locally, in the corner shop or newsagents, so that if you are followed home, you are never more than a few yards from help.
- Consider the possibility of carrying a 'screech' alarm and hold it in your hand so that you can activate it instantly.
- Always be sure that somebody knows where you are. In the event of an attack, at least you would know that within a short time someone may raise the alarm.
- If you are in digs and are going out alone, tell your landlady when you expect to be home. If sharing, tell your flatmates.

This can be very irksome but unfortunately, attacks do happen, people are abducted and you have to consider your own safety first.

A course of lessons in self-defence can be good fun and will enable you to meet new people. The idea of these is not to enable you to overpower an 18-stone psychopath armed with a knife, but to give you the confidence to cope in the first split second of the attack. Then you can kick, shout, punch, scream and, possibly, run away. Attackers prey on the fact that their victims are so paralysed with terror, that they are unable to move or shout.

Always keep a list of taxi telephone numbers with you and never go out without making sure you can get home safely.

The problem of unwanted attention

Sexual harassment is victimisation through unwanted sexual advances or abusive reference to sexual orientation which threaten a worker's job or state of mind. It takes many forms including persistent touching, suggestive remarks or other verbal abuse, leering or demands for sexual favours.

Sometimes temps are considered 'fair game' as they are not established staff in the workplace but, temp or not, there is no need to put up with conduct which makes you uncomfortable.

If you encounter sexual harassment, which you cannot handle just by ignoring it, state openly that you find such conduct oppressive. Make sure that there are witnesses to your statement because, if you should decide to take the case further, the presence of witnesses will strengthen your case.

Home, sweet home

It has been said time and again in the press, on television and by well-meaning advisers that accommodation in London and the South East is not only very difficult to find, but also very expensive.

And the boring fact is that it is true. The importance of fixing accommodation before starting work cannot be overestimated.

You may be lucky enough to stay with friends while you get a job but once you start temping your homeseeking time will be severely limited and it may take you a long time to find somewhere congenial to live.

The area you choose will depend on your requirements. You may want to live near to friends or family. But the most likely consideration will be the need to combine habitable accommodation that you can afford with a convenient journey to the area in which you are seeking work. Sit down with a map and transport timetable and, with the aid of a column of newspaper adverts to give you a rough guide as to what is available at what cost, work out which areas might be worth looking at.

Where to live and what it costs

In general, the areas closer to the centre tend to be more expensive than those further out. But there are expensive outer suburbs and bargains to be had in the more fashionable areas. Also, a property might have an upmarket address, but itself be on the border between the smart and the rundown, so you will have to make a few reconnaissance trips to see for yourself.

- Always visit a particular area in daylight and figure out how you would get home at night. Can you get home quickly from the bus stop or tube station without having to cross lonely waste ground or go down unlit alleyways?
- Does the area look well cared-for or are there flyblown shreds of net curtain hanging from peeling window frames? Are Neighbourhood Watch stickers visible on many windows? These can give you the clues as to whether the local inhabitants care about their area or whether they are demoralised and depressed. All this can make a big difference to your feeling of security.
- Ask a few well-chosen questions in the local newsagent's shop

> to find out more information about the area: amenities, the sort of people who live there: for instance, is it a family-orientated area, which may be pleasant but dreary on Sunday? Or an area full of bedsitters, which, with its 'drifting population' might be livelier but less attractive from the security point of view.

The presence of builders' skips in the street is a good sign as it often denotes owner-occupation, ie., people who care about their homes and the area itself.

If you can arrange to do your snooping when people are returning from work, so much the better. You can see whether they are people amongst whom you think you would feel comfortable.

There are various types of accommodation which you might like to consider. These are lodgings, or 'digs'; a shared flat, single or double bedsitter or hostel. Whatever type of accommodation you choose, try not to let it absorb more than 30 per cent of your net income. The first port of call for women looking for accommodation in London should be the London Council for the Welfare of Women and Girls (LCWWG) and London YWCA Accommodation and Advisory Service at 57 Great Russell Street, London WC1B 3BD, tel: 01-430 1524, 10 am — 4 pm (7 pm Thursdays). You can drop in any time from 11 am to 3 pm (7 pm Thursdays). Here you can obtain help with any problem you may have (not only accommodation) and can obtain lists of accommodation, names of agents and a range of useful booklets.

Helpful guidelines

These include: 'Coming to London?', which gives an outline budget (reckon on £100 a week minimum) and other useful advice; 'A Place to Stay', giving general guidelines on seeking a privately rented flat or bedsit and 'Temporary Accommodation in London', which lists addresses and prices of accommodation for stays of one night to four weeks.

For these, just send a stamped addressed foolscap envelope. There is no charge for using the service, although a small donation if you can manage it would help those coming along after you.

LCWWG also publishes 'Hostels in London', listing 150 hostels (some of which also take men). This costs £1.50, direct sale or £2.00 by post. Cheques/postal orders should be made payable to LCWWG at 57 Great Russell Street, London WC1B 3BD.

Short stay accommodation is also available from the London Tourist Board, Victoria Station, London SW1V 1JT, tel: 01-730 3488. The Board's booklet *'Where to Stay in London'* is available at most bookstalls.

Get digging

Finding digs is easier than finding a flat, so may be a good choice to start with. Here you have a bedroom in a family house, usually use the family's bathroom and have an arrangement either to eat with the family or use the kitchen at certain times to prepare your own food.

The rent is normally inclusive, although you might have to use a slot-meter for heating, but at least you will not have utilities bills to worry about. The best time of year to find digs is June/July, when the students have gone home and you can expect to pay a minimum of £35 a week. Having identified an area you think you might like to live in, look at newsagents' boards and the local paper.

If you are leaving home for the first time and enjoying your first taste of freedom, it may tempting to reject accommodation in which the landlady seems rather fussy and you may be hedged with petty restrictions.

But if you are new to London, it might pay you to be a little wary until you find your feet. If the house is clean and cared-for, it may mean that the family and other lodgers treat each with consideration. If you have to clean the bath after use and keep your radio turned down, then so does everybody else. In a house where nobody cares about anybody, you can be sure nobody will care about your needs.

Sharing

A shared flat or house will give you more freedom, but can lead to trouble if you fall out with the other tenants. It is said that 'you don't really know someone until you've lived with them' and this is only too true.

Issues like the apportionment of housework, who does the shopping, or cooking can lead to trouble and then there are other problems like what to do if someone brings a friend home for a week, or a month, and he/she not only outstays his/her welcome, but doesn't even contribute to the bills.

Then there are those who fail to pay their share of the bills, promising the money always 'next week' and leaving the other tenants out of pocket. Sharing can be enormous fun, but if you are on your own, again it might be better to wait until you make some real friends and then get a place together, with a written, albeit informal agreement about basic matters of co-existence.

Despite the trials and tribulations, there is great competition for places in shared properties and the best ones are usually passed on through friends. However, they are also advertised on notice boards, newspapers, *Time Out* magazine and accommodation agencies. Or you can pick up the Capital Radio flatshare list, published every Tuesday morning at 11 am and available from Capital Radio, Euston Tower, Euston Road, London NW1. The best time of year to find a flat to rent is winter/early spring as tourists tend to occupy them on short lets during the summer.

Self-reliance

A word of warning: only use accommodation agencies as a last resort. Some, which will be listed in the Yellow Pages, charge no fees to landlords — which means they DO charge tenants, so ascertain exactly what the fees are before committing yourself.

A single bedsitter on your own will cost around £45 a week minimum. It avoids the irritations of sharing but you must be very self-reliant and have a great capacity to enjoy your own company. If you want to build a social life you will have to make a determined effort, otherwise you can slide into loneliness and depression. Temping for a big company can pay dividends here as you may be able to join its sports and social activities.

If you are seeking your fortune in the metropolis with a companion, you may be able to rent a double bedsitter for around £60 to £75 a week. This may or may not include bills.

Look ahead

It can also be worth advertising under the Accommodation Wanted section of the local newspaper of the area you want to live in. Outside London, try notice boards, local papers and in smaller communities you could do worse than mention what you are looking for in the local village shop or pub.

And, of course, if you are already working, spread the word around that you are looking for somewhere else to live and ask your colleagues if they know of anywhere suitable.

Whatever type of accommodation you choose, you will almost certainly be asked to supply references and to pay a week or a month's rent in advance, according to whether the rent is paid weekly or monthly, plus a further sum as a deposit against damage caused while you are there. This means that your last month's accommodation will, in effect, be 'free' as you will already have paid for it, but it is a hefty sum to find at the start, so be sure to obtain a receipt.

Hostels

Hostels are listed in the Yellow Pages. Best-known are the YMCA and YWCA, which publish a handbook of hostels, and 'the Y' has, over the years, provided a welcome stepping stone for newcomers to cities all over the world. The big snag here is the waiting list, which can be from, three to six months.

If you are fortunate enough to get a room at a hostel, a single room, with shower will cost £55.54 per week for the first month, reducing to £49.74 thereafter. Twin and double rooms are also available and some have access to a communal kitchen.

Having secured your accommodation, be sure that all payments are recorded in a rent book. If your landlord is reluctant to provide one, you can buy one from a newsagent and ensure that each payment of rent is dated and signed for so that in the event of a dispute, you have evidence of having paid your rent on time.

If you send cheques to your landlord, still keep a rent book with the recorded cheque numbers and dates. Again, if there is a dispute, it will save you looking through all your cheque stubs to ascertain what you paid and when.

Buying a home

Most temps will be either renting property or living in the family home. For many people the ultimate wish is to own their own property. This way, rather than paying rent which only goes to line the pocket of the landlord, the monthly mortgage payments are being invested in property, considered to be one of the most secure forms of investment available.

As a temp you might be inclined to think that buying a home is something you will have to put off for the future. However, that doesn't have to be the case. Although your employment may only be on a temporary basis, most mortgage lenders will still consider an application if you can show that you are in a sound financial situation and have a good record of regular past temporary employment, which would indicate a strong likelihood of regular future employment. A lender will primarily be concerned with your ability to repay the loan. The onus will be on you to prove that you are a reputable character. Evidence of regular earnings, either by your pay slips, or bank statements, will be looked for. Some agencies will provide mortgage reference forms indicating length of service and average earnings, which will be an additional help.

The amount you can borrow will probably be related to your average earnings. Most lenders have 'income multiples' which will be used, eg. three times your income. These are only a guideline, and the ability to repay is still the most important concern.

Many books are available on the subject of buying a home and banks and building societies provide general booklets. Although being a temp will make buying your own home harder, it does not make it impossible.

A way of life

Although temping can be exciting, and being a rolling stone means you are always moving on to pastures new, the lack of involvement with an organisation can become stressful. You may get the feeling of being with the company but not of it — this succession of superficial relationships may begin to pall. Perhaps after some months, you will find your niche and join the permanent staff. Only you can decide for how long temping will continue to be your way of life.

Answers

1 NO! Your coats may not be your sexiest clothing investment but their quality, style and condition say a lot about you. You need at least three — a hardwearing raincoat, a classic wool full-length design and a jacket (three quarter length is most versatile and practical). Buy the best quality you can afford and rest them between wearings on padded, not wire, hangers.

2 YES! Women who have a polished, groomed look with appropriate make-up and hairstyle feel more confident. Don't cheat the effort of a great outfit by not bothering with the final touches. Spend 15 minutes minimum, on make-up and hair each day.

3 YES! Of course! To receive a compliment you don't need to be flashy or dress in designer clothes. The key is to learn how to dress your best so that people notice you.

4 NO! If something doesn't suit you don't wear it. You'll look and feel uncomfortable. Save the blouse to wear when Aunt Sophie visits or give it to charity.

5 YES! Your hosiery is an essential finishing touch. Take pride and pleasure in choosing elegant shades which blend with your work clothes. Avoid overly-patterned, colourful or sexy styles for work.

6 YES! It's important to know what looks are appropriate for different occasions, audiences and work placements.

7 YES! You may think a belt is a belt. Not so. Select the best quality accessories you can afford. If they are well chosen you can wear them with most of your wardrobe. You don't need drawers full of scarves, belts and costume jewellery, only a few contemporary styles which will help you update from previous seasons.

8 NO! You will find your clothes will go further if you use them in different ways. Spend a spare hour looking through the wardrobe to see how you can make alternative combinations by using the same clothes. Don't be boring — use your imagination.

The Survivor's Checklist

Armed with the right attributes, information and a good measure of common sense you will be able to survive the life of a London Temp. Keep the following points in mind:

- Accept that there will be lean times and budget for them.
- Build a good relationship with your temp controller.
- Make sure you're qualified for your assignments.
- Be flexible in terms of lunches and overtime, but always check with the agency before accepting extra work.
- Dress well and make a good impression.
- Check your travel routes to work and don't be late! See the tube map on page 230.
- Eat well and take some exercise — swimming or yoga are painless and fulfilling.
- Make sure home is a haven. It's crucial to have somewhere you feel safe, comfortable and relaxed.

Chapter 4

Money Matters

Your income will probably be earned on an irregular basis which means that the management of your money is extremely important.

For example, you may enjoy several weeks continuous work and begin to feel quite well off. The temptation to indulge in a few luxuries may just be too great — and why not? — you have worked hard enough for the money. Then, suddenly, several bills all arrive at once. Some are a little larger than you thought possible and one you had forgotten about. We all know the situation. It starts with the familiar — 'if only I'd ....' and ends with a few difficult weeks trying to save on more essential spending to make ends meet.

But this need not the be case. Financial institutions — banks and building societies in particular — can be helpful. They can help you budget properly and ensure that the rainy days aren't so bad after all. Current accounts with cheque books and cash cards are an easy way to pay and receive money. Savings and deposit accounts will earn you interest on your money. Then, when you need to dip into the red, there is a whole range of borrowing and credit schemes, one of which will no doubt be tailored to your needs.

Bank on it

In today's world, a bank or building society account is essential. But having opened an account, keeping control of your finances is also important.

From time to time, bank managers meet customers who admit to being 'hopeless with money' and let their finances get into a real mess. The problems often arise, not simply through overspending, but because the customer has no system for checking and controlling their day-to-day finances.

Most people gradually evolve their own method of looking after their money and if you have a system that works, then stick to it. But, for those who have recently started work and for those who receive an irregular income and regularly find that they have 'too many days left before the next payment is received' here are a few tips.

Working it out

A certain amount of self discipline is, of course, essential. But how do you know how much you can spend? Well, the first thing to do is ask your bank for a regular statement, perhaps a monthly one two days after any major regular bills are paid, eg. your mortgage or rent. When you get the statement, devote a little time, say five minutes, to what is called a bank account reconciliation. It sounds complicated, but is really quite simple. Here's what to do:

a Go through your cheque book and tick on the cheque stubs all cheques that have been debited on your statement, cross ticking the cheque on your statement.

b Add up all the cheques you have issued but that have not yet been prepared.

c List all the payments you know you will have to make during the rest of the month for example, outstanding bills, standing orders.

d Add the totals of (b) and (c) and deduct the final balance of your bank statement. If the bank statement already shows you are overdrawn this total should be added on, increasing the overdraft — in which case go and see the bank quickly!

Hopefully, however, there will still be a credit balance — what you might call your spending money!

If the system is to work it is essential that you not only fill in all your cheque book stubs, but that you also carefully note all withdrawals you make from automatic cash dispensers. Why not record these on your cheque book stub when you make the withdrawal?

Some people like to note the 'revised' bank balance on their cheque book stub and keep a running total throughout the month by deducting any cheques made out or withdrawals made. This 'revised' figure will give you a starting point. It shows you where you are.

The budget action plan

A rough budget plan will be useful, setting out your income against likely expenses over a set period, such as a month. A week will be too short a span to be of use. If one week you are faced with a major cost — the gas bill for example — it will ruin a plan for that week. A plan that spreads over a month is more realistic, as the ups or downs of one week can be balanced out. Below are two situations.

Plan A — Copy Typist earning £5 per hour

Monthly work schedule

2 weeks full-time work	70 hours
1 week — 4 days only	28 hours
1 week — 2 days only	14 hours
TOTAL	112 hours

Income		£
Gross Pay:	112 hours @ £5 per hour	560.00
Deductions:	National Insurance 9%	50.40
Taxable pay:	(£560 — £200 = £360); tax at 25%	90.00
TOTAL DEDUCTIONS		140.40
Net pay		419.60

Expenditure		£
Rent		160
Travel pass Rent		35
Bills		40
Shopping:	food	60
	clothes	75
TOTAL		370
Balance remaining £44.60		

Plan B — Word processor operator £8 per hour

Monthly work schedule

Three weeks full-time	105 hours
One week — one day	7 hours
TOTAL	112 hours

Income £
Gross pay:	112 hours @ £8 per hour	896.00
Deductions	National Insurance 9%	80.64
Taxable pay	(£896 — £200 = £696); tax at 25%	174.00
TOTAL DEDUCTIONS		254.64
Net pay		641.36

Expenditure £
Rent	200
Travel	40
Bills	50
Shopping: food	70
clothes	40
Access bill	50
Entertainment	80
TOTAL	530

Balance remaining £111.36	£50 to savings account
	£40 driving lesson
	£21.36 surplus

Budget plans explained

Working out from your gross salary how much you will be paid can be a mystery. There are two main deductions:

- National Insurance — 9% of gross salary
- Income Tax — everybody is allowed to earn a certain amount each year before they have to pay tax. For most temps this will be the single person's allowance which at present is £2,600, or £50 per week. So in a four week budget plan, £200 will be tax-free. Deduct £200 from gross salary to find your taxable pay. This amount will be taxed at 25%.

If you are not employed for the whole of a tax year, you won't use

> up all of your single person's allowance. In that case you will be entitled to a tax refund, which can be arranged through your tax office.

How much do you need?

As a temp, you cannot guarantee full-time work, so base your budget plan on a reasonable estimate of the amount of work you will get. In these examples, a couple of weeks of full-time work and a couple of weeks with only a few days' work are used.

Some outgoings are easy to predict, others are not so. Travel and rent are likely to be much the same from month to month, so put a regular amount aside. As we all know, bills, like buses, come in groups. But if you put aside £40 per month, some bills can be paid in the next month, or else you can save up extra to pay two or three bills in one go.

The amount needed for entertainment will vary widely from person to person. A drinking, smoking, car-owning, night-clubber is going to need much more than a more reserved counterpart.

Convenience cash

When choosing a cheque account, be careful on the overdrafts policy. It is reasonable to assume that as a temp you will often be overdrawn, perhaps when the weekly cheque is paid late because of a bank holiday. You will be expected to have held an account for a little while before being allowed a large overdraft, but you will be given some leeway without permission. Don't push it though. If the bank or building society starts bouncing cheques, they will make charges for this and life starts to get difficult. See the section on borrowing for further thoughts on overdrafts.

The other thing you will want is convenience. These days money is available through cash machines, or ATMs (automated teller machines) as they are known in industry jargon.

Money anytime, anyplace

In a rush of good sense, banks and building societies have woken up to the fact that what the customer wants is as many cash machines in as many different places as possible. So, as well as adding more of their own machines, expansion has been hastened by joining the networks of rivals. Amongst the major institutions, it means that Barclays' and Lloyds' customers can use each other's machines; National Westminster, Midland and TSB have a similar arrangement; more recently, all the building societies, along with Girobank and the Co-Op Bank, have joined together to become the third largest network.

These three major networks of machines should fit most people's requirements. Which one you opt for is up to you — choose the one which has a machine nearest to your home, station, or bus stop.

Though most people have a cash machine card as part of their cheque account, cards can be attached to other accounts, such as savings accounts. Improvements in the design of cash machines means that they can provide a range of services other than just cash withdrawals — paying cash or cheques, providing statements, even payment of bills is now possible through some ATMs.

Life savings

Savings accounts are useful. They will pay a better rate of interest than is provided by a current account, but unless you have thousands of pounds to save, the interest is unlikely to far outstrip inflation. The advantage of a savings account is that it will help you put money aside for a holiday, a car or simply for future emergencies. Hopefully you won't spend it until you really need it. Try saving a certain amount each month — an amount which should be not too large, nor too small.

The type of savings accounts you have depends on two things — the amount of money and the length of time for which you are prepared to commit it. Building societies and banks will have a basic account which can be opened with £1 and pay in and take out of, when you like. If you have a larger lump sum with which to open the account, say £500; if you can put money away and give one month or three months' notice to withdraw, again you will probably find more interest by shopping around.

Borrowing money

The 1980's has been the decade of massive expansion in credit. The number of people borrowing money has grown; the average amount being borrowed has increased. Two factors have caused this change.

- There are more financial institutions making loans, marketing them more aggressively and making credit more widely available.
- Growing economic confidence and prosperity have encouraged people to borrow more. If people are happy that their job will exist, and that their pay will be higher, this time next year, then they will see credit as a useful, even a sensible option.

It is the second point that should particularly concern any temp thinking of borrowing. If you have doubts about being able to repay the loan then don't take it on in the first place. For the temp with job security of no more than a week, careful thought is necessary.

If careful thought doesn't deter you, then ensure your finances are well planned. As a rule of thumb, keeping loans at less than two weeks typical net salary may prove useful. If the future prospects for regular work look hazy, then reduce that to one week.

In considering borrowing options, scrutinise the APR (annual percentage rate). All lenders are required by law to display the APR on advertising or promotional material relating to loans.

What can I do if I overspend?

Where are times when money simply won't go the distance, even with the best intentions — your rail or bus season ticket could go rocketing up in price, for example.

That's when you'll find your local branch can be very helpful. You should contact the staff who are very experienced in dealing with all types of money problems and they will be happy to talk to you.

If you need to arrange an overdraft to tide you over a period of peak expenditure, then advice can be given to you on how to handle your budget to deal with the problem.

Overdrafts

There will be times when some borrowing is necessary, and an overdraft on your cheque account may be the most useful way of dealing with this. If you have an account that makes no charges when you are overdrawn, the only cost you will have on the overdraft is interest on the amount borrowed. Check this interest rate carefully: it shouldn't exceed the amount you would have been charged for a personal loan.

Most companies will prefer you to have operated your account smoothly, ie. without going overdrawn too often, before granting overdrafts.

Typically, overdrafts will be charged at an interest rate of 7% above base rate, though this will be subject to negotiation and individual circumstances. Remember, always ask before you issue cheques that will create an overdraft and try to present your case in a logical way showing that you have carefully considered how repayment is to be made. A few notes and figures on a piece of paper often help to clarify the position.

NatWest has a new type of overdraft facility which is a permanent standing overdraft known as Credit Zone. It can cost you less than normal overdraft charges and there are no specific repayment arrangements. As long as you stay within your personal limit, you can normally repay the Bank as and when you want. Interest is charged at 1.7% per month on the balance outstanding and there is a £5 per quarter usage fee should you dip into the Credit Zone facility.

Personal loans

For a lump sum purchase, a personal loan can be considered. If you want to buy a car, or an expensive holiday, a personal loan of £1,000 over two years might look attractive and within the scope of your budget. But it will be a long-term commitment, so taking on a personal loan may not be a wise move for temps.

Credit cards

Taking a loan by deferring payments via a credit card is probably the simplest and most flexible approach open to the temp. You can delay payment for up to seven weeks without paying interest. This means that for this period you have extra money in the account. In effect, a free loan.

The world of credit cards is dominated by Access and Visa, the two most widely distributed cards. With these, a bill is sent once a month detailing payments made on the cards. Twenty five days or so are usually allowed for payment, after which time the balance on the card starts to incur interest. Interest will be calculated from the date the item went on the bill, not the end of the interest expiry period.

Access and Visa cards are issued by a broad range of financial companies, who introduce differing approaches — a Lloyd's Access card is not the same as a Midland Access card. New institutions are differentiating their cards, by linking them with donations to charity or charging markedly lower interest rates. There are some simple rules to follow:

- Every time you use your card you are given a receipt for payment. Keep this so that you can keep track of how much you are spending.
- At the end of the month carry out a credit card account reconciliation using your statement just as you did with your cheque account.
- Always take into account the amount of money you spend on your credit card when working out your 'where am I now' position and your budgets.

Charge cards

Many retail chains issue their own brand credit cards, known as charge cards. Usually the rate charged will be higher than other credit cards. Two considerations therefore apply. The store card may bring other privileges such as a discount on items or a member's magazine. If you are a regular user of that particular store, the advantages may outweigh the penalty of higher interest rates. Secondly, certain stores only accept their own charge card. Marks & Spencer is the most notable example. In these cases, if you are a moderate user of the store, their card may be a sensible option.

Don't forget that the day-to-day expenditure for the week will also be considerable. Papers, magazines, bars of chocolate, stamps and the variety of things you buy without thinking about it will be £5 and £10 per week.

A plan is pointless if it is not kept to. If the budget says only £40 a month for clothes, then only spend £40. Note that each plan leaves a surplus amount, around £20 a month. You will always need a little extra to fall back on. Naturally, over a period of months, you may want to adapt the plan. You might discover that in one category you have been overspending, another underspending, so re-adjust to meet these circumstances.

What to do with your pay cheque

The last thing you need as a temp is trouble with your money — being unable to get cash when you want it, cheques being bounced or charges on your account. Two prime considerations apply:

- Convenience — you need to be able to get to money without problems.
- Flexibility — you need to be unrestricted by the threat of charges if you stray a little overdrawn.

Fortunately in this last respect, things have been getting a little easier.

Building societies led the way with cheque accounts that offered the full range of services — cheque book, cheque card, cash machine card, standing orders and direct debits — but with two additional features: interest paid on balances and no charges for transactions, even when overdrawn. Not surprisingly these accounts, first offered by Nationwide Anglia and Abbey National, were extremely popular. The banks have responded with similar services.

This is all good news for the temp of course. The policy of making no charges, even when the account goes into overdraft, has particular appeal. Usually you will only be charged interest on the amount you have overdrawn.

Credit checking

When applying for a credit card or even a cheque guarantee card, your application will be subject to a process of credit checking; ie. looking through your details, finding out if you have any bad debts, asking your bankers if you are regularly overdrawn, etc. You must meet certain criteria before the application will be approved.

This is often a source of worry for people, who conjure up images of Big Brother. Under the Data Protection Act you are entitled to find out all the information that is held about you on computer files. If you find yourself rejected for a card, ask the organisation to put you in touch with the credit rating company, who for a fee of £1 will supply the full details held about you.

Being rejected for a particular credit card does not necessarily mean that you have a permanent 'no' against your name. Some of the new lower interest cards are only available on particular minimum incomes, which as a temp you may not qualify for. Try and find out if there are particular conditions to qualify before applying for the card.

Credit rating systems will keep close records on you. So, if you do get a reputation as a bad payer then it may be hard to shake this off. Becoming a bad payer does not mean just being late with one month's payments, you may find yourself not only in trouble with the credit card company, but in difficulties in getting credit from other firms for several years to come.

The Money Matters Checklist

It is essential that you learn to manage your money well — the following points may help you:

1. Choose a bank or building society which offers the range of services that meet your needs.
2. Work out a budget action plan to help you manage your money, on a regular basis.
3. Carry out a regular bank account reconciliation exercise.
4. However irregular your income, always try to put something away into a savings account.
5. Assess the various options and costs of borrowing money.
6. Aim to live within your earning power.

Chapter 5

Business Organisation

If you have read the first four chapters, you've got a good idea how to make a success of the temping life, from budgets to home building, from your agency to your health. But what about the environments you'll be working in? This chapter tells you about the types of organisation which exist and the ones you'll be working in.

As a temp, you do face the disadvantage of not knowing about the place you work in. Unlike permanent staff you won't have an induction course, but the next few pages can at least guide you through general aspects of the organisations you'll be working in.

The Business spectrum

Basically organisations may be split into profit-making and non-profit making concerns. The former includes both manufacturing/trading concerns and service industries like banking and insurance while the latter will cover things like hospitals and educational establishments.

Organisations also fall into what are known as the public or private sectors. The public sector can be divided into two categories — state-owned or nationalised undertakings like the Bank of England and British Rail, and municipal undertakings in which the services are operated by local authorities for the benefit of the community in general. The private sector is made up of the rest.

A lot of choice

The aspect of temping which is so different from a permanent post is the variety of organisations in which you will work. Literally all kinds of organisations seek the help of temporary staff — from the small business which normally relies on one person to run the office to the multinational corporation employing hundreds of office personnel.

Obviously there will be considerable differences in the type and range of work on offer and it is important to give some thought to your own preferences and where you think would best fit in, given your experience and personality.

For example, you may have previously worked for a particular type of firm or you may have special skills such as foreign languages, or legal knowledge which make you marketable for certain types of vacancy. Your own profile will, therefore, have a bearing on the type of agencies you sign up with (many specialise in filling particular types of vacancy) and the type of work you would ideally like to do.

Small businesses

Recent years have seen the resurgence of the small business and consequently the need for office support staff. Small firms are concerned with a range of business, from the manufacture of, for example, small industrial components to the design and manufacture of clothes, jewellery, toys and craft items. They can be small scale catering outlets, or providers of business, professional or consultancy services. Whatever the enterprise, office and secretarial support of some kind will be required.

Flexibility

Perhaps the main quality sought in someone working for a small business is flexibility and a willingness to turn your hand to anything and everything as required. Remember that many small businesses operate on a fairly tight budget so premises may be less sumptuous than large offices with fewer staff amenities and they may be situated further away from shops and other facilities — perhaps even on one of the many new small industrial complexes.

Also, there may be relatively few staff which means that less instant help is available if you get stuck, and you could be left to your own devices fairly quickly. In a small business you must feel confident enough to act more on your own initiative than you would in a larger firm.

Claire spent 2 months working as a temp for a small publishing company in South London. 'The work was varied and pressurized and I found myself doing lots of different tasks on the same day. I had to be flexible because there weren't any other secretaries — just me! It was great fun though, because you were a team working together toward the same goals. I have worked in big banks and large city businesses and found them too impersonal.'

Partnerships

Many partnerships operate within what can loosely be termed 'the professions', eg. lawyers, accountants, architects, surveyors, estate agents and financial consultants. So, the nature of the work frequently carries a high degree of confidentiality. The organisation depends on its relationship with its clients and business is frequently secured on a reputation for a high quality, reliable service.

There will be certain expectations within this sort of organisation in terms of the level of professionalism provided by all staff — permanent and temporary. In this respect 'professionalism' will include things like:

- Accuracy of work presented
- Attention to detail
- Good communication and interpersonal skills
- Appropriate self-presentation
- Tact and discretion
- Maintenance of strict confidentiality at all times
- Ability to reflect the image of the organisation.

Can you keep a secret?

Confidentiality was the key to Sarah's success when she took up a temporary assignment with a firm of solicitors. 'I have always prided myself in my ability to keep quiet when it matters,' says Sarah, 'though I confess, some of the work was so interesting I wanted to talk about it. I often go back to temp for the firm because they know I'm efficient and trustworthy.'

Companies

Limited companies are set up for all types of businesses. They may be private, where the maximum number of shareholders is restricted and where shares are not offered for sale on the open market. They may be public liability companies, where there is no upper limit in terms of the number of shareholders and where shares are quoted on the Stock Exchange.

The local or national dimension?

If you are temping in your own area it is likely that you will know something about the company in which you are to work. It may, for example, be a long-established firm with a sound reputation as a good employer. You may even know people who work there and something about its line of business, of course, this can be an advantage. Alternatively, you may be sent to work for a company which has branches nationwide, with perhaps even an international scale of operations.

In both instances it is helpful to try to find out something about the nature of the business either in advance or at least as soon as you start to work there, particularly if you're on a long assignment. A little background knowledge not only helps make your work more interesting, but it enables you to build up a file of your temping appointments and this can prove useful later.

Manufacturing or service industries?

Most organisations are concerned with the manufacture of goods or the provision of services. While the former can easily be described as 'product producing' in that the main function is to produce goods and sell them at a profit, service industries cover a wider field. They may or may not be motivated by profit. For example, they may be providing a service whereby the nature of the office work is concerned with what might usefully be termed as 'people processing'. Here people are the main focus of attention and are put through some programme of activity for their own benefit, as in the case of a hospital or some form of welfare service. Alternatively, service industries exist to add to the quality of life as in the case of libraries, museums, theatres, leisure industries, hotels, restaurants, travel agents and retail stores.

The nature of an organisation's activities will affect the way in which it operates and the scale and nature of office and administrative support that it requires.

Categories of organisation

A quick glance through the job pages of any newspaper will provide a useful indication of the types of organisation in which you might be placed and, broadly speaking, they will fall into one of the 20 general categories listed below:

Manufacturing
Construction and property
Engineering
Scientific
Electricity, oil and gas
Education
Government
Technology
Retail and distribution
Import and export
Legal
Medical
Banking and finance
Accounting
Hotel and catering
Leisure
Media and publishing
Travel
Advertising and public relations
Registered charities.

Obviously, some will be instantly more appealing and attractive to you than others. However, you should guard against jumping to the wrong conclusions.

Don't judge a book by its cover

There is a danger in labelling some organisations as 'likely to be boring' and others as 'bound to be interesting and exciting'. For example, the hotel and fashion industries are invariably less glamorous behind the scenes than you would imagine. Remember that money is more likely to be injected into what is seen by the customer than into the offices which serve to support the front of house operation. On the other hand a company manufacturing steel tubes or electrical components may have very modern, well-equipped offices with excellent staff facilities. Many heavy or light industrial concerns boast the latest in office technology. It is often through the efficiency of their office support that they are able to operate effectively in a very competitive market.

Here's what some temps have to say about assignments they've had.

Tina thought it was a dream come true when she got a long-term assignment with a fashion house. 'It turned out to be very dull,' says Tina. 'All the glamour was for the models and the shows none of which I was involved in.'

Sarah groaned when she was asked to turn up bright and early on a Monday at an engineering company. 'I thought it would be dull and noisy, but far from it, the offices had the latest equipment and I loved the work.'

Banking was tough work for Andrea. 'The hours were very long and breaks were at a minimum. I ended up earning a lot though.'

'Medical secretarial work was fascinating, I was so glad I had the skills for the work,' says Amanda.

A language of its own

Every type of work has its own specialist vocabulary and it can sometimes take a while to get the hang of it. You will encounter words which you have never heard of before let alone know what they mean and this takes a bit of getting used to. Always be sure to ask if you are in doubt about anything and note it down somewhere so that you will know the next time. It's surprising how quickly you will become accustomed to completely new language and, of course, once you have acquired a certain type of expertise it can prove useful for other jobs with similar firms in the near future.

The family tree

When you work for a small firm it is relatively easy to figure out who's who and how things are done. However, when you work for a large organisation it can be difficult to visualise just how it is set up and where the department, in which you are to be placed, fits into the general scheme of things.

Looking at a large organisation on paper is a bit like looking at the family tree of the Royal Family. There are many branches and many inter-relationships. Many large companies actually have formal organisation charts drawn up and a typical one is shown in Figure 1.

This chart shows the breakdown of a typical manufacturing organisation with separate divisions for the production, service and marketing functions. As you can see from the diagram each division is sub-divided into departments or areas of working activity. Just like the branches of a family tree these departments can be further sub-divided into sections of activity within the department and yet again into actual roles within the sections.

In fact, the sub-dividing can continue until individuals are each in a position to distinguish where exactly, within the total organisation, they fit in. An example of this sub-division is provided in the diagram, Figure 2, (page 94) illustrating the breakdown of work in an Administration Department within virtually any type of organisation you can think of whether in the manufacturing or service industries.

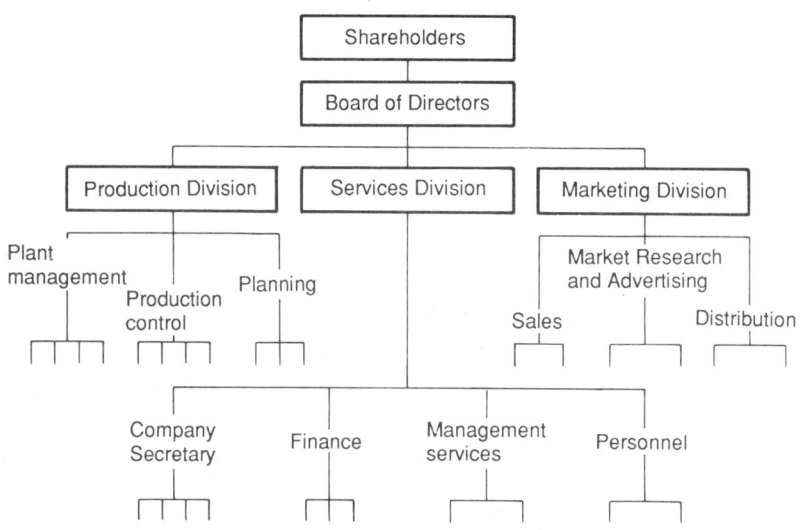

Figure 1 Organisation chart

Workplace hierarchy

Organisation charts tend to be shaped rather like pyramids, ie. they are narrow at the top and broad at the bottom, with the 'boss' represented at the apex of the pyramid and the workforce forming the base line. Throughout the pyramid individuals will have different degrees of authority and levels of responsibility in accordance with their position in what is termed the 'hierarchy'. (See Figure 3 page 95).

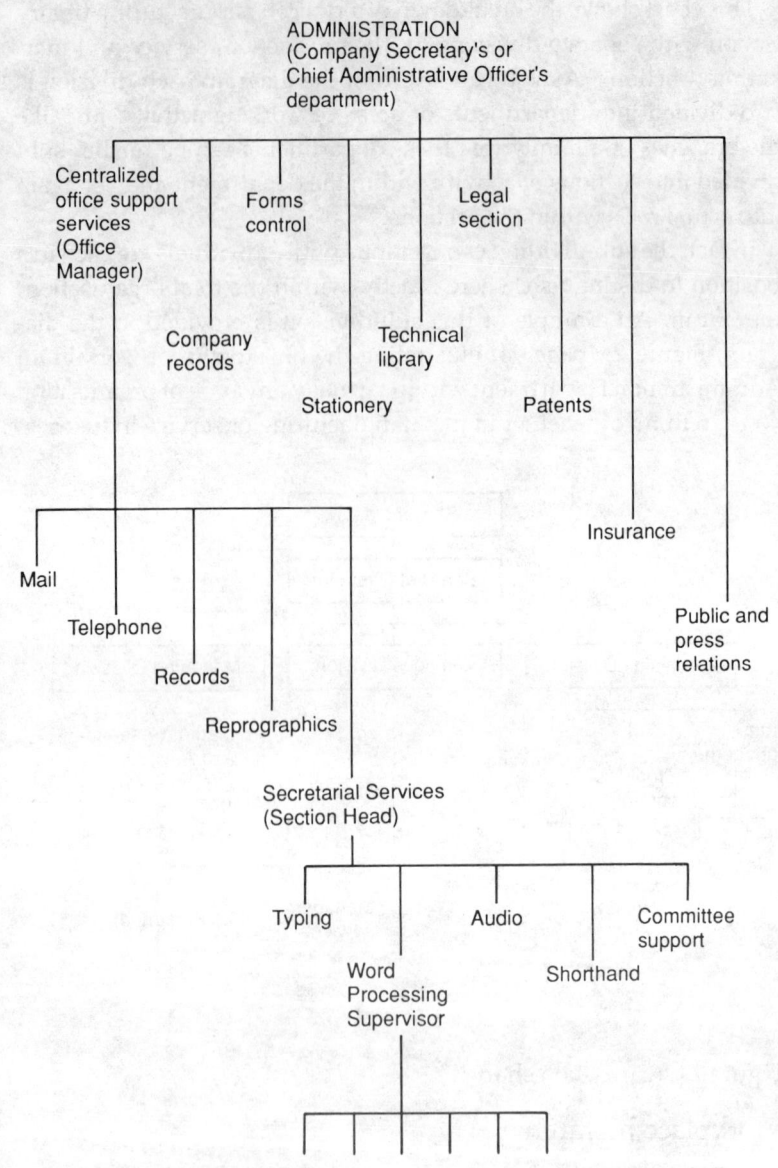

Figure 2 The administration function

Every organisation needs to be structured in such a way that duties, tasks and responsibilities can be carried out effectively so that the organisation achieves its objectives. This means that certain individuals will occupy positions of authority with the right to exercise control over others. Typically authority rests with top management who determines overall policy for the company and decides how it may best be put into practice. Clearly, however, one or two individuals at senior management level within a large company cannot undertake all managerial functions. Therefore a system of what is known as delegation results with middle management and supervisory roles emerging further down the pyramid.

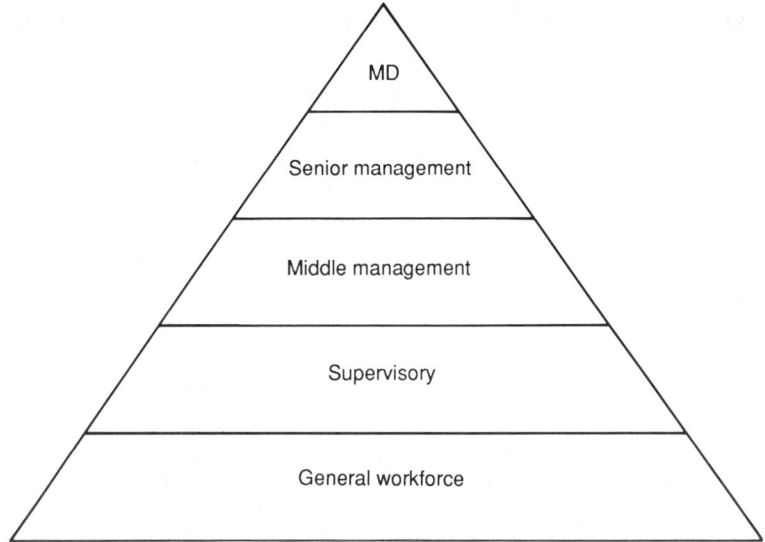

Figure 3 Organisational pyramid

Delegation

At its simplest authority may be passed in a straight line from the top to the bottom of an organisation rather like in the armed forces. However, it is more likely to be spread widely across an organisation according to the functions carried out and the expertise possessed by different departmental managers. For example the Sales Manager would have authority over all the Sales personnel while the Company Secretary of Chief Administrative Officer would have authority over all those working within the Administration function.

However, where these departments are large in themselves they will be broken into different sections and authority will be delegated to respective section heads or supervisors. Such a structure obviously makes sense as it would be impossible if every single instruction had to come from the Managing Director — nothing would ever get done!

Who's your boss?

When you take on a temping job you are, of course, paid by the agency and any major problem you may experience with regard to the placement will ultimately need to be taken up with the temp controller who has placed you. This might, for example, be in relation to the type of work you are being asked to do or it may be something to do with your hours or working conditions.

However, as far as the actual work itself is concerned you will be taking instructions from someone in the firm which is hiring your services. It is important to establish at the outset the identity of this person (or perhaps it may be more than one person) because it is to him or her that you will be accountable on a day to day basis for the work you are doing. Some firms are more accustomed to dealing with temporary staff than others so it will be useful to study the Survival Tips given earlier.

Work load

The level of responsibility that you can reasonably expect to be given will depend on the type of placement and its duration. Where you are filling in for say a couple of days, you are probably providing emergency cover of some kind and all that can reasonably be expected of you is that you perform to the best of your ability, submitting accurate, neat work of a standard that reflects well on you and your agency. Where, on the other hand, your placement may be for a longer period it is likely that a much more clearly defined workplan will have been drawn up in advance, and consequently it is possible that the position may call for a much higher level of responsibility with more opportunity to demonstrate your range of skills and abilities.

Around the company

Since organisations can be of many different kinds offering a range of alternative structures, the variations in terms of departments and sections and what they are called will be equally diverse.

If we were to take the lid off a typical manufacturing company the following represent the main areas of activity and provide details of their main functions and responsibilities, together with an indication of the particular kind of office work that is likely to be found.

Purchasing department

In most large organisations the purchasing function tends to be centralised with one department responsible for buying all goods used by the organisation from raw materials, to plant, machinery and equipment, to fixtures and fittings, to office stationery, to food for the canteen.

The functions and responsibilities of the department will include the following:

- Researching markets and suppliers.
- Negotiating the best prices and terms.
- Drawing up and placing contracts.
- Monitoring stock levels and maintaining stock control procedures.
- Checking goods received against invoices and dealing with any discrepancies.
- Matching deliveries to production schedules.

A lot of documentation and record keeping will be involved in this work and many strict procedures will need to be adhered to. Special forms will be used for different aspects of the work.

Production department

This department is primarily concerned with the manufacture of goods and will usually be a mix of engineering, planning and control sections. It is the heart of the organisation and almost represents a business in its own right as the range of duties and responsibilities can be very wide and are likely to include some of the following:

- Matching orders and sales forecasts to the workforce, materials and machines available.
- Ensuring that delivery dates can be met.

- Batching orders to ensure economic production.
- Working to specified standards, eg. BSI specifications or EEC regulations.
- Maintaining safety standards.
- Carrying out work study exercises.
- Designing special tools for use in the manufacturing process.
- Setting up and carrying out quality control tests.
- Controlling stock levels.
- Monitoring and recording machine breakdowns.
- Rescheduling work where necessary.
- Liaising with other departments to ensure the product range is appropriate.
- Diversifying as necessary to comply with innovation and change.

Once again there will be a lot of form-filling, peculiar to the production activity involved as well as accurate figure work and record keeping and inter-departmental meetings.

Research and development department

Sometimes viewed as part of the Production Department itself, this is the area which is concerned with improving the company's existing products and developing new ones. It is very much the area of technological innovation and as such is an expensive area for any organisation to fund but an essential one where companies wish to retain a competitive edge. The functions and responsibilities will include:

- Designing, developing and testing new products.
- Making short term improvements or modifications to existing products.
- Setting up long term research projects.
- Engaging in pure or applied research.
- Suggesting ways in which an organisation might diversify its activities.

There is likely to be a certain amount of secret or classified work going on in such departments and consequently temporary staff are unlikely to be directly involved. However, it may be that permanent office support is thin on the ground and where proposals, specifications and bills of quantity need to be submitted to meet tight deadlines it is possible that agency staff may be called in to help.

Marketing department

This can be a very large section and one which is central to any organisation. For convenience it can be split into three principal areas of activity: research, sales and distribution.

Research embraces things like market research, advertising and customer relations and will include the following:

- Preparing mail shots.
- Distributing samples.
- Processing questionnaires.
- Organising sales promotion exercises and exhibitions.
- Processing complaints.
- Providing after sales advice and service.
- Disseminating product information.

Sales, which includes both home and export sales, is the focal aspect of the marketing function in that it involves selling the actual goods or services to the consumer. The work will include:

- Processing all documentation.
- Monitoring and analysing sales.
- Routing queries to appropriate sales personnel.
- Preparing statistics in relation to sales figures.
- Communicating with branches, agents and overseas outlets.

Distribution is also an important aspect of marketing as there is little point in a company producing a good product which customers want if it cannot reach the market in good condition and in the fastest possible time. The areas of activity involved include:

- Warehousing.
- Transport.
- Overseas freight handling.
- Wholesaling.
- Franchising.

All these areas of activity involve a considerable amount of communication and paperwork. Staff supporting the marketing function is an administrative capacity will be required to complete a wide range of forms and specialist documents. Marketing departments sink or swim on latest sales figures so there is usually a high level of pressurised activity with peaks and troughs associated with the work.

It is also worth remembering that while it is easier to associate the concept of marketing with goods, it is perfectly feasible to market all manner of services, as well as less tangible commodities like places and entertainment. So you could easily find yourself working in the marketing department of your local authority offices!

Finance and accounting department

All organisations ultimately measure the extent of their success or failure in financial terms and so all will have departments dealing with financial matters. Finance is important to a company at all stages of its operation from the raising of initial funds, through its day to day running to the production of final results in terms of profit or loss. The nature and size of the organisation will determine the type of financial procedures and systems which operate and the way in which the work is divided. Whatever the organisation financial and accounting functions and responsibilities will be likely to include:

- Preparing company accounts.
- Keeping accurate financial records.
- Analysing all receipts and payments.
- Calculating and paying out wages and salaries.
- Preparing departmental budgets.
- Carrying out cost control exercises.
- Setting up and monitoring credit control systems.
- Checking financial transactions within the company via a system of internal audits and checks.
- Investigating alternative sources of funding.
- Dealing with tax matters.
- Introducing computerised systems of financial management.

If you are going to work in this area, it is helpful if you have an interest in financial matters and you don't feel threatened by figures. There are growing and well paid opportunities for secretarial and office personnel in finance offices generally.

In any case, we are no longer talking about your skills in mental arithmetic and your ability to fully understand the intricacies of double entry book-keeping. Such are the advances in computer assisted techniques that a lot of the routine work is done for you. So never pass over the opportunity to learn to use any of the financial software packages, such as spreadsheets, and be sure that you are competent in the use of an electronic calculator. Above all, qualities such as good concentration, painstaking checking and accurate proof reading are needed where figure work is involved.

Administration department

This is the principal paperwork department in any organisation and as such it will deal with the day to day running of all office type activities. In today's world it would be impossible for the organisation to survive without the high level of administrative assistance that it relies on to support its main activity, whether that be manufacturing baked beans or running a hospital.

Regardless of the talk of paperless offices it is virtually impossible to conceive of a business operating without the mass of forms, returns and records that need to be processed every day – not to mention the internal memoranda that circulate!

As far as describing what is classified as administration, this will vary enormously depending on the organisation concerned, although it is likely to resemble the breakdown of activities given in Figure 2. Functions and responsibilities are, therefore, likely to include:

- Dealing with all aspects of mail handling and processing.
- Providing a telephone service.
- Typing and word processing.
- Shorthand and audio dictation services.
- Duplicating and photocopying.
- Maintaining filing and record systems.
- Controlling and issuing stationery supplies.
- Maintaining up-to-date technical libraries.
- Cataloguing work.
- Providing committee support for meetings.

Many temping jobs will fall into this broad general category of activity, although, as has been stressed earlier, it is the nature of the organisation's activities which will determine the actual content of the work you do and in which department you do it. Nonetheless, general office work within an administration department will tend to be similar throughout many different organisations. The main things to remember will be to:

- Use the house style for all letters, memoranda, minutes, reports and other communication.
- Observe the standard conventions in terms of number and perhaps colours of copies.
- Follow the standard procedures in operation.
- Ask when in doubt.

Personnel department

The Personnel Department is responsible for everything to do with staff and broadly speaking will be concerned with recruitment and selection, training, welfare and industrial relations. Clearly small firms will not have a personnel department and staff matters will be dealt with directly by the boss. In larger organisations, however, the work will be undertaken by a specialist department. It is a particularly important area of work in that any organisation is only as good as its staff who need to be well motivated and committed to achieving the objectives set by the company they work for.

As far as temping is concerned any work undertaken for a personnel department would usually be of a relatively routine nature, given the confidentiality associated with personnel files and records. An exception might be perhaps where extra staff are required to help out during an intensive period of special interviews like, for example, the Milk Round, where large numbers of university students are interviewed for a small number of vacancies and there is a lot of paperwork to be processed in a relatively short space of time.

In general, however, the nature of much of the more interesting aspects of personnel work is such that the need for confidentiality and a certain element of specialist knowledge would rule out the likelihood of many openings.

Management services department

The term management services is taken to include the more recent range of specialist services and provisions which many organisations have introduced to support management and secure improved performance in the areas of planning, policy-making and general organisation. Where smaller companies may need to rely on outside consultants and agencies to provide such services, larger organisations find it more economical to set up their own support units. These may range from computing and data processing, to organisation and methods, to security services and facilities management — to name but a few of the possibilities.

Developments in technology have played a major part in the build up of such specialist services. Also the recognition that computer power can now be applied to so many areas of a company's activities to provide fast, accurate, up-to-date, quality information for management purposes, has brought about the introduction of many new kinds of expertise.

All this has meant that a lot of new job titles have appeared with a lot of interesting possibilities for those who enjoy the challenge of solving problems and introducing new procedures, frequently supported by modern office technology. Working for a management services unit is likely to involve contact across an organisation as the unit will provide a centralised facility for all departments who wish to make use of the provision. This means that the assignments will be varied with opportunities to get a feel for the work of the organisation as a whole.

These are the eight principal functional areas of activity which go to make up most organisations. Different types of company will select different titles to describe them in ways appropriate to their particular line of business, but in broad terms they should be reflected in the ones selected here.

Job satisfaction

Two of the common reasons people give for temping are that it gives them useful experience and provides them with opportunities to sample a variety of different organisations before looking for a permanent position.

If these are your reasons for temping, it is worth taking some simple steps to ensure that you get the most out of your jobs. Temping certainly provides you with a wealth of useful experience as well as building your confidence to tackle a selection of different jobs, and perhaps in areas you had previously dismissed.

It will be useful to keep a file listing your different placements as it soon becomes difficult to remember detail with any degree of accuracy once you have had a variety of different jobs. You should record the type of work you did, the systems and procedures you found in operation and the equipment you used, as well as the type of work carried out by the firm, the sort of organisation structure that existed and your own views of the placement in general.

This sort of information can be very helpful when you are preparing to be interviewed, either by agencies or for a permanent position. It will enable you to build up a profile of your experience and help you to elaborate on certain aspects of that experience.

As all school and college leavers soon find out, organisations want practical experience as well as theoretical knowledge and good qualifications. Therefore it is a bonus if you are able to provide a prospective employer with insight into the sort of experience you have had. The following checklists show the items you should record in your file for future reference.

Checklist of equipment you have used

Make a note of the equipment you have used including:
- Models of typewriter
- Types of word processing system
- Types of audio system
- Types of photocopier
- Models of duplicating machine
- Telephone systems and switchboards
- Telex machines
- Fax machines
- Details of any computer systems you are familiar with
- Details of any software packages, eg database, spreadsheet, desktop publishing.

Checklist of particular experiences you have had

Aim to record details of:
- Any specialist work, eg. medical, legal, financial, engineering, exporting
- Extensive telephone work undertaken
- Minute taking and committee work
- Any travel arrangements you have been responsible for
- Filing systems you have set up and/or used
- Statistical or figure work
- Anything you have done which called upon your organisational abilities
- Dealing with the general public
- Working for more than one person
- Handling money.

Chapter 6

Taking Off

As with any career, hard work and highly developed skills pay dividends and temping is no exception. So far we have discussed the pros of being a temp and how to deal with the cons. With confidence, grooming and a passion for technology your success is well within reach.

Where to now?

Decide where you are heading. If the temping world continues to hold you spellbound, stick with it. The more established you are as a reliable temporary worker, the more work will come your way as you will be one of your agency's favourites.

If you decide you want a change then don't worry because as a temp change is easy. We've already established that temping gives you the flexibility to look for new job prospects and choose a varied work environment, if you so wish.

Prospecting

If you want a career change, or have a clear ambition for greater temping success, self-development is essential and there are some rules to guide you.

Assess yourself

It is important that you assess your strengths and weaknesses when you come to consider a career change.

- What do you enjoy doing?
- Which assignment did you enjoy most and why?
- What good qualities have your clients and your temp controller commented on?
- What weaknesses do you acknowledge and what weaknesses have others pointed out?
- What aspects of work scare you the most?
- Can you cope with a 9 to 5 job, in the same environment everyday?

The crucial factor is knowing exactly, what you want to do and then giving it a 'temporary' whirl. Be honest with your temp controller, tell her what you want a career in, for example, publishing. She will do her best to find you assignments in a publishing field and you will get a taste of what's in store.

Once may be enough to decide yes or no, but remember every company is different, so it's worth sampling a few before drawing those final conclusions.

On the wanted list

You can rest assured that there is a market for office skills and over the past five years the image of the temp and the secretary have altered considerably.

With the skills you've mastered as a temporary worker, you could go on to be a top London secretary commanding a salary in excess of £15,000 a year — plus perks and bonuses.

These 'executive secretaries' range in age from late twenties to mid forties — in short, its not the age that counts, but the attitude. Employers want:

- Assertiveness
- Confidence
- Career planners
- Good personal presentation

- Good communication skills
- Motivation
- Excellent skills.

Take off with training

It is the last of these points which can be your touchstone to a key job. Training literally pays — if you put yourself onto a diploma course you will demand a higher salary and if you master new technology the story is much the same. The more software packages you are familiar with the better: Rapid File, DisplayWrite, Lotus 123 — should all be plan sailing to he high-flying career prospector in the office field.

Always remember, there's nothing to be afraid of and use your temping time well to learn about different equipment.

Self-improvement

Annie Haywood, a PA with a leading pharmaceutical company believes that temping was the springboard to her success. 'I temped for two years and loved every minute of it but for me personally there always was a time to move on. In this instance it was a conscious decision to settle down in one work environment.

'My time as a temp was invaluable. I had an excellent temp controller who did her best to develop my abilities whilst also keeping me in work. I would like to think I never wasted a single assignment. You can do your job well and take the chance to learn.'

Annie not only learnt about different types of company and work environment, she also mastered a range of equipment and wherever possible, tried to use a new software package and the latest hardware.

'Don't be afraid to say you don't know how to do something — that's your first step to knowledge. The majority of clients will be quite happy to spend 20 minutes explaining how something works and will always help you out when things go wrong.

'The placements where I met hostility and no help were in the minority,' says Annie.

Further qualifications

Temping will give you a great chance to develop a range of skills, but what about further qualifications? Private secretarial colleges could be the answer because many are running short term courses to boost skills and develop office techniques further.

The Pitman College in Southampton Row offers a six week typing, computing and office technology course and a three week computer applications course. Also on offer is a three week Wordstar 2000 and typewriting course. So there is a short answer to skill development.

It's a case of grasping the nettle. Your abilities may have been tried and tested, literally, as a temp and the fact that you can type, word process and use computers will be a forgone conclusion to you, but is it on paper? Some firms will want those magic certificates, so if you've got a big bucks career in mind, be prepared to get them.

The colleges listed in our Directory will be a starting point for you and you get help advice from Pitman Examinations Institute (PEI), The Royal Society of Arts (RSA) and the Industrial Society. Some colleges may want 'O' and 'A' levels before they'll allow you to do a course, but both PEI and the RSA take work experience and practical skills into account.

Nice and easy

Self-development need not be a slog, but don't leave everything till the last minute. You should be planning now — even if you're happy with a full-time career as a temp. Don't stint on gaining knowledge and improving your own abilities; every day is the right time to take stock and keep planning.

With the right attitude and a dash of confidence you can make temping a triumph and move on to work full-time on a high note. When it comes to your own progress just remember — the only way is up.

Chapter 7

The London Temp's Directory

Our Directory of the main recruitment agencies in and around the London area is dividend into two listings. The alphabetic listing allows you to quickly locate the details of a particular agency you know by name. If however, you are interested in working in a specific area — either one of the counties or a London postal district — you should refer to the geographical listing.

Alphabetic listing of recruitment agencies

A
Access Personnel Ltd
Industries: All
Placements: Accounts clerks, bilingual operators, computer operators, receptionists, secretaries and personal assistants, telephone and telex operators.
Qualifications: None required
Skills: Computer, shorthand, typing, word processing.
Comments: Technical and commercial permanent and temporary placements.
103 Victoria Street
St Albans
Hertfordshire AL1 3TJ
Tel: 0727 43255
Fax: 0727 41916

Ace Foster Beazley Associates
Industries: All, media and bilingual.
Placements: Bilingual operators, receptionists, secretaries and personal assistants, telephone and telex operators, word processingoperators.
Qualifications: Typing 45 wpm, shorthand 80 wpm.
Skills: Shorthand, typing, word processing.
Comments: We are a secretarial recruitment agency, placing staff in permanent and temporary assignments, from clerk typist to senior PA level. We also specialise in the world of media and bilingual positions.
London Area: C
23 Red Lion Street
London WC1R 4PS
Tel: 01-242 8844
Fax: 01-404 4212

Acme Appointments
Industries: All
Placements: Accounts clerks, receptionists, secretaries and personal assistants, telephone and telex operators, word processing operators.
Qualifications: Typing 45/60+ wpm, shorthand 100/60 wpm, audio 60+ wpm.
Skills: Shorthand, typing, word processing.
Comments: A privately owned family led group established over 40 years. Always looking for good temporaries for interesting and well-paid bookings.
London Area: E
122 Middlesex Street
London E1 7HY
Tel: 01-375 1441

Moorgate Station
29 Moorfields
London EC2 9AE
Tel: 01-638 4397

20 Wormwood Street
London EC2M 1RQ
Tel: 01-256 5191

158 Bishopsgate
London EC2M 4LN
Tel: 01-247 9701

2nd Floor
88 Cannon Street
London EC4N 6HT
Tel: 01-220 7550

London Area: C
315 Oxford Street
London W1R 2HH
Tel: 01-629 7232

Head Office
315 Oxford Street
London W1R 2HH
Tel: 01-493 4000
Fax: 01-493 4383

Adair International
Industries: All, specialising in City work, legal, hotel & catering, media.
Placements: Computer operators, bilingual operators, receptionists, secretaries and personal assistants, word processing operators, overseas placements related to hotel and catering.
Qualifications: None required. Skills matched to client requirements.
Skills: Shorthand, word processing.
Comments: Favouritism to Australians and New Zealanders. The company has 5

divisions of recruitment with an office in Sydney.

London Area: C
5 Sherwood Street
London W1V 7RA
Tel: 01-734 9582
Fax: 01-439 1395

Adventure Personnel Ltd
Industries: Media
Placements: Receptionists, secretaries and personal assistants, word processing operators.
Qualifications: None required
Skills: Shorthand, typing, word processing.
London Area: C
12 South Moulton Street
London W1Y 1DF
Tel: 01-629 5747
Fax: 01-499 0841

Advisory Employment Agency
Industries: All
Placements: Accounts clerks, bilingual operators, computer operators, receptionists, secretaries and personal assistants, telephone and telex operators.
Qualifications: None required. All levels of applicants considered.
Skills: Computer, shorthand, typing, word processing.
Comments: Deal with permanent and temporary office staff. Look for WP skills, good typing and if possible, also experienced telephonists.

London Area: N
9 Regency Parade
Finchley Road
London NW3 5EG
Tel: 01-722 8851
Fax: 01-483 4162

15 Watford Way
Hendon Central
London NW4 3JL
Tel: 01-202 3677
Fax: 01-202 1754

London Area: C
Third Floor
67-68 New Bond Street
London W1Y 9DF
Tel: 01-408 2313
Fax: 01-495 1111

Albany Appointments Ltd
Industries: Media, publishing
Placements: Accounts clerks, receptionists, secretaries and personal assistants, telephone and telex operators, word processing operators.
Qualifications: Typing 45 wpm, knowledge of WP, minimum o'levels, 6 months work experience.
Skills: Computer, shorthand, typing, word processing.
Comments: A small temporary division of 50-80 Temps, looking for loyalty and flexibility.
London Area: C
5 Dering Street
London W1R 9AB
Tel: 01-493 8611
Fax: 01-493 8216

Alexis Personnel
Industries: All
Placements: Accounts clerks, bilingual operators, computer operators, receptionists, secretaries and personal assistants, telephone and telex operators, word processing operators.
Qualifications: Typing 25/60 wpm. Accuracy most important.
Skills: Shorthand, typing, word processing.
Comments: Alexis Personnel is a small, professional employment consultancy which specialises in finding the right person with the right skills and personality for their select client base.
London Area: C
Radnov House
93 Regent Street
London W1R 7TF
Tel: 01-439 2777
Fax: 01-437 0470

Alfred Marks Bureau Limited
Industries: All

Placements: Accounts clerks, bilingual operators, computer operators, receptionists, secretaries and personal assistants, telephone and telex operators, word processing operators.
Qualifications: None required
Skills: Shorthand, typing, word processing.
Comments: As one of the major temp agencies, Alfred Marks recruits a variety of staff with a range of qualifications.

London Area: C
ADIA House, PO Box 1AL
84/86 Regent Street
London W1A 1AL
Tel: 01-437 7855
Fax: 01-734 2538

Amanda Barrington Recruitment Consultants

Industries: All, media, publishing.
Placements: Bilingual operators, receptionists, secretaries and personal assistants, word processing operators. Overseas placements are made.
Qualifications: Typing 60 wpm, shortand 80/100 wpm.
Skills: Shorthand, typing, word processing.
Comments: Amanda Barrington seeks flexible, efficient, temps with varied WP experience.

London Area: C
13 Upper St Martins Lane
London WC2H 9DL
Tel: 01-379 7007
Fax: 01-379 3267

Angela Mortimer Ltd

Industries: All
Placements: Receptionists, secretaries and personal assistants.
Qualifications: Typing 50 wpm, shorthand 90 wpm. Experience on Monarch/Herald/Plessey. 5 O' levels or more.
Skills: Typing, word processing, shorthand or audio, computer useful.
Comments: Privately owned, quality secretarial recruitment consultancy. We look for committed, reliable secretarial temps who either want a career in temping or a permanent job.

London Area: E
1/3 Frederick's Place
London EC2
Tel: 01-726 8491

London Area: C
22/23 Princes Street
London W1
Tel: 01-408 1461

Foxglove House
166 Piccadilly
London W1
Tel: 01-629 9686

Anglia Recruitment

Industries: All
Placements: Accounts clerks, bilingual operators, computer operators, receptionists, secretaries and personal assistants, telephone and telex operators, word processing operators.
Qualifications: None required
Skills: Computer, shorthand, typing, word processing.
Comments: Anglia Recruitment is a small, independent agency with 2 offices.

31 Hills Road
Cambridge
Cambridgeshire CB2 1NW
Tel: 0223 461526
Fax: 0223 67403

24 King Street
Saffron Walden
Essex CB10 1ES
Tel: 0799 21761/25699
Fax: 0799 513473

Ann Warrington Secretarial Careers

Industries: All
Placements: Receptionists, secretaries and personal assistants, telephone and telex operators, word processing operators.
Qualifications: Typing 45 wpm, shorthand 90 wpm, 2 good references, 6 month's secretarial experience.
Skills: Computer, shorthand, typing, word processing.
Comments: As we specialise in the placement of permanent office staff we

are always interested in 'temp to perm' posts and inshort term relief staff who are really seeking permanency on finding the right position.

London Area: E
52 Bow Lane
London EC4M 9DS
Tel: 01-248 2014
Fax: 01-248 6770

Aquarius Employment Bureau Ltd
Industries: All
Placements: Accounts clerks, computer operators, receptionists, secretaries and personal assistants, telephone and telex operators,word processing operators.
Qualifications: None required. We test all applicants - permanent and temporary.
Skills: Computer, shorthand, typing, word processing.
Comments: We have been established for 15 years. All temporaries are welcome, providing they can supply three references.

London Area: N
Aquarius House
Archway Corner
London N19 3TD
Tel: 01-272 6252
Fax: 01-263 2485

Arena Staff Agency
Industries: All
Placements: Accounts clerks, computer operators, receptionists, secretaries and personal assistants, telephone and telex operators,word processing operators.
Qualifications: Typing 40+ wpm, shorthand 80+ wpm, minimum of 3 O' levels.
Skills: Computer, shorthand, typing, word processing.
Comments: We concentrate on secretarial and general office skills including book-keeping, VDU, as well as good qualifiedsecretaries, WP operators and accounts staff.

54b Leys Avenue
Letchworth
Hertfordshire SG6 3EQ
Tel: 0462 678202
Fax: 0462 672576

Argosy Employment Group
Industries: All
Placements: Accounts clerks, bilingual operators, computer operators, receptionists, secretaries and personal assistants, telephoneand telex operators, word processing operators.
Qualifications: None required
Skills: Computer, shorthand, typing, word processing.
Comments: We recruit a wide range of temps eg., manual labourers, secretarial staff, professionals, etc.

57 High Street
Ashford
Kent TN24 8SG
Tel: 0233 37700

38 High Street
Canterbury
Kent CT1 2RY
Tel: 0227 762170

2a Batchelor Street
Chatham
Kent ME4 4BJ
Tel: 0634 406031

7 Castle Street
Dover
Kent CT16 1PT
Tel: 0304 216432/203946

108 High Street
Edenbridge
Kent TN8 5AR
Tel: 0732 864141

33 Bouverie Square
Folkestone
Kent CT20 1BA
Tel: 0303 850567

11 Pudding Lane
Maidstone
Kent ME14 1PA
Tel: 0622 688488

6/7 Cecil Square
Margate
Kent CT9 1BD
Tel: 0843 297112

The Shambles
Sevenoaks
Kent TN13 1AL
Tel: 0732 451331/2

93/95 High Street
Tonbridge
Kent TN9 1DR
Tel: 0732 770282

14 Dyke Road
Brighton
Sussex East BN1 3FE
Tel: 0273 24883/24282

30 Terminus Road
Eastbourne
Sussex East BN21 3LP
Tel: 0323 643417/8/9

7 Havelock Road
Hastings
Sussex East TN34 1BP
Tel: 0424 720117

8 The Broadway
1st Floor
Crawley
Sussex West RH10 1DS
Tel: 0293 27131

Constructive Services Division
6 The Broadway (1st Floor)
Crawley
Sussex West RH10 1DS
Tel: 0293 21896

Management Recruitment Division
6 The Broadway (First Floor)
Crawley
Sussex West RH10 1DS
Tel: 0293 29014

Armstrong Staff Bureau
Industries: All, law, media, medical, publishing.
Placements: Accounts clerks, bilingual operators, computer operators, receptionists, secretaries and personal assistants, telephoneand telex operators, word processing operators.
Qualifications: Typing 50 wpm, shorthand 100 wpm.
Skills: Computer, shorthand, typing, word processing.
Comments: A privately owned employment agency which aims to match the right skills to the right job.

221a Banbury Road
Summertown
Oxford
Oxfordshire OX2 7HQ
Tel: 0865 310416
Fax: 0865 310652

8a Market Square
Witney
Oxfordshire OX8 7BB
Tel: 0993 778541
Fax: 0993 702012

Arron Employment Ageney
Industries: All
Placements: Accounts clerks, bilingual operators, computer operators, receptionists, secretaries and personal assistants, telephoneand telex operators, word processing operators.
Qualifications: Junior shorthand 35/70 wpm; shorthand 55/90 wpm; secretary 60/100 wpm, WP 55 wpm, audio 50 wpm. A generallygood standard of education, appearance, skills and telephone manner will be taken into account.
Skills: Shorthand, typing, word processing.
Comments: A one office, privately owned company, established over 23 years, concerned with secretarial and office applicants.
223 Imperial Drive
Rayners Lane
Harrow
Middlesex HA2 7HE
Tel: 01-868 0044
Fax: 01-868 0301

Ashton Staff Bureau
Industries: All
Placements: Accounts clerks, bilingual operators, computer operators, receptionists, secretaries and personal assistants, telephoneand telex operators, word processing operators.
Qualifications: Typing 50 wpm, shorthand 80 wpm.
Skills: Computer, shorthand, typing, word processing.
Comments: Principally a secretarial agency. It also places drivers, warehouse

workers and catering staff.
52 High Street
Orpington
Kent BR6 0JQ
Tel: 0689 78574
Fax: 0689 78574

Atlas Employment Agency Ltd
Industries: All
Placements: Accounts clerks, bilingual operators, computer operators, receptionists, secretaries and personal assistants, telephone and telex operators, word processing operators.
Qualifications: Typing 45 wpm, shorthand 80 wpm, 1 year's WP experience, 1 year's legal secretarial experience.
Skills: None required
Comments: We are a high street employment agency looking for all types of temporaries, both skilled and unskilled. We need hardworking, reliable applicants for a variety of positions.

London Area: N
154 High Road
Wood Green
London N22 6EB
Tel: 01-888 8490

68 High Street
Harlesden
London NW10 4SJ
Tel: 01-965 8181

237 Kentish Town Road
London NW5 2JS
Tel: 01-284 1818

London Area: E
106c High Street
Walthamstow
London E17 7JY
Tel: 01-520 0214

'Roundhouse'
213 Old Street
London EC1V 9PG
Tel: 01-253 4355

152/154 Bishopsgate
London EC2M 4LN
Tel: 01-247 7444

14 Eldon Street
London EC2M 7LA
Tel: 01-588 7184

13 Eastcheap
London EC3M 1BU
Tel: 01-929 1758

London Area: S
18 Borough High Street
London SE1 9QG
Tel: 01-406 8311

74 Denmark Hill
Camberwell Green
London SE5 4RZ
Tel: 01-733 6101

14 Streatleigh Parade
Streatham High Road
London SW16
Tel: 01-677 5327

17a Kings Road
London SW3 4RP
Tel: 01-823 5122

London Area: C
104 Baker Street
London W1M 2AR
Tel: 01-486 0542

52 James Street
London W1M 5HS
Tel: 01-486 5225

71 Oxford Street
London W1R 1RB
Tel: 01-636 4000

71 Oxford Street
London W1R 1RB
Tel: 01-636 4000

275 Regent Street
London W1R 9BR
Tel: 01-493 2021

7 Harewood Place
London W1R 9HA
Tel: 01-629 1904

31/33 High Holborn
London W1V 6AX
Tel: 01-831 0012

108 High Holborn
London WC1V 9JS
Tel: 01-242 1811

London Area: W
84 Uxbridge Road
Shepherds Bush
London W12 8LR
Tel: 01-749 2171

126 The Broadway
West Ealing
London W13 0SY
Tel: 01-579 5451

38 The Broadway
Ealing
London W5 2NP
Tel: 01-579 2971

1st Floor
4 Hammersmith Broadway
London W6 7AL
Tel: 01-748 9434

4 Hammersmith Broadway
London W6 7AL
Tel: 01-741 4771

43 Kensington High Street
London W8 5ED
Tel: 01-938 3011

6 Windsor Road
Slough
Berkshire SL1 2EJ
Tel: 0753 822424

95 Cranbrook Road
Ilford
Essex IG1 4TG
Tel: 01-514 8600

11 Holywell Hill
St Albans
Hertfordshire AL1 1EZ
Tel: 0727 40531

12 Market Street
Watford
Hertfordshire WD1 7AD
Tel: 0923 49936

17a High Street
Bromley
Kent BR1 1LG
Tel: 01-460 2121

202a Station Road
Edgware
Middlesex HA8 7AR
Tel: 01-958 1311

25a Church Street
Enfield
Middlesex EN2 6AF
Tel: 01-367 7567

374 Station Road
Harrow
Middlesex HA1 2DE
Tel: 01-863 6011

20 Station Road
Hayes
Middlesex UB3 4DA
Tel: 01-573 9660

600 High Road
Wembley
Middlesex HA0 2AF
Tel: 01-903 0381

6 Park Lane
Wembley
Middlesex HA9 YRP
Tel: 01-900 2144

22/26 George Street
Croydon
Surrey CR0 1PB
Tel: 01-686 8314

28 London Road
Croydon
Surrey CR0 2TA
Tel: 01-686 4631

64 Fife Road
Kingston
Surrey KT1 1SP
Tel: 01-541 5511

164 High Street
Sutton
Surrey SM1 1LX
Tel: 01-642 0640

Aylesbury Staff Bureau

Industries: All, medical
Placements: Accounts clerks, bilingual operators, computer operators, receptionists, secretaries and personal assistants, telephone and telex operators, word processing operators.
Qualifications: Elementary typing, shorthand 80 wpm, 4 GCSE's including English.
Skills: Shorthand, typing, word processing.
Comments: We are a high street employment agency looking for all types of temporaries, both skilled and unskilled. We need hardworking, reliable applicants for a variety of positions.

12 Temple Square
Aylesbury
Buckinghamshire HP20 2QL
Tel: 0296 87371

B

Baileys Employment Bureau
Industries: All
Placements: Accounts clerks, computer operators, receptionists, secretaries and personal assistants, telephone and telex operators, word processing operators.
Qualifications: Typing 45 wpm, shorthand 80/90 wpm.
Skills: Computer, shorthand, typing, word processing.
Comments: We recruit for both long term and short term bookings in all categories.
36a White Rock
Hastings
Sussex TN34 1JL
Tel: 0424 444555

Belle Secretarial Ltd
Industries: All
Placements: Accounts clerks, computer operators, receptionists, secretaries and personal assistants, telephone and telex operators, word processing operators.
Qualifications: Typing, copy and audio 50 wpm, shorthand 90 wpm, general clerical/accounts experience.
Skills: Computer, shorthand, typing, word processing.
Comments: Provides temps to a variety of companies in the West End and the City. Established for 26 years.
London Area: C
24 Chancery Lane
London WC2A 1LS
Tel: 01-404 4655

Bertram Personnel Group
Industries: Media
Placements: Accounts clerks, computer operators, receptionists, secretaries and personal assistants, telephone and telex operators, word processing operators.
Qualifications: Typing 50 wpm for secretaries, 35 wpm for juniors, shorthand 90/100 wpm, O' levels dependant upon the client.
Skills: Computer, shorthand, typing, word processing.

Comments: We are always looking for good temps to fill a variety of positions.
London Area: E
12-14 Devonshire Row
London EC3
Tel: 01-247 0367

Body Bank, The
Industries: All
Placements: Accounts clerks, bilingual operators, computer operators, receptionists, secretaries and personal assistants, telephoneand telex operators, word processing operators.
Qualifications: None required
Skills: Computer, shorthand, typing, word processing.
Comments: The Body Bank employ a variety of temps from secretaries to casual staff. It looks for enthusiastic, flexible personnelwith outgoing personalities.
117 High Street
Barnet
Hertfordshire EN5 5UZ
Tel: 01-441 6868
Fax: 01-441 6915

485 High Road
Wembley
Middlesex HA9 7AG
Tel: 01-900 2877
Fax: 01-902 6784

Boxmoor Bureau (Staff Recruitment) Ltd
Industries: All
Placements: Accounts clerks, bilingual operators, computer operators, receptionists, secretaries and personal assistants, telephoneand telex operators, word processing operators.
Qualifications: A good level of proficiency in the particular skills offered by each individual.
Skills: Computer, shorthand, typing, word processing.
Comments: We have been established for over 17 years and supply staff to a wide range of local businesses. Our temps receiveholiday pay from day one.

5a Marlowes
Hemel Hempstead
Hertfordshire HP1 1LA
Tel: 0442 50437
Fax: 0442 68174
6 Spencer Street
St Albans
Hertfordshire AL3 5EG
Tel: 0727 41102
Fax: 0727 64966

Bridge Street Bureau Ltd, The
Industries: All
Placements: Accounts clerks, computer operators, receptionists, secretaries and personal assistants, telephone and telex operators, word processing operators.
Qualifications: Typing 50 wpm, shorthand 80 wpm.
Skills: Computer, shorthand, typing, word processing.
Comments: Deals with office staff and serves local businesses within a 10 mile radius. Provides WP and computer training.
34 Bridge Street
Walton on Thames
Surrey KT12 1AJ
Tel: 0932 228420
Fax: 0932 232141

Brook Street
Industries: All
Placements: Accounts clerks, receptionists, secretaries and personal assistants, telephone and telex operators, word processingoperators.
Qualifications: Typing 40/50 wpm, shorthand 80/100 wpm, 2 GCSE's including English.
Skills: Shorthand, typing, word processing.
Comments: We are looking for PA's, secretaries, copy typists, clerks, account clerks, switchboard operators, receptionists, cateringstaff, industrial staff.
London Area: N
119 High Road
Wood Green
London N22 6BB
Tel: 01-888 1101

80 Kilburn High Road
London NW6 4HS
Tel: 01-328 7121
London Area: E
Business Efficiency Centre
3-4 Limeharbour
London E14 9TQ
Tel: 01-538 0232
56 Broadway
Stratford
London E15 1NG
Tel: 01-555 8261
238 Hoe Street
Walthamstow
London E17 3AX
Tel: 01-520 7324
172 Bishopsgate
London EC2M 4NQ
Tel: 01-283 7935
108 Fenchurch Street
London EC3M 5JJ
Tel: 01-481 8441
131/133 Cannon Street
London EC4N 5AX
Tel: 01-623 3966
London Area: S
52 Lewisham High Street
London SE13 5JH
Tel: 01-852 4454
84a Rye Lane
Peckham
London SE15 4RZ
Tel: 01-639 6417
64 St John's Road
Clapham Junction
London SW11 1PS
Tel: 01-228 7891
71 Putney High Street
London SW15 1SR
Tel: 01-789 5021
71 Streatham High Road
London SW16 1PH
Tel: 01-677 2641
139 Victoria Street
London SW1E 6RD
Tel: 01-834 5745
Catering Section
139 Victoria Street
London SW1E 6RD
Tel: 01-630 6112

Alphabetical Listing

Stockley House
130 Wilton Road
London SW1V 1LQ
Tel: 01-630 1311
Fax: 01-630 1877

167 Earls Court Road
London SW5 9RF
Tel: 01-373 7822

London Area: C

136 Baker Street
London W1M 1FH
Tel: 01-496 6144

63 Oxford Street
London W1R 1FA
Tel: 01-493 8531

230 High Holborn
London WC1V 7DA
Tel: 01-242 6991

32 The Strand
London WC2N 6MA
Tel: 01-930 7399

Catering Section
32 Strand
London WC2N 6MA
Tel: 01-930 9933

London Area: W

14 Pembridge Road
London W11 3Hl
Tel: 01-229 9234

320 Chiswick High Road
London W4 5TA
Tel: 01-995 2311

11 The Broadway
Ealing
London W5 2NH
Tel: 01-567 7799

14 Kensington Church Street
London W8 4EP
Tel: 01-937 5115

Dudley House
High Street
Bracknell
Berkshire RG12 1[l
Tel: 0344 59118

49/51 High Street
Maidenhead
Berkshire SL6 1JT
Tel: 0628 73187

138 High Street
Slough
Berkshire SL1 1DN
Tel: 0753 34747

47 Cranbrook Road
Ilford
Essex IG1 4PG
Tel: 01-478 1116

50a South Street
Romford
Essex RM1 1RJ
Tel: 0708 67211

6a London Street
Basingstoke
Hampshire RG21 1NU
Tel: 0256 471242

76 High Street
Watford
Hertfordshire WD1 2BP
Tel: 0923 42377

187 The Broadway
Bexleyheath
Kent DA6 7ER
Tel: 01-303 5651

155 High Street
Bromley
Kent BR1 1JD
Tel: 01-464 1166

1a Grosvener Road
Tunbridge Wells
Kent TN1 2AH
Tel: 0892 44826

97-99 Station Road
Edgware
Middlesex HA8 7JG
Tel: 01-952 8441

17 College Road
Harrow
Middlesex HA1 1BA
Tel: 01-863 1082

45 Station Road
Hayes
Middlesex UB3 4BE
Tel: 01-573 1866

82 High Street
Hounslow
Middlesex TW3 1NH
Tel: 01-570 0111

Industrial Section, Victor House
Norris Road
Staines
Middlesex TW18 4DS
Tel: 0784 56441

Victor House
Norris Road
Staines
Middlesex TW18 4DS
Tel: 0784 62381

425 High Road
Wembley
Middlesex HA9 7AB
Tel: 01-902 3636

16 High Street
Oxford
Oxfordshire OX1 4AG
Tel: 0865 722571

47a High Street
Camberley
Surrey GU15 3RB
Tel: 0276 66451

6 George Street
Croydon
Surrey CR0 1PA
Tel: 01-686 7312

96 High Street
Guildford
Surrey GU1 3HU
Tel: 0483 302979

9 Eden Street
Kingston-upon-Thames
Surrey KT1 1BQ
Tel: 01-546 4586

51a George Street
Richmond on Thames
Surrey TW9 1HJ
Tel: 01-948 1481

99 High Street
Sutton
Surrey SM1 1JF
Tel: 01-642 4493

4a Commercial Way
Woking
Surrey GU21 1ET
Tel: 04862 26167

77/78 North Street
Brighton
Sussex BN1 1ZE
Tel: 0273 202991

Bryman Personnel
Industries: All
Placements: Accounts clerks, computer operators, receptionists, secretaries and personal assistants, telephone and telex operators, word processing operators. Overseas placements are made.
Qualifications: None required
Skills: Computer, shorthand, typing, word processing.
Comments: A commercial and technical recruitment agency, handling permanent, temporary and contract vacancies in the UK and overseas.

Bryman House
16 Weston Road
Southend-on-Sea
Essex SS1 1AS
Tel: 0702 353990

Business Back-Up Ltd
Industries: All
Placements: Accounts clerks, bilingual operators, computer operators, receptionists, secretaries and personal assistants, telephone and telex operators, word processing operators, legal, accountancy and catering positions.
Qualifications: None required
Skills: Computer, shorthand, typing, word processing.
Comments: We are a small, privately owned agency and place good quality, well presented, honest and reliable temps at all levels.

1 King Street
Maidenhead
Berkshire SL6 1DZ
Tel: 0628 770124
Fax: 0628 784412

C

Carwell Employment Bureau
Industries: All
Placements: Accounts clerks, bilingual operators, computer operators, receptionists, secretaries and personal assistants, telephone and telex operators.
Qualifications: None required
Skills: Computer, shorthand, typing, word processing.

Comments: Established for over 20 years providing all aspects of temporary staff to office, industrial and professionalcompanies.

13 Market House
The High
Harlow
Essex CM20 1BL
Tel: 0279 33033/32727/450220
Fax: 0279 450210

Catch 22 Employment Agency Limited
Industries: All
Placements: Receptionists, secretaries and personal assistants, telephone and telex operators, word processing operators.
Qualifications: None required. Consider most people at all skill levels.
Skills: Computer, shorthand, typing, word processing.
Comments: London Area: S
199 Victoria Street
London SW1E 5NE
Tel: 01-821 1134
Fax: 01-630 6660

Catherine Johnstone Recruitment
Industries: All
Placements: Accounts clerks, bilingual operators, computer operators, receptionists, secretaries and personal assistants, telephoneand telex operators, word processing operators.
Qualifications: None required. Those offering qualifications bring certificates. References will be undertaken.
Skills: Computer, shorthand, typing, word processing.
Comments: Small privately owned Croydon based company serving most aspects of commercial recruitment.
Saffron House
15 Park Street
Croydon
Surrey CR0 1YD
Tel: 01-680 5777

Centacom Staff Agency
Industries: All
Placements: Accounts clerks, computer operators, receptionists, secretaries and personal assistants, telephone and telex operators, word processing operators.
Qualifications: None required
Skills: Computer, shorthand, typing, word processing.
Comments: Small agency with branches in Australia and New Zealand.
London Area: C
15 Adam Street
Strand
London WC2
Tel: 01-938 2921
London Area: W
30 Kensington Church Street
London W8 4EP
Tel: 01-937 6525
Fax: 01-938 2921

Central Recruitment
Industries: All
Placements: Accounts clerks, computer operators, receptionists, secretaries and personal assistants, telephone and telex operators, word processing operators.
Qualifications: None required
Skills: Computer, shorthand, typing, word processing.
Comments: We have four specialist sections in accountancy, law, insurance and general office vancancies, and consider anyone withoffice experience.
Hampstead House
New Town Centre
Basingstoke
Hampshire RG21 1LG
Tel: 0256 844228
Fax: 0256 844257
31 Gabriels Hill
Maidstone
Kent ME15 6HX
Tel: 0622 688391
Fax: 0622 688394
9 Bank Plain
Norwich
Norfolk NR2 4SF
Tel: 0603 620203
Fax: 0603 619965

Chequers Employment
Industries: All

Placements: Accounts clerks, bilingual operators, computer operators, receptionists, secretaries and personal assistants, telephone and telex operators, word processing operators. Overseas placements are made.

Qualifications: Typing 40 wpm, shorthand 80 wpm.

Skills: Computer, shorthand, typing, word processing.

Comments: Established 1962, specialising in permanent and temporary office staff.

129 St Albans Road
Watford
Hertfordshire WD1 1RA
Tel: 0923 241077/34233
Fax: 0923 818226

Computer Help

Industries: All

Placements: Accounts clerks, bilingual operators, receptionists, secretaries and personal assistants, telephone and telex operators.

Qualifications: Typing 45 wpm, minimum 1 year's work experience, standard education.

Skills: Computer, word processing.

Comments: We specialise in the computer field: VDU, WP operations and programming. Seek high calibre staff.

12a Bushey Hall Road
Bushey
Hertfordshire WD2 2EA
Tel: 0923 817595
Fax: 0923 246447

Computer Help

Industries: Media, publishing

Placements: Accounts clerks, bilingual operators, receptionists, secretaries and personal assistants, telephone and telex operators.

Qualifications: Typing 45 wpm, minimum 1 year's work experience, standard education.

Skills: Computer, word processing.

Comments: We specialise in the computer field: VDU, WP operations and programming. Seek high calibre staff.

1a Elmside Rod
Wembley Park
Middlesex HA9 8JA
Tel: 01- 903 9344
Fax: 01- 903 6803

Covent Garden Bureau

Industries: Media, publishing

Placements: Receptionists, secretaries and personal assistants, telephone and telex operators, word processing operators.

Qualifications: None required

Skills: Shorthand, typing, word processing.

Comments: Convent Garden Bureau offers an interesting and wide choice of temporary bookings in the creative fields. All ages are welcome.

London Area: E
Ludgate House
107-110 Fleet Street
London EC4
Tel: 01- 353 7696

Crest Employment Bureau

Industries: All

Placements: Receptionists, secretaries and personal assistants, telephone and telex operators, word processing operators.

Qualifications: Typing 45 wpm, Shorthand 80 wpm.

Skills: Computer, shorthand, typing, word processing.

Comments: Mainly secretarial and clerical, but also seek packers, porters and manual workers.

14 Market Parade
Hampton Road West
Hanworth
Middlesex TW7 4BX
Tel: 01-898 4051

461 London Road
Isleworth
Middlesex TW13 6AL
Tel: 01-568 9611
Fax: 01-569 7861

Crown Personnel Ltd

Industries: All

Placements: Accounts clerks, bilingual operators, computer operators, receptionists, secretaries and personal assistants, telephone and telex operators, word processing operators.
Qualifications: Typing 50 wpm, shorthand 45 wpm, GCSE's in Maths and English preferred.
Skills: Computer, shorthand, typing, word processing.
Comments: We are a successful agency providing temporary staff for a wide range of organisations in and around South Bucks who require skills in all secretarial disciplines.

58 High Street
Aylesbury
Buckinghamshire HP20 1SE
Tel: 0296 436001
Fax: 0296 392938

D

Davis Secretarial Recruitment

Industries: Media, property
Placements: Receptionists, secretaries and personal assistants, telephone and telex operators, word processing operators.
Qualifications: Typing 50 wpm, shorthand for top PA bookings at least 80 wpm, WP experience, Good GCSE education, good speaking voice for reception work.
Skills: Computer, shorthand, typing, word processing.
Comments: Small established consultancy specialising in temporary and permanent appointments with design, advertising, PR and sales promotion companies. Our clients look for bright, bubbly individuals for long or short term bookings.

London Area: C
13-14 Dean Street
London W1V 5AH
Tel: 01-437 6419

Diamond Staff Bureau

Industries: All
Placements: Receptionists, secretaries and personal assistants, telephone and telex operators, word processing operators.
Qualifications: Minimum qualifications: the ability to read and write, but obviously the more skills and experience one has, the better.
Skills: Computer, shorthand, typing, word processing.
Comments: We provide all categories of office temporaries from junior clerical to senior PAs, as well as accounts and computer staff.

Neville House
High Street
Bracknell
Berkshire RG12 1DE
Tel: 0344 55321
Fax: 0344 51606

Directors' Temporaries Ltd

Industries: All
Placements: Accounts clerks, bilingual operators, receptionists, secretaries and personal assistants, telephone and telex operators, word processing operators.
Qualifications: Typing 60 wpm and shorthand 85 wpm are the minimum requirements.
Skills: Shorthand, typing, word processing.
Comments: We recruit staff to suit director-level assignments.

London Area: C
Standbrook House, (4th Floor)
2-5 Old Bond Street
London W1X 3TB
Tel: 01-493 2545
Fax: 01-629 4255

Downtown Burea, The

Industries: All
Placements: Accounts clerks, computer operators, receptionists, secretaries and personal assistants, telephone and telex operators, word processing operators.
Qualifications: None required
Skills: Computer shorthand, typing, word processing.
Comments: Independent bureau looking for reliable temps with good skills, keen to recruit those returning to work.

11 Friday Court
24 North Street
Thame
Oxfordshire OX9 3GA
Tel: 0864 421 6976/7459

Drake International
Industries: All
Placements: Accounts clerks, computer operators, receptionists, secretaries and personal assistants, telephone and telex operators, word processing operators.
Qualifications: Typing 50 wpm, shorthand 80 wpm, 6 -- 12 months office experience required for all temps hired.
Skills: Computer shorthand, typing, word processing.
Comments: An international recruitment consultants, placing permanent and temporary staff in all industries. As well as the obvious office skills, Drake looks for flexibility and loyalty in its recruits.

London Area: C
(Office Overload - Temp Division)
223 Regent Street
London W1
Tel: 01-734 0911
Fax: 01-734 7751

Drayton Secretarial
Industries: All
Placements: Accounts clerks, computer operators, receptionists, secretaries and personal assistants, telephone and telex operators, word processing operators.
Qualifications: Typing 50/90 wpm, shorthand 50/90 wpm.
Skills: Computer shorthand, typing, word processing.
Comments: Covers all office, warehouse and industrial temps.

2-6 Horton Road
West Drayton
Middlesex UB7 8ED
Tel: 0895 448141
Fax: 0895 444639

E
Eastern Staff Services
Industries: All
Placements: Accounts clerks, computer operators, receptionists, secretaries and personal assistants, telephone and telex operators, word processing operators.
Qualifications: None required
Skills: Computer shorthand, typing, word processing.
Comments: Seek reliable, office, secretarial and executive temps for a wide range of vacancies throughout the East Anglian region.

62 Sidney Street
Cambridge
Cambridgeshire CB2 3JW
Tel: 0223 63567
Fax: 0223 63550

1 Bank Passage
Colchester
Essex CO1 1HZ
Tel: 0206 560460
Fax: 0206 763307

49 Abbeygate Street
Bury St Edmunds
Suffolk IP33 1LB
Tel: 0284 67561
Fax: 0284 750031

157 Hamilton Road
Felixstowe
Suffolk IP11 7DR
Tel: 0394 279111
Fax: 0394 670181

10 Northgate Street
Ipswich
Suffolk IP1 3BZ
Tel: 0473 219755
Fax: 0473 231217

Euro Personnel Services
Industries: All
Placements: Computer operators, receptionists, secretaries and personal assistants, telephone and telex operators, word processing operators.
Qualifications: Typing 50 wpm, shorthand 70 wpm.
Skills: Computer shorthand, typing, word processing.

Comments: London Area: S
268 The Colonnade
Waterloo Road
London SE1 85F
Tel: 01-620 1121
Fax: 01-401 2545

F

Faithfold Travel Personnel
Industries: Travel
Placements: Retail travel agencies, business travel agencies.
Qualifications: Two years IATA experience, gained in the UK or overseas.
Skills: Experience in the travel industry.
Comments: Faithfold recruit purely for the travel industry. Clients require temps who can fit immediately into a travel consultantposition. Previous travel administrative experience is essential.

London Area: C
Suite 220, Linen Hall
162-168 Regent Street
London W1R 5TB
Tel: 01-439 0482
Fax: 01-439 4276

Femco Employment Agency Ltd
Industries: All
Placements: Accounts clerks, computer operators, receptionists, secretaries and personal assistants, telephone and telex operators, word processing operators.
Qualifications: A range of qualifications is acceptable, from GCSE to degree level; also general clerical, secretarial, accounting, technical and engineering skills.
Skills: Computer, shorthand, typing, word processing.
Comments: Recruitment of permanent and temporary staff in a range of work areas including: secretarial, administration, clerical, accounts, VDU, computers, catering, technical and engineering.
24-25 Stonehills House
Stonehills
Welwyn Garden City
Hertfordshire AL8 6NH
Tel: 0707 323067/329858
Fax: 0707 323067

Find-A-Job (East Anglia) Ltd
Industries: All
Placements: Accounts clerks, bilingual operators, computer operators, receptionists, secretaries and personal assistants, telephoneand telex operators, word processing operators.
Qualifications: None required
Skills: Computer, shorthand, typing, word processing.
Comments: 8a Queen Street
Ipswich
Suffolk IP1 1SS
Tel: 0473 58277

First Personnel
Industries: All
Placements: Accounts clerks, receptionists, secretaries and personal assistants, telephone and telex operators, word processingoperators.
Qualifications: Typing 40 wpm, shorthand 75 wpm. Accuracy is more important than speed.
Skills: Computer, shorthand, typing, word processing.
Comments: A privately owned agency providing permanent and temporary staff in the commercial sector. Looking for presentable, reliable staff with accurate skills.
42a Longbridge Road
Barking
Essex IG11 8RT
Tel: 01-594 2666
92c High Street
Billericay
Essex CM12 9BT
Tel: 0277 657000
57a Orsett Road
Grays
Essex RM17 5HJ
Tel: 0375 391111
Fax: 0375 390151

Forest Employment Ltd
Industries: All
Placements: Accounts clerks, bilingual operators, computer operators, receptionists, secretaries and personal

assistants, telephone and telex operators, word processing operators.

Qualifications: Typing 40 wpm, minimum. Forest look for a positive attitude and good presentation both of which count as qualifications in their book.

Skills: Computer, shorthand, typing, word processing.

Comments: A multi -- disciplined agency with a strong secretarial, commercial division, which always has assignments for good WP operators.

21 York Road
Maidenhead
Berkshire RG1 2JI
Tel: 0628 73242
Fax: 0628 770745

11/12 Gun Street
Reading
Berkshire
Tel: 0734 587272
Fax: 0734 391404

Futures Recruitment Advisors

Industries: All

Placements: Bilingual operators, receptionists, secretaries and personal assistants, word processing operators.

Qualifications: Typing 40+ wpm, shorthand 90 wpm, GCSE English or equivalent, a knowledge of commerce preferred.

Skills: Shorthand, typing, word processing.

Comments: Futures specialises in office staff. It is attached to a private secretarial college and can arrange training for candidates.

28 Commercial Road
Guildford
Surrey GU1 4SX
Tel: 0483 302201
Fax: 0483 34777

G

Gordon Turner Appointments

Industries: All

Placements: Secretaries, PA's, clerical, receptionists, bilingual operators, WP operators, computer operators, accounts clerks and technical placements.

Qualifications: Secretarial temps need O'levels, typing 45 wpm, shorthand 80 wpm. Typists: 45 wpm and multi -- machine knowledge. WP: 6 months experience and ideally a knowledge of a minimum of three packages.

Skills: Computer, shorthand, typing, word processing.

Comments: Deal in high calibre secretarial staff and all kinds of office vacancies. Applicants tested and references taken before employing. Very careful matching procedures.

40-42 Hobson Street
Cambridge
Cambridgeshire CB1 1NL
Tel: 0223 359614

Graduate Appointments Ltd

Industries: All

Placements: Accounts clerks, receptionists, secretaries and personal assistants, word processing operators.

Qualifications: Typing 50 wpm, shorthand 80 wpm; A' levels.

Skills: Computer, shorthand, typing, word processing.

Comments: Look for good secretaries with a flexible approach to temping, for long and short assignments.

London Area: C
7 Princes Street
London W1R 7RB
Tel: 01-629 7262
Fax: 01-434 2055

Gregorys Staff Agency Ltd

Industries: All

Placements: Accounts clerks, computer operators, receptionists, secretaries and personal assistants, telephone and telex operators, word processing operators.

Qualifications: Typing 45 wpm, shorthand 80 wpm, GCSE Maths and English preferred, common sense.

Skills: Computer, shorthand, typing, word processing.

Comments: Seeks temps for commercial, technical and secretarial placements.

20 Station Road
West Drayton
Middlesex UB7 7BY
Tel: 0895 443181
Fax: 0895 422565

H
Hall Placements
Industries: All
Placements: Accounts clerks, bilingual operators, computer operators, receptionists, secretaries and personal assistants, telephone and telex operators, word processing operators.
Qualifications: Minimum typing 35 wpm, minimum shorthand 80 wpm, educated to O' level standard.
Skills: Computer, shorthand, typing, word processing.
Comments: We only use temps with proven skills and have built up a reputation of supplying high calibre personnel both in permanent and temporary placements.
Hall Place
South Street
Havant
Hampshire P0G 1DA
Tel: 0705 475541
Fax: 0705 473851

Hazell Staton Associates Ltd
Industries: All
Placements: Receptionists, secretaries and personal assistants.
Qualifications: Typing 40 wpm, shorthand 80 wpm, PA speeds shorthand 100 wpm, typing 60 wpm. 5 GCSE's minimum, A'level candidates preferred.
Skills: Computer, shorthand, typing, word processing.
Comments: Specialise in high calibre assignments for high calibre temps.

London Area: E
12 St Michaels Alley
Cornhill
London EC3V 9DS
Tel: 01-621 0686
Fax: 01-621 9907

London Area: C
8 Golden Square
London W1R 3AF
Tel: 01-439 6021
Fax: 01-494 0609

Head Start Appointments Ltd
Industries: Secretarial, clerical and admin in anything office based.
Placements: Accounts clerks, receptionists, secretaries and personal assistants, telephone and telex operators, word processing operators.
Qualifications: LCC qualification for senior secretarial positions (or equivalent) RSA and Pitman Typing qualifications for non-senior secretarial positions (or equivalent), WP qualification for WP operators (or equivalent).
Skills: Shorthand, typing, word processing.
Comments: We deal broadly with office-based staff. This mainly covers secretarial, clerical and admin vacancies, but we do also deal with accounts bookings.
64 High Street
Harpenden
Hertfordshire AL5 2SP
Tel: 0582 460415
Fax: 0582 62601

64 High Street
Harpenden
Hertfordshire AL5 2SP
Tel: 0582 460415
Fax: 05827 62601

20 London Road
St Albans
Hertfordshire AL1 1NG
Tel: 0727 60195
Fax: 0727 45015

83a High Street
Stevenage
Hertfordshire SG1 3HR
Tel: 0438 745555
Fax: 0438 740299

38/40 Stonehills
Welwyn Garden City
Hertfordshire AL8 6PD
Tel: 0707 321196
Fax: 0707 321187

Hendersons Recruitment
Industries: All
Placements: Accounts clerks, bilingual operators, computer operators, receptionists, secretaries and personal assistants, telephone and telex operators, word processing operators.
Qualifications: None required
Skills: Computer, shorthand, typing, word processing.
Comments: We try to help those with fewer skills where possible.
London Area: S
118 Cromwell Road
London SW7 4EG
Tel: 01-370 5066/7/8
Fax: 01-370 4706

High Flyers
Industries: All
Placements: Accounts clerks, computer operators, receptionists, secretaries and personal assistants, telephone and telex operators, word processing operators.
Qualifications: None required. Attitude and personal qualities are important.
Skills: Computer, shorthand, typing, word processing.
Comments: A local, friendly, professional agency offering personal service to everyone locally, from filing clerks to senior managers.
2 Dukes Place
Marlow
Buckinghamshire SL7 2QH
Tel: 06284 75703
Fax: 06284 75707

Hodge Recruitment
Industries: All
Placements: Accounts clerks, bilingual operators, computer operators, receptionists, secretaries and personal assistants, telephone and telex operators, word processing operators.
Qualifications: Typing 50 wpm minimum. Accuracy as important as speed. A good standard of education.
Skills: Computer, shorthand, typing, word processing.
Comments: A small firm with a client base covering all industries.
London Area: C
Bond House
19/20 Woodstock Street
London W1R 1HF
Tel: 01-629 8863
Fax: 01-408 0961

I

Info-Tech Employment Agency
Industries: All
Placements: Receptionists, secretaries and personal assistants, telephone and telex operators, word processing operators.
Qualifications: None required
Skills: Shorthand, typing, word processing.
Comments: A flexible agency looking for reliable staff.
9 Park End Street
Oxford
Oxfordshire OX1 1HH
Tel: 0865 791558

J

J & M Group
Industries: All, medical
Placements: Accounts clerks, computer operators, receptionists, secretaries and personal assistants, telephone and telex operators, word processing operators.
Qualifications: None required
Skills: Computer, shorthand, typing, word processing.
Comments: A group of companies dealing in industrial, commercial, secretarial, engineering, electronics, mechanical, civil, building and nursing staff.
102 High Street
Southend-on-Sea
Essex SS1 1JN
Tel: 0702 614451
Fax: 0702 460951

Jane Crosthwaite Recruitment Ltd
Industries: All
Placements: Receptionists, secretaries and personal assistants.

Qualifications: Typing 40 wpm.
Skills: Typing
Comments: JCR is a small and friendly recruitment consultancy.

London Area: S
21 Beauchamp Place
London SW3 1NQ
Tel: 01-581 2977
Fax: 01-581 1766

Jane Wynne Recruitment Ltd
Industries: All
Placements: Accounts clerks, bilingual operators, computer operators, receptionists, secretaries and personal assistants, telephoneand telex operators and word processing operators.
Qualifications: None required. Basic GCSE's preferred.
Skills: Computer, shorthand, typing and word processing.
Comments: Jane Wynne seeks intelligent well rounded individuals who will offer an excellent service to our clients.

London Area: E
2nd Floor, Ludgate House
107/111 Fleet Street
London EC4A 2AB
Tel: 01 - 353 9694
Fax: 01 - 583 1784

Jigsaw Limited
Industries: All, medical
Placements: Bilingual operators, receptionists, secretaries and personal assistants, word processing operators.
Qualifications: Typing 50 wpm, shorthand 80 wpm.
Skills: Shorthand, typing, word processing.
Comments: Clients in PR, banking, manufacturing and advertising.

London Area: C
5 Margaret Street
London W1N 7LG
Tel: 01-631 0902
Fax: 01-637 8620

Jonathan Wren & Co Ltd
Industries: Finance and banking

Placements: Accounts clerks, bilingual operators, computer operators, receptionists, secretaries and personal assistants, telephoneand telex operators, word processing operators.
Qualifications: Speeds 50/90 wpm, some clients seek O' and A' level standard of education.
Skills: Computer, shorthand, typing, word processing.
Comments: A financial recruitment consultants, seeking applicants with international banking experience. to work in the City.

London Area: E
1 New Street
London EC2
Tel: 01-623 1266
Fax: 01-626 5258

Judy Fisher Associates
Industries: Media
Placements: Receptionists, secretaries and personal assistants.
Qualifications: None required
Skills: Shorthand, typing, word processing.
Comments:

London Area: C
2 Princes Street
Hanover Square
London W1R 7RA
Tel: 01-493 0238
Fax: 01-499 3649

K

Kelly Temporary Services
Industries: All
Placements: Accounts clerks, bilingual operators, receptionists, secretaries and personal assistants, telephone and telex operators, word processing operators.
Qualifications: Qualifications relevant to specific assignments required.
Skills: Shorthand, typing, word processing.
Comments: Established in the USA in 1946, 800 branches worldwide, over 30 in the UK. We are always looking for competent, conscientious temporary staff, preferably with work experience.

London Area: C
European Headquarters
87-91 New Bond Street
London W1Y 0HQ
Tel: 01-493 7843
Fax: 01-499 1793

Kemp Recruitment
Industries: All
Placements: Accounts clerks, receptionists, secretaries and personal assistants, telephone and telex operators, word processing operators.
Qualifications: None required
Skills: Shorthand, typing, word processing.
55a Northbrook Street
Newbury
Berkshire RG13 1AN
Tel: 0635 41464
Fax: 0635 521481

Kent Personnel Services Ltd
Industries: All
Placements: Accounts clerks, computer operators, receptionists, secretaries and personal assistants, telephone and telex operators, word processing operators.
Qualifications: Typing 40 wpm, shorthand 80 wpm. 1 year's office experience essential.
Skills: Computer, shorthand, typing, word processing.
Comments: We offer a wide variety of office related work and serve most commercial and industrial companies in Kent.
53 High Street
Maidstone
Kent ME14 1SY
Tel: 0622 673351/2/3/4

Kerr Staff Ltd
Industries: All
Placements: Accounts clerks, bilingual operators, computer operators, receptionists, secretaries and personal assistants, telephone and telex operators, word processing operators.
Qualifications: None required
Skills: Shorthand, typing, word processing.
Comments: We are able to place a range of people from school leavers to executive levels.
London Area: W
41 Haven Green
Ealing
London W5 2NX
Tel: 01-998 4086
Fax: 01-991 5228

Keynes Personnel Ltd
Industries: All
Placements: Accounts clerks, bilingual operators, computer operators, receptionists, secretaries and personal assistants, telephone and telex operators, word processing operators.
Qualifications: Typing 50 wpm, shorthand 80 wpm.
Skills: Computer, shorthand, typing, word processing.
Comments: We only supply computing staff. Skills, attitude and appearance are important.
356 Silbury Boulevard
Milton Keynes
Buckinghamshire MK9 2LR
Tel: 0908 668385
Fax: 0908 662615

Enterprise House Business Centre
Ocean Village
Southampton
Hampshire SO1 1XB
Tel: 0703 331666
Fax: 0703 332050

Kingsway Recruitment Consultants
Industries: All
Placements: Accounts clerks, bilingual operators, computer operators, receptionists, secretaries and personal assistants, telephone and telex operators, word processing operators.
Qualifications: Typing 50 wpm, minimum 6 month's experience for WP operators.
Skills: Shorthand, typing, word processing, computer.
Comments: We are part of the Adia Group and pride ourselves in being honest with both our clients and applicants

alike. All applicants including office juniors are welcome to register and we will advise on career choice.

London Area: E
11 Ludgate Circus
London EC4M 7lQ
Tel: 01-489 8032
Fax: 01-329 0210

London Area: C
145 Oxford Street
London W1R 1TV
Tel: 01-434 9644
Fax: 01-287 0580

1 Kingsway
London WC2B 6XF
Tel: 01-836 9272
Fax: 01-497 9142

5a Town Centre
Hatfield
Hertfordshire AL10 0JZ
Tel: 07072 75411
Fax: 07072 62730

2 High Street
Kingston-upon-Thames
Surrey KT1 1EY
Tel: 01-549 5501
Fax: 01-547 1918

Knight Benton
Industries: All
Placements: Accounts clerks, bilingual operators, computer operators, receptionists, secretaries and personal assistants, telephone and telex operators, word processing operators.
Qualifications: Typing 40 wpm, shorthand 70/90/100 wpm, audio stages 2 and 3. We look for good grammar and numeracy skills. Tests given at interview.
Skills: Computer, shorthand, typing, word processing.
Conwell House
42 East Street
Chichester
Sussex West PO19 1HX
Tel: 0243 776310

Kompass Ltd
Industries: All
Placements: Accounts clerks, bilingual operators, receptionists, secretaries and personal assistants, telephone and telex operators, word processing operators.
Qualifications: Typing 50+ wpm, shorthand 50+ wpm, audio 50+ wpm. Good standard of English. Professional qualifications where applicable.
Skills: WP, VDU, shorthand, typing.
Comments: Recruitment consultancy dealing with both permanent and temporary vacancies at all levels.

London Area: E
127 Cheapside
1st Floor
London EC2
Tel: 01-600 8091
Fax: 01-726 4290

London Area: S
170 Sloane Street
London SW1
Tel: 01-245-1267
Fax: 01-235-5003

London Area: C
10 Hills Place
London W1
Tel: 01-734 2921
Fax: 01-494 2273

L
L.M.S
Industries: Law, media, medical, clerical/secretarial, publishing.
Placements: Accounts clerks, bilingual operators, computer operators, receptionists, secretaries and personal assistants, telephone and telex operators, word processing operators.
Qualifications: Typing 40/60+ wpm, shorthand 90+ wpm, Less skilled applicants such as school leavers also considered, but must have a good standard of education, be articulate and well groomed.
Skills: Computer, shorthand, typing, word processing.
Comments: We are a small agency giving a very personal service to our candidates and clients. We spend a lot of time with the former and latter alike, establishing the requirments of each party to ensure

that our temps are placed correctly.
24 Cheap Street
Newbury
Berkshire RG14 5DB
Tel: 0635 45612
Fax: 0635 43623

La Creme
Industries: All
Placements: Receptionists, secretaries and personal assistants, word processing operators.
Qualifications: Typing 55/60 wpm, shorthand 90 wpm, WP experience an advantage.
Skills: Shorthand, typing, word processing.
Comments: We are a consultancy specialising in the recruitment of all levels of temporary and permanent secretarial and wordprocessing staff. We are looking for temporary staff who have a good educational background and proficient secretarial skills.

London Area: C
4 Princes Street
London W1R 7RA
Tel: 01-491 1868
Fax: 01-495 6171

Lewis Recruitment
Industries: All
Placements: Accounts clerks, bilingual operators, computer operators, receptionists, secretaries and personal assistants, telephoneand telex operators, word processing operators.
Qualifications: Clerk/typists 40 wpm typing, 2 O'levels. Copy/audio typists 50 wpm, 2 O'levels, including English Language.Shorthand/typists 50 wpm typing, 80+ wpm shorthand, O'levels.
Skills: Shorthand, typing, word processing.
55 High Street South
Dunstable
Bedfordshire LU6 2SF
Tel: 0582 601391
Fax: 0582 661793

Link Recruitment Services
Industries: All
Placements: Accounts clerks, bilingual operators, computer operators, receptionists, secretaries and personal assistants, telephoneand telex operators, word processing operators.
Qualifications: Typing 30 wpm, minimum. Shorthand 60 wpm.
Skills: Shorthand, typing, word processing.
Comments: We look for temps who enjoy a varied work environment.

71 London Road
East Grinstead
Sussex West RH19 1EQ
Tel: 0342 313234 (5 lines)

London Town Staff Bureau
Industries: All, mainly publishing
Placements: Receptionists, secretaries and personal assistants, word processing operators.
Qualifications: Typing 40 wpm, shorthand 70/80 wpm.
Skills: Typing
Comments: We specialise in publishing and non-commercial companies.

London Area: C
19 Broad Court
London WC2B 5QN
Tel: 01-836 0627
Fax: 01-836 1997

LRS Ltd
Industries: All, law
Placements: Accounts clerks, bilingual operators, computer operators, receptionists, secretaries and personal assistants, telephoneand telex operators, word processing operators.
Qualifications: Minimum O' level standard. Typing and shorthand speeds depends upon demands of temporary positions.
Skills: Computer, shorthand, typing, word processing.
Comments: We are an independent agency dealing with a variety of temporary and permanent vacancies, including legal secretaries,audio typists, general clerks and VDU and WP operators.

31 Beach Road
Littlehampton
Sussex West BN17 5JA
Tel: 0903 716782
Fax: 0903 726318

Luton Secretarial Staff Bureau
Industries: All
Placements: Accounts clerks, bilingual operators, computer operators, receptionists, secretaries and personal assistants, telephone and telex operators, word processing operators.
Qualifications: No minimum qualification. Personality and attitude are seen as being important.
Skills: Computer, shorthand, typing, word processing.
Comments: Independent bureau which aims to match the requirements of the company with those of the worker.
6 Union Street
Luton
Bedfordshire LU1 3AN
Tel: 0582 451588
Fax: 0582 22069

M

Mackay Personnel
Industries: All
Placements: Receptionists, word processing operators, secretaries and personal assistants.
Qualifications: Typing 40+ wpm, shorthand 80+ wpm.
Skills: Shorthand, typing, word processing.
Comments: We need solid, reliable temps and staff with good WP experience.

London Area: C
70/71 New Bond Street
London W1A 4DY
Tel: 01-491 0383
Fax: 01-409 2555

Manpower plc
Industries: All
Placements: Accounts clerks, bilingual operators, computer operators, receptionists, secretaries and personal assistants, telephone and telex operators, word processing operators.
Qualifications: We use our own skill measurement tests.
Skills: Shorthand, typing, word processing, computer.
Comments: Market leader in all forms of temporary work, specialising in office automation. We provide free training to our field staff.
Manpower House
272 High Street
Slough
Berkshire SL1 1LJ
Tel: 0753 73111
Fax: 0753 824524

Mediad
Industries: All
Placements: Receptionists, secretaries and personal assistants.
Qualifications: Typing 50 wpm, shorthand 80 wpm, WP skills preferred. O' and A' level standard education desirable.
Skills: Typing, word processing, shorthand useful.
Comments: Professional, secretarial recruitment consultancy specialising in jobs in media and advertising. We provide quality tempwork for people looking to work short or long term.

London Area: S
Finland House
56 Haymarket
London SW1
Tel: 01-925 0139

Medical & General, The
Industries: Medical
Placements: Receptionists, secretaries and personal assistants, word processing.
Qualifications: Minimum typing speed of 40 wpm, shorthand 80 wpm.
Skills: Shorthand, typing, word processing.
Comments: London Area: C
6 Paddington Street
London W1M 4BE
Tel: 01-935 9426/4061

Meridian Associates Ltd
Industries: All, media, medical, publishing.
Placements: Accounts clerks, bilingual operators, receptionists, secretaries and personal assistants, telephone and telex operators, word processing operators. Occasional overseas placements.
Qualifications: Depends entirely on the assignment.
Skills: Shorthand, typing, word processing.
Comments: Small, privately owned consultancy. Limited temporary department, on avarage 40 temps put out.
London Area: S
1st Floor, 7 Belgrave Road
Victoria
London SW1V 1QB
Tel: 01-828 5757
Fax: 01-828 5569

London Area: C
Museum House
25 Museum Street
London WC1A 1JT
Tel: 01-255 1555
Fax: 01-487 3018

Merrow Employment Agency Ltd
Industries: All, specialising in linguistics.
Placements: Accounts clerks, bilingual operators, receptionists, secretaries and personal assistants, telephone and telex operators, word processing operators. Overseas placements in Europe only.
Qualifications: Typing 45 wpm minimum, shorthand 90 wpm, audio 45 wpm. A' level standard of education preferred, especially in language subjects.
Skills: Computer, shorthand, typing, word processing.
Comments: We specialise in temps with 2 or more languages.
London Area: C
7 Henrietta Place
London W1M 9AG
Tel: 01-408 1286

Michele Zarak Recruitment
Industries: Advertising, PR and design
Placements: Receptionists, secretaries and personal assistants, word processing operators.
Qualifications: Typing 50 wpm.
Skills: Typing, word processing and switchboard skills.
Comments: London Area: C
10a James Street
London WC2E 8BT
Tel: 01-240 5931
Fax: 01-240 5759

Middleton Jeffers Recruitment Ltd
Industries: All, except medical secretaries
Placements: Bilingual operators, computer operators, receptionists, secretaries and personal assistants, telephone and telex operators, word processing operators.
Qualifications: Typing 50 wpm and some experience of word processing an advantage.
Skills: Shorthand, typing, word processing, computer.
Comments: We are a recruitment consultancy with a high calibre profile and a wide and varied client base. We have a small successful team of good reliable temps who take on short, long and temporary to permanent assignments.
London Area: E
15 Devonshire Row
London EC2M 4RQ
Tel: 01-377 6777
Fax: 01-377 5079

Milton Staff
Industries: All
Placements: Accounts clerks, computer operators, receptionists, secretaries and personal assistants, telephone and telex operators, word processing operators.
Qualifications: None required
Skills: Computer, shorthand, typing, word processing.
Comments: We are a small, personal agency with a very good reputation, both with our applicants and with our clients. Temp secretaries are always in demand. We recruit school leavers.

London Area: E
76 Watling Street
London EC4M 9BJ
Tel: 01-248 8141

Mison Recruitment Services Ltd
Industries: All
Placements: Accounts clerks, bilingual operators, computer operators, receptionists, secretaries and personal assistants, telephone and telex operators and word processing operators.
Qualifications: None required. Basic GCSE's preferred.
Skills: Computer, shorthand, typing and word processing.
Comments: Mison seeks intelligent well rounded individuals who will offer an excellent service to our clients.

London Area: E
Ludgate House
107/111 Fleet Street
London EC4A 2AB
Tel: 01-583 5441
Fax: 01-583 1784

Miss Reception
Industries: All
Placements: Receptionists
Qualifications: Minimum of one year's reception and switchboard experience.
Skills: Switchboards
Comments: We only handle reception duties, therefore temps must be very well presented and well spoken with switchboard experience.

London Area: C
2nd Floor, Wells House
79 Wells Street
London W1P 3RE
Tel: 01-580 5522

Mistprestige Recruitment Consultants
Industries: All
Placements: Bilingual operators, receptionists, secretaries and personal assistants, telephone and telex operators, word processing operators. Placements also made for Dublin, Ireland.
Qualifications: Every vacancy has a different minimum requirement.
Skills: Shorthand, typing, word processing, audio.
Comments: Predominately have secretarial vacancies for temps and offer long and short term bookings.

London Area: E
5 London Wall Buildings
London EC2M 5NT
Tel: 01-528 7248
Fax: 01-588 8012

London Area: S
197 Knightsbridge
London SW7 1RB
Tel: 01-581 9799
Fax: 01-581 9411

London Area: C
4 Denman Street
London W1V 7RH
Tel: 01-439 2308
Fax: 01-437 1637

25 South Moulton Street
London W1Y 1DB
Tel: 01-408 1117
Fax: 01-629 2031

Multilingual Services
Industries: All
Placements: Bilingual operators, receptionists, secretaries and personal assistants.
Qualifications: Typing 50 wpm and shorthand 90+ wpm and word processing preferrable. For secretary/linguists A' level standard minimum in relevant language.
Skills: Shorthand, typing, WP.
Comments: We look for bilingual secretaries at all levels with good languages and skills. A lesser demand for translators who must also be able to type their work and preferably also use a word processor. We test all languages as well as secretarial skills.

London Area: C
22 Charing Croos Road
London WC2H 0HR
Tel: 01-836 3794
Fax: 01-836 6755

N
Norton Staff Agency Ltd
Industries: All

Placements: Accounts clerks, computer operators, receptionists, secretaries and personal assistants, telephone and telexoperators.

Qualifications: Typing 35+ wpm, shorthand 80 wpm (preferrably not Teeline), RSA I and Audio, Secretarial course (BTEC National,etc), knowledge of at least 1 word processor.

Skills: Computer, shorthand, typing, word processing.

Comments: We are an independent agency, establised for over 25 years. We offer a personalised service to both applicant and client.We are looking for all kinds of temps, from junior secretaries to senior PA's, and warehouse staff.

26 Park Place
Stevenage
Hertfordshire SG1 7BR
Tel: 0438 314501
Fax: 0438 742233

O
Office Angels
Industries: All

Placements: Accounts clerks, computer operators, receptionists, secretaries and personal assistants, telephone and telexoperators.

Qualifications: None required

Skills: Computer, shorthand, typing, word processing.

Comments: Medium sized, personalised recruitment consultants dealing in permanent and temporary placements in all categories.Unskilled applicants also catered for.

London Area: E
128 Cheapside
London EC2V 3PD
Tel: 01-606 0011

60 Cornhill
London EC3V 3PD
Tel: 01-621 9363

12 Groveland Court
Bow Lane
London EC4M 9EH
Tel: 01-606 0011

London Area: S
71 The Broadway
London SW19 1QE
Tel: 01-542 6688

189 Victoria Street
London SW1E 5NE
Tel: 01-630 0844

London Area: C
111 Baker Street
London W1M 1FE
Tel: 01-935 7248

Wells House
79 Wells Street
London W1P 4AX
Tel: 01-734 1200

12 Swallow Street
London W1R 1RF
Tel: 01-434 0683

25 Oxford Street
London W1R 1RF
Tel: 01-434 9545

311 Regent Street
London W1R 5AJ
Tel: 01-629 0777

115 High Holborn
London WC1V 6JJ
Tel: 01-430 2531

Angel House
28 Friar Street
Reading
Berkshire RG1 1DP
Tel: 0734 508001

274 High Street
Slough
Berkshire SL1 1NB
Tel: 0753 691484

Sovereign Court
203 Witan Gate East
Milton Keynes
Buckinghamshire MK9 2HP
Tel: 0908 678600

72 South Street
Romford
Essex RM1 1RX
Tel: 0708 24718

72 South Street
Romford
Essex RM1 1RX
Tel: 0708 24718

81 Church Street
Basingstoke
Hampshire RG21 1QT
Tel: 0256 464744

112 The Parade
Watford
Hertfordshire WD1 2AU
Tel: 0923 55626

25 The Mall
Bromley
Kent BR1 1TR
Tel: 01-464 5225

76 College Road
Harrow
Middlesex HA1 1BQ
Tel: 01-861 2949

251 High Street
Hounslow
Middlesex TW3 1EA
Tel: 01-572 8787

12 Suffolk House
College Road
Croydon
Surrey CR0 1PF
Tel: 01-681 3039

18 Jeffries Passage
Guildford
Surrey GU1 4AP
Tel: 0483 578989

89/91 Clarence Street
Kingston-upon-Thames
Surrey KT1 1QY
Tel: 01-541 0544

Office People Recruitment Consultants
Industries: All
Placements: Accounts clerks, computer operators, receptionists, secretaries and personal assistants, telephone and telexoperators.
Qualifications: Equivalent RSA I Typing for clerk typists (35 wpm), equivalent RSA II for anything secretarial(typing 45 wpm,shorthand 80 wpm). GCSE or good CSE in English and Mathematics useful.

Skills: Computer, shorthand, typing, word processing.
Comments: 3-5 North Street
Chichester
Sussex West PO19 1LB
Tel: 0243 778021

Omegar Personnel Limited
Industries: All,
Placements: Accounts clerks, computer operators, receptionists, secretaries and personal assistants, telephone and telex operators,word processing operators.
Qualifications: Typing or word processing 45/50 wpm, shorthand 35/40 wpm. GCSE's in Maths and English.
Skills: Computer, shorthand, typing, word processing.
Comments: We cater for local industry and commerce and seek reliable and well presented temps.

London Area: N
74a Belsize Lane
Hampstead
London NW3 5BJ
Tel: 01-435 7492

London Area: E
125-129 Middlesex Street
London E1
Tel: 01-929 4133

27a High Street
Andover
Hampshire SP10 1LJ
Tel: 0264 57629
Fax: 0264 333350

Osborne Richardson Ltd
Industries: All, law, banking
Placements: Receptionists, secretaries and personal assistants, telephone and telex operators, word processing operators.
Qualifications: Typing 50 wpm, shorthand 80 wpm. GCSE or CSE level education.
Skills: Shorthand, typing, word processing.
Comments: Small consultancy specialising in secretarial staff, but covering many different industries.

London Area: C
110 New Bond Street
London W1Y 3AA
Tel: 01-409 2393
Fax: 01-491 3993

OV Selection
Industries: All
Placements: Accounts clerks, bilingual operators, receptionists, secretaries and personal assistants, telephone and telex operators, word processing operators.
Qualifications: Reasonable presentable people with skills appropriate to the job.
Skills: Shorthand, typing, word processing.
Comments: Single branch recruitment office.

London Area: S
Ashford House
15 Wilton Road
London SW1V 1LT
Tel: 01-828 8345

P

Paragons Personnel
Industries: All, law, banking
Placements: Accounts clerks, bilingual operators, receptionists, secretaries and personal assistants, telephone and telex operators, word processing operators. Overseas placements.
Qualifications: None required
Skills: Computer, shorthand, typing, word processing.
Comments: Independent agency operating a Commercial and Industrial Division. Looking for temps to cover all aspects of officework.

9 Latimer Street
Romsey
Hampshire SO51 8DF
Tel: 0794 524212

Part Time Careers Limited
Industries: All
Placements: Accounts clerks, receptionists, secretaries and personal assistants, telephone and telex operators, word processing operators.
Qualifications: Typing 50 wpm, shorthand 100 wpm, word processing and audio useful. Minimum of 6 O'levels.
Skills: Shorthand, typing, word processing.
Comments: We look for high calibre personnel and specialize in part-time, permanent and temporary office staff.

London Area: C
10 Golden Square
London W1R 3AF
Tel: 01-437 3103
Fax: 01-494 1154

Personnel Support
Industries: All
Placements: Accounts clerks, bilingual operators, computer operators, receptionists, secretaries and personal assistants, telephone and telex operators, word processing operators.
Qualifications: Qualifications relevant to the position sought.
Skills: Computer, shorthand, typing, word processing.
Comments: We supply a wide range of office staff.

London Area: E
Brushfield House
12 Brushfield Street
London E1 6AN
Tel: 01-528 8877
Fax: 01-375 1045

Peters & Smyth Staff Bureau Ltd
Industries: All
Placements: Executive secretarial appointments only.
Qualifications: None required
Skills: Computer, shorthand, typing, word processing.
Comments: An employment agency with all grades of temporary workers.

Senior Executive Secretaries Div
4 The Green
Richmond
Surrey TW9 1PL
Tel: 01-332 2999

Peters & Smyth Staff Bureau Ltd
Industries: All

Placements: Accounts clerks, bilingual operators, computer operators, receptionists, secretaries and personal assistants, telephone and telex operators, word processing operators.
Qualifications: None required
Skills: Computer, shorthand, typing, word processing.
Comments: An employment agency with all grades of temporary workers.

London Area: W
44 The Mall
Ealing
London W5 3TJ
Tel: 01-840 3130

1 The Bridge
Wealdstone
Harrow
Middlesex HA3 5AB
Tel: 01-861 1311

Head Office, Pharmacia House
Prince Regent Street
Hounslow
Middlesex TW3 1NE
Tel: 01-569 4242

2a Kingsley Road
Hounslow
Middlesex TW3 1NP
Tel: 01-577 3434

53a Church Street
Staines
Middlesex TW18 4EN
Tel: 0784 65575

Portman Recruitment Services Ltd
Industries: Law, banking, computer and general.
Placements: Accounts clerks, computer operators, receptionists, secretaries and personal assistants, telephone and telex operators, word processing operators.
Qualifications: Typing 40 wpm, shorthand 80 wpm, good presentation and speech. Also relevant requirements for specialist areas of law, computing and banking.
Skills: Computer, shorthand, typing, word processing.
London Area: E
15 Great St Thomas Apostle
London EC4V 2BB
Tel: 01-236 1113
Fax: 01-489 8991

London Area: C
Ilford House
133-135 Oxford Street
London W1R 1TD
Tel: 01-494 2596
Fax: 01-493 1585

Q

QED (Quest Employment Development Services)
Industries: All
Placements: Accounts clerks, bilingual operators, computer operators, receptionists, secretaries and personal assistants, telephone and telex operators, word processing operators.
Qualifications: Typing 55 wpm, shorthand 80 wpm. 5 O' levels but A' levels preferred.
Skills: Computer, shorthand, typing, word processing.
Comments: Temps must be skilled and reliable.

London Area: C
37 Dover Street
Mayfair
London W1X 3RB
Tel: 01-409 1343
Fax: 01-409 1525

R

Recruitment Company, The
Industries: All
Placements: Receptionists, secretaries and personal assistants.
Qualifications: None required
Skills: Computer, shorthand, typing, word processing.
Comments: Independent agency with clients in the West End and City. Seeks a wide range of temps in the secretarial field.

London Area: C
5 Garrick Street
London WC2E 9AR
Tel: 01-831 1220
Fax: 01-379 4558

Reed Employment

Industries: All

Placements: Accounts clerks, bilingual operators, computer operators, receptionists, secretaries and personal assistants, telephone and telex operators, word processing operators.

Qualifications: None required. All potential candidates are fully screened and tested.

Skills: Computer, shorthand, typing, word processing.

Comments: Reed Employment recruits permanent and temporary staff in the following areas: secretarial, WP operators and all office skills, accountancy, nursing, industrial, insurance and computing.

London Area: N
152 Fore Street
London N18 2XA
Tel: 01-803 2166

30 High Road
London N22 6RX
Tel: 01-888 5214

376 Holloway Road
London N7 6RN
Tel: 01-607 8763

141 Camden High Street
London NW1 7JR
Tel: 01-267 4091

London Area: E
76 Broadway
Stratford Centre
London E15 1NG
Tel: 01-555 0313

10 Leather Lane
London EC1N 7RA
Tel: 01-831 7685

192 Bishopsgate
London EC2M 4NR
Tel: 01-283 0066

192 Bishopsgate
London EC2M 4NR
Tel: 01-283 0066

47 Liverpool Street
London EC2M 7PR
Tel: 01-621 0155

34 Wormwood Street
London EC2N 1RE
Tel: 01-638 1666

65 Fenchurch Street
London EC3M 4BE
Tel: 01-481 2661

23 Lime Street
London EC3M 7AE
Tel: 01-623 2213

Cannon Street Station
Cannon Street
London EC4N 6AP
Tel: 01-929 7959

London Area: S
19 Borough High Street
London SE1 9SE
Tel: 01-403 0171

68 Lewisham High Street
London SE13 5JH
Tel: 01-852 7411

112 Powis Street
London SE18 6LU
Tel: 01-317 8591

44 Denmark Hill
London SE5 8RZ
Tel: 01-733 2173

176 Putney High Street
London SW15 1RS
Tel: 01-788 2432

9 Wimbledon Bridge
London SW19 7NW
Tel: 01-947 4473

181 Victoria Street
London SW1E 5NE
Tel: 01-828 2401

143 Victoria Street
London SW1E 5NH
Tel: 01-834 1801

London Area: C
197 Regent Street
London W1R 7WA
Tel: 01-439 0303

54 South Molton Street
London W1Y 1HF
Tel: 01-491 4610

5 High Holborn
London WC1V 6DR
Tel: 01-405 6525

80 Kingsway
Holborn
London WC2B 6AE
Tel: 01-404 9542

159 Charing Cross Road
London WC2H 0EN
Tel: 01-734 8694

65 The Strand
London WC2N 5LR
Tel: 01-836 8815

London Area: W

62 Nottinghill Gate
London W11 3HT
Tel: 01-229 9452

202 Uxbridge Road
London W12 7JP
Tel: 01-749 2283

116 The Broadway
London W13 0SY
Tel: 01-579 4465

94 High Street
Acton
London W3 9QX
Tel: 01-992 8984

402 Chiswick High Road
London W4 5TF
Tel: 01-994 0106

41 St John's Road
London W4 5TF
Tel: 01-223 8484

26 The Broadway
London W5 2NP
Tel: 01-579 3481

Reed House
65 Westcroft Square
London W6 0TA
Tel: 01-748 3511
Fax: 01-748 2417

81 George Street
Luton
Bedfordshire LU1 2AT
Tel: 0582 417979

19 High Street
Bracknell
Berkshire RG12 1DL
Tel: 0344 486777

19 High Street
Bracknell
Berkshire RG12 1DL
Tel: 0344 486777

103 High Street
Maidenhead
Berkshire SL6 1JX
Tel: 0628 73656

70 Broad Street
Reading
Berkshire RG1 2AF
Tel: 0734 573464

164 High Street
Slough
Berkshire SL1 1JP
Tel: 0753 25062

304 Farnham Road
Slough
Berkshire SL1 4XL
Tel: 0753 34141

114 Peascod Street
Windsor
Berkshire SL4 1DN
Tel: 0753 857624

456 Midsummer Boulevard
Milton Keynes
Buckinghamshire MK9 2EA
Tel: 0908 660057

19 Station Parade
Barking
Essex IG11 8EA
Tel: 01-591 6900

35 Cranbrook Road
Ilford
Essex IG1 4PA
Tel: 01-514 3777

148 High Street
Southend-on-Sea
Essex SS1 1JX
Tel: 0702 612511

22 Wote Street
Basingstoke
Hampshire RG21 1NL
Tel: 0256 463385

2 Newnham Parade
College Road
Cheshunt
Hertfordshire EN8 9NU
Tel: 0992 38121

24 Maidenhead Street
Hertford
Hertfordshire SG14 1DR
Tel: 0992 583251

11 Market Place
St Albans
Hertfordshire AL3 5DR
Tel: 0727 43410

68 High Street
Watford
Hertfordshire WD1 2BS
Tel: 0923 56269

104 The Broadway
Bexleyheath
Kent DA6 7DE
Tel: 01-304 8211

20 High Street
Bromley
Kent BR1 1EA
Tel: 01-460 2123

11 High Street
Dartford
Kent DA1 1DT
Tel: 0322 29531

7 The Town
Church Street
Enfield
Middlesex EN2 6LE
Tel: 01-367 6699

22 The Centre
Feltham
Middlesex TW13 4UA
Tel: 01-890 7156

52 The Broadway
Greenford
Middlesex UB6 9QA
Tel: 01-578 6853

310 Station Road
Harrow
Middlesex HA1 2DX
Tel: 01-863 0244

267 Station Road
Harrow
Middlesex HA1 2TB
Tel: 01-863 9211

42 Station Road
Hayes
Middlesex UB3 4DD
Tel: 01-573 6272

178 High Street
Hounslow
Middlesex TW3 1HL
Tel:

352 Bath Road
Hounslow
Middlesex TW4 7HW
Tel: 01-572 1821

91 High Street
Staines
Middlesex TW18 4PQ
Tel: 0784 58526

12 King Street
Twickenham
Middlesex TW1 3SN
Tel: 01-892 9107

20 High Street
Uxbridge
Middlesex UB8 1JN
Tel: 0895 51665

4 Ealing Road
Wembley
Middlesex HA0 4TL
Tel: 01-903 0151

451 High Road
Wembley
Middlesex HA9 7AF
Tel: 01-902 6111

1 Cambridge Walk
Camberley
Surrey GU15 3SW
Tel: 0276 691547

36 George Street
Croydon
Surrey CR0 1PB
Tel: 01-688 3498

115 North End Road
Croydon
Surrey CR0 1TG
Tel: 01-686 7803

23 high Street
Epsom
Surrey KT19 8DD
Tel: 03737 43522

51 High Street
Guildford
Surrey GU1 3DY
Tel: 0483 300428

68 Clarence Street
Kingston-upon-Thames
Surrey KT1 1NN
Tel: 01-570 2300

64 London Road
Morden
Surrey SJ4 5BE
Tel: 01-640 5426

74 High Street
New Malden
Surrey KT3 4ET
Tel: 01-949 1935

21 George Street
Richmond on Thames
Surrey TW9 1HY
Tel: 01-948 2151

24 Victoria Road
Surbiton
Surrey KT6 4JZ
Tel: 01-399 5367

101 High Street
Sutton
Surrey SM1 1JF
Tel: 01-643 6331

20 High Street
Walton-on-Thames
Surrey KT12 1DA
Tel: 0932 231414

3 Harland House
44 Commerical Way
Woking
Surrey GU21 1HW
Tel: 04862 24284

18 The Martlets
Crawley
Sussex RH10 1ES
Tel: 0293 547455

Ridgeway Employment Agency Limited
Industries: All
Placements: Accounts clerks, bilingual operators, computer operators, receptionists, secretaries and personal assistants, telephoneand telex operators, word processing operators.
Qualifications: None required. All potential candidates are fully screened and tested.
Skills: Computer, shorthand, typing, word processing.
Comments: C I Tower - St George's Square
High Street
New Malden
Surrey KT3 4HH

Tel: 01-336 2666
Fax: 01-336 1981

RNW Recruitment Ltd
Industries: Law, media, medical, publishing, office, secretarial, catering.
Placements: Accounts clerks, receptionists, secretaries and personal assistants, telephone and telex operators, word processingoperators.
Qualifications: Typing 40 wpm+, for secretarial bookings. Shorthand and WP skills an advantage, but not essential. Good level ofeducation and work experience preferred.
Skills: Shorthand, typing and word processing.
Comments: RNW Recruitment is part of the RNW group -others cover contract engineering, recruitment, executive search andselection, accounting services and debt collection. Looking for temps in these fields - secretarial, WP, admin, accounts and catering.
7 Church Street
Staines
Middlesex TW18 4EN
Tel: 0784 57513/5

S
Scan-Tec Employment Service
Industries: All
Placements: Accounts clerks, bilingual operators, computer operators, receptionists, secretaries and personal assistants, telephoneand telex operators, word processing operators.
Qualifications: Clerk typist 35 wpm, copy typist 45 wpm, junior shorthand 80 wpm and 40 wpm typing.
Skills: Computer, shorthand, typing, word processing.
Comments: The secretarial/clerical division is one of three divisions in this agency. Looking for workers in all office disciplines but especially secretaries, typists and word processor operators.
Scan-Tec House
19 Church Street
Bishop's Stortford
Hertfordshire CM23 2LY
Tel: 0279 58362

Secretaries Plus
Industries: All
Placements: Receptionists, secretaries and personal assistants, telephone and telex operators, word processing operators.
Qualifications: Typing 50 wpm, shorthand 80 wpm.
Skills: Shorthand, typing, word processing.
Comments: We are valued by companies in the City and West End of London. Our temporary controllers have a Personnel Management background which ensures that the assignments match your skills and requirements as well as meeting the client's needs.

London Area: E
146 Bishopsgate
London EC2M 4JX
Tel: 01-377 8600
Fax: 01-375 1950

London Area: C
44 Conduit Street
London W1R 9FB
Tel: 01-439 4344
Fax: 01-434 4423

Situations Vacant Ltd
Industries: All
Placements: Accounts clerks, computer operators, receptionists, secretaries and personal assistants, telephone and telex operators, word processing operators.
Qualifications: None required. Experience preferred.
Skills: Computer, shorthand, typing, word processing.
Comments: 3/5 George Street West
Luton
Bedfordshire LU1 2BJ
Tel: 0582 405888

Solution Bureau
Industries: All
Placements: Accounts clerks, computer operators, receptionists, secretaries and personal assistants, telephone and telex operators, word processing operators.
Qualifications: Typing 45 wpm, shorthand 80 wpm, 5 O' levels and a full driving licence.
Skills: Computer, shorthand, typing, word processing.
Comments: Small employment bureau dealing with a wide range of temporary and permanent staff.

London Area: C
29 Maddox Street
London W1R 9LD
Tel: 01-491 3130

St Stephen's Secretariat Limited, The
Industries: All
Placements: Accounts clerks, receptionists, secretaries and personal assistants, telephone and telex operators, word processing operators.
Qualifications: Typing 45+ wpm.
Skills: Shorthand, typing, word processing.
Comments: A small agency which aims to offer an efficient and friendly service.

London Area: S
316 Vauxhall Bridge Road
London SW1V 1AA
Tel: 01-834 0031
Fax: 01-828 9317

Staffline Employment Agency
Industries: All
Placements: Accounts clerks, computer operators, receptionists, secretaries and personal assistants, telephone and telex operators, word processing operators.
Qualifications: None required
Skills: Computer, shorthand, typing, word processing.
Comments: We also recruit industrial, driving, commercial and technical staff on a temporary or permanent basis.

83-85 Cranbrook Road, Ilford
Essex IG1 4PG
Tel: 01-514 8544
Fax: 01-553 5135

Stilton Staff (ER) Ltd
Industries: All
Placements: Accounts clerks, computer operators, receptionists, secretaries and personal assistants, telephone and telex operators.

Qualifications: None required
Skills: Computer, shorthand, typing, word processing.
Comments: 32 Long Causeway
Peterborough
Cambridgeshire PE1 1YJ
Tel: 0773 60531/2

Stirling Recruitment
Industries: All
Placements: Accounts clerks, bilingual operators, computer operators, receptionists, secretaries and personal assistants, telephone and telex operators.
Qualifications: None required
Skills: Computer, shorthand, typing, word processing.
Comments: Mainly concerned with secretarial/office recruitment area, with a specialist temporary division.
36 Station Road
Redhill
Surrey RH1 1PH
Tel: 0737 768847
Fax: 0737 766938

Susan Beck Recruitment
Industries: All
Placements: Accounts clerks, receptionists, secretaries and personal assistants, telephone and telex operators, word processing operators.
Qualifications: Good secretarial skills, smart appearance and flexible manner important.
Skills: Shorthand, typing, word processing.
Comments: We give practical career counselling and advice if needed. Applicants dealt with on a personal basis.
London Area: S
10 Beauchamp Place
Knightsbridge
London SW3 1NQ
Tel: 01-584 6242/3/4
Fax: 01-584 2184

Susan Hamilton Personnel Services
Industries: All

Placements: Bilingual operators, receptionists, secretaries and personal assistants, telephone and telex operators, word processing operators.
Qualifications: Typing 50 wpm, shorthand 80 wpm. Education to O'level standard.
Skills: Shorthand, typing, word processing.
Comments: Small, personalised consultancy.
London Area: C
33 St Georges Street
London W1R 9FA
Tel: 01-629 9157
Fax: 01-499 4878

Swift Employment
Industries: All
Placements: Accounts clerks, bilingual operators, computer operators, receptionists, secretaries and personal assistants, telephone and telex operators, word processing operators.
Qualifications: The ability to liaise with the client.
Skills: Computer, shorthand, typing, word processing.
Comments: We are a single branch high street agency operating on high principles and personal relationships, established almost 9 years. We are fully computerised.
3 Homesdale Road
Reigate
Surrey RH2 0BA
Tel: 0737 22531
Fax: 0737 249253

Swift Personnel
Industries: All
Placements: Accounts clerks, computer operators, receptionists, secretaries and personal assistants, telephone and telex operators, word processing operators.
Qualifications: Typing 40 wpm, shorthand 80 wpm, minimum 2 O' levels - English and Maths.
Skills: Computer, shorthand, typing, word processing.
Comments: We are part of Swift Personnel, Swift Technical and Swift Nursing. We

look for temporary staff in all office work. Our nursing section look for part-time nurses and our Technical Division look for contract workers in off-shore and building services.

49 High Street
Barnet
Hertfordshire EN5 5UW
Tel: 01-441 5991
Fax: 01-441 7160

T
Tate Appointments
Industries: All
Placements: Accounts clerks, receptionists, secretaries and personal assistants, telephone and telex operators.
Qualifications: Typing 50 wpm, shorthand 70 wpm, 5 'O' levels or equivalent, friendly and outgoing personality.
Skills: Shorthand, typing, word processing.
Comments: Small independent consultancy that specialises in secretarial, general office and management recruitment both for permanent and temporary vacancies.

London Area: C
70/71 New Bond Street
London W1Y 9DE
Tel: 01-408 0424
Fax: 01-493 8790

TAV Staff Agency Limited
Industries: All
Placements: Accounts clerks, bilingual operators, computer operators, receptionists, secretaries and personal assistants, telephone and telex operators, word processing operators.
Qualifications: None required. All applicants are tested in spelling, filing, arithmetic, shorthand, typing and audio to determine their relevant skill level.
Skills: Shorthand, typing, word processing.
Comments: The secretarial division of our organisation is TAV office team, and is able to place all levels of temporary and permanent applicants in all areas of commerce and industry.

17a Church Street
Basingstoke
Hampshire RG21 1PG
Tel: 0256 471717

67 Leigh Road
Eastleigh
Hampshire SO5 4DF
Tel: 0703 614711

201 West Street
Fareham
Hampshire PO16 OEN
Tel: 0329 282016

12 East Street
Havant
Hampshire PO9 1AQ
Tel: 0705 476731

34a-42a Market Parade
Havant
Hampshire PO9 1QF
Tel: 0705 471711

237 Commercial Road
Portsmouth
Hampshire PO1 4BJ
Tel: 0705 819341

8 Bargate
Southampton
Hampshire SO1 0DP
Tel: 0703 634534

56 High Street
Camberley
Surrey GU15 3RS
Tel: 0276 691930

62 Chapel Road
Worthing
Sussex BN11 1BN
Tel: 0903 820911

Team-Sel
Industries: All
Placements: Accounts clerks, computer operators, receptionists, secretaries and personal assistants, telephone and telex operators, word processing operators.
Qualifications: None required
Skills: Computer, shorthand, typing, word processing.
Comments: We have four specialist divisions: Offshore, Overseas, Computer and Secretarial/administrative.

Team-Sel House
148 King Street
Great Yarmouth
Norfolk
Tel: 0493 851611
Fax: 0493 854833

Teamwork Recruitment
Industries: All
Placements: Accounts clerks, computer operators, receptionists, secretaries and personal assistants, telephone and telex operators, word processing operators.
Qualifications: Typing 45 wpm.
Skills: Shorthand, typing, word processing.
Comments: Local to Banbury and its ten mile radius.

Tintern House
37 High Street
Banbury
Oxfordshire OX16 8EQ
Tel: 0295 53440
Fax: 0295 69188

The City Word Processing Centre
Industries: All
Placements: Word processing operators.
Qualifications: None required
Skills: None required - WP training available.
Comments: We are a word processing centre, involved in anything related to WP training, temporary and permanent recruitment, bureau facilities and WP consultancy. We look for people who have, or can be trained to have good WP ability.

London Area: E
6 Long Lane
London EC1A 9HA
Tel: 01-600 8391
Fax: 01-600 4207

Times Computer Services Limited
Industries: All
Placements: Accounts clerks, computer operators, receptionists, secretaries and personal assistants, telephone and telex operators, word processing operators.
Qualifications: Typing 45 wpm. We will consider people with any experience in the office/computer market.
Skills: Computer, shorthand, typing, word processing.
Comments: Place workers into the computer industry. Specialise in computer operators, VDU operators, typists and word processor operators.

London Area: C
95 York Street
London W1H 1DU
Tel: 01-258 1878
Fax: 01-724 5617

Tops Personnel Services
Industries: All
Placements: Accounts clerks, bilingual operators, computer operators, receptionists, secretaries and personal assistants, telephone and telex operators, word processing operators.
Qualifications: None required
Skills: Computer, shorthand, typing, word processing.
Comments: Deal with commercial and industrial vacancies from junior clerks to PA executive secretaries and from an assembler to an HGV 1 Driver.

London Area: W
82a High Street
Acton
London W3
Tel: 01-993 8201
Fax: 01-993 9518

18 the Green
Ealing
London W5 5DA
Tel: 01-840 5888
Fax: 01-579 2970

Townselection
Industries: All
Placements: Accounts clerks, bilingual operators, receptionists, secretaries and personal assistants, word processing operators.
Qualifications: None required
Skills: Computer, shorthand, typing, word processing.

Comments: We look for general office staff and marketing staff, including senior managers.

London Area: S
Unity Wharf
Mill Street
London SE1 2BH
Tel: 01-252 0127
Fax: 01-252 0277

Types Recruitment
Industries: All
Placements: Secretaries and personal assistants, word processing operators.
Qualifications: Typing 45 wpm.
Skills: Shorthand, typing, word processing.
Comments: We are a small private agency which specializes in WP staff, especially CPT operators. We offer free training on a wide range of systems to candidates who can type at least 45 wpm.

London Area: W
1a The Parade
Haven Green, Ealing
London W5 2PB
Tel: 01-997 5604/991 1734

U

Unique Freelance Secretaries
Industries: All
Placements: Computer operators, receptionists, secretaries and personal assistants, word processing operators.
Qualifications: None required
Skills: Computer, shorthand, typing, word processing.
Comments: We specialise in part-time workers and returners to work.

London Area: N
766 Finchley Road
London NW11 7TH
Tel: 01-455 8187/1266
Fax: 01-455 5335

Uptown Personnel Services Ltd
Industries: All
Placements: Accounts clerks, bilingual operators, computer operators, receptionists, secretaries and personal assistants, telephone and telex operators, word processing operators.
Qualifications: None required
Skills: Computer, shorthand, typing, word processing.
Comments: We specialise in placing both permanent and temporary staff in the secretarial and administrative sectors. Staff should be multi-skilled and flexible in approach. Word processing is an asset.

London Area: S
1 The Arcade
Victoria Station
London SW1E 8ND
Tel: 01-828 2727
Fax: 01-630 6318

London Area: C
61 Oxford Street
London W1R 1RB
Tel: 01-734 6425
Fax: 01-734 8772

V

Valentine Staff Services Ltd
Industries: All
Placements: Accounts clerks, computer operators, receptionists, secretaries and personal assistants, telephone and telex operators, word processing operators.
Qualifications: None required
Skills: Computer, shorthand, typing, word processing.
Comments: Mainly secretarial/office vacancies, plus a small number of accounting, drawing office, surveying vacancies. Their two other divisions are permanent office employment and managerial and technical personnel.
30a East Street
Horsham
Sussex West RH12 1HL
Tel: 0403 64811/2

W

West End Staff Bureau (Intl) Ltd
Industries: All
Placements: Accounts clerks, computer operators, receptionists, secretaries and personal assistants, telephone and telex operators, word processing operators.

Qualifications: Typist 50 wpm, shorthand 80 wpm. Attitude and appearance count.

Skills: Computer, shorthand, typing, word processing.

Comments: London Area: C
Chesham House
150 Regent Street
London W1R 5FA
Tel: 01-629 0538/439 6288
Fax: 01-434 2469

Whitehead Recruitment Ltd

Industries: Law, media, medical, publishing.

Placements: Accounts clerks, computer operators, receptionists, secretaries and personal assistants, telephone and telex operators, word processing operators.

Qualifications: Typing 40 wpm, shorthand 80 wpm, 3 O' levels.

Skills: Computer, shorthand, typing, word processing.

Comments: Our aim is to offer local companies a professional recruitment service with an understanding of local business needs. Wecover all personnel requirements but concentrate primarily on administrative, secretarial and accounts staff.

Still House
29 East Street
Farnham
Surrey GU9 7SW
Tel: 0252 725934
Fax: 0252 713691

Comments: Family owned agency specialising in office recruitment. Looking for experienced office workers with energy andenthusiasm.

2 Green's End
Woolwich
Horsham
Sussex West SE18 6HX
Tel: 01-854 7651

Woolwich Staff Agency Limited

Industries: All

Placements: Accounts clerks, receptionists, secretaries and personal assistants, telephone and telex operators, word processingoperators.

Qualifications: None required

Skills: Shorthand, typing, word processing.

Geographical listing of recruitment agencies

North London

Advisory Employment Agency
Industries: All
Placements: Accounts clerks, bilingual operators, computer operators, receptionists, secretaries and personal assistants, telephone and telex operators.
Qualifications: None required. All levels of applicants considered.
Skills: Computer, shorthand, typing, word processing.
Comments: Deal with permanent and temporary office staff. Look for WP skills, good typing and if possible, also experienced telephonists.

9 Regency Parade
Finchley Road
London NW3 5EG
Tel: 01-722 8851
Fax: 01-483 4162

15 Watford Way
Hendon Central
London NW4 3JL
Tel: 01-202 3677
Fax: 01-202 1754

Aquarius Employment Bureau Ltd
Industries: All
Placements: Accounts clerks, computer operators, receptionists, secretaries and personal assistants, telephone and telex operators, word processing operators.
Qualifications: None required. We test all applicants - permanent and temporary.
Skills: Computer, shorthand, typing, word processing.
Comments: We have been established for 15 years. All temporaries are welcome, providing they can supply three references.

Aquarius House
Archway Corner
London N19 3TD
Tel: 01-272 6252
Fax: 01-263 2485

Atlas Employment Agency Ltd
Industries: All
Placements: Accounts clerks, bilingual operators, computer operators, receptionists, secretaries and personal assistants, telephone and telex operators, word processing operators.
Qualifications: Typing 45 wpm, shorthand 80 wpm, 1 year's WP experience, 1 year's legal secretarial experience.
Skills: None required
Comments: We are a high street employment agency looking for all types of temporaries, both skilled and unskilled. We need hardworking, reliable applicants for a variety of positions.

154 High Road
Wood Green
London N22 6EB
Tel: 01-888 8490

68 High Street
Harlesden
London NW10 4SJ
Tel: 01-965 8181

237 Kentish Town Road
London NW5 2JS
Tel: 01-284 1818

Brook Street
Industries: All
Placements: Accounts clerks, receptionists, secretaries and personal assistants, telephone and telex operators, word processing operators.
Qualifications: Typing 40/50 wpm, shorthand 80/100 wpm, 2 GCSE's including English.
Skills: Shorthand, typing, word processing.
Comments: We are looking for PA's, secretaries, copy typists, clerks, account clerks, switchboard operators, receptionists, catering staff, industrial staff.

119 High Road
Wood Green
London N22 6BB
Tel: 01-888 1101

80 Kilburn High Road
London NW6 4HS
Tel: 01-328 7121

Omegar Personnel Limited
Industries: All, law, banking
Placements: Receptionists, secretaries and personal assistants, telephone and telex operators, word processing operators.
Qualifications: Typing or word processing 45/50 wpm, shorthand 35/40 wpm. GCSE's in Maths and English.
Skills: Shorthand, typing, word processing.
Comments: We cater for local industry and commerce and seek reliable and well presented temps.

74a Belsize Lane
Hampstead
London NW3 5BJ
Tel: 01-435 7492

Reed Employment
Industries: All
Placements: Accounts clerks, bilingual operators, computer operators, receptionists, secretaries and personal assistants, telephone and telex operators, word processing operators.
Qualifications: None required. All potential candidates are fully screened and tested.
Skills: Computer, shorthand, typing, word processing.
Comments: Reed Employment recruits permanent and temporary staff in the following areas: secretarial, WP operators and all office skills, accountancy, nursing, industrial, insurance and computing.

152 Fore Street
London N18 2XA
Tel: 01-803 2166

30 High Road
London N22 6RX
Tel: 01-888 5214

376 Holloway Road
London N7 6RN
Tel: 01-607 8763

141 Camden High Street
London NW1 7JR
Tel: 01-267 4091

Unique Freelance Secretaries
Industries: All
Placements: Computer operators, receptionists, secretaries and personal assistants, word processing operators.
Qualifications: None required
Skills: Computer, shorthand, typing, word processing.
Comments: We specialise in part-time workers and returners to work.

766 Finchley Road
London NW11 7TH
Tel: 01-455 8187/1266
Fax: 01-455 5335

East London

Acme Appointments
Industries: All
Placements: Accounts clerks, receptionists, secretaries and personal assistants, telephone and telex operators, word processing operators.
Qualifications: Typing 45/60+ wpm, shorthand 100/60 wpm, audio 60+ wpm.
Skills: Shorthand, typing, word processing.
Comments: A privately owned family led group established over 40 years. Always looking for good temporaries for interesting and well-paid bookings.

122 Middlesex Street
London E1 7HY
Tel: 01-375 1441

Moorgate Station
29 Moorfields
London EC2 9AE
Tel: 01-638 4397

20 Wormwood Street
London EC2M 1RQ
Tel: 01-256 5191

158 Bishopsgate
London EC2M 4LN
Tel: 01-247 9701

2nd Floor
88 Cannon Street
London EC4N 6HT
Tel: 01-220 7550

Angela Mortimer Ltd
Industries: All
Placements: Receptionists, secretaries and personal assistants.
Qualifications: Typing 50 wpm, shorthand 90 wpm. Experience on Monarch/Herald/Plessey. 5 O' levels or more.
Skills: Typing, word processing, shorthand or audio, computer useful.
Comments: Privately owned, quality secretarial recruitment consultancy. We look for committed, reliable secretarial temps who either want a career in temping or a permanent job.
1/3 Frederick's Place
London EC2
Tel: 01-726 8491

Ann Warrington Secretarial Careers
Industries: All
Placements: Receptionists, secretaries and personal assistants, telephone and telex operators, word processing operators.
Qualifications: Typing 45 wpm, shorthand 90 wpm, 2 good references, 6 month's secretarial experience.
Skills: Computer, shorthand, typing, word processing.
Comments: As we specialise in the placement of permanent office staff we are always interested in 'temp to perm' posts and in short term relief staff who are really seeking permanency on finding the right position.
52 Bow Lane
London EC4M 9DS
Tel: 01-248 2014
Fax: 01-248 6770

Atlas Employment Agency Ltd
Industries: All
Placements: Accounts clerks, bilingual operators, computer operators, receptionists, secretaries and personal assistants, telephone and telex operators, word processing operators.
Qualifications: Typing 45 wpm, shorthand 80 wpm, 1 year's WP experience, 1 year's legal secretarial experience.
Skills: None required
Comments: We are a high street employment agency looking for all types of temporaries, both skilled and unskilled. We need hardworking, reliable applicants for a variety of positions.
106c High Street
Walthamstow
London E17 7JY
Tel: 01-520 0214
'Roundhouse'
213 Old Street
London EC1V 9PG
Tel: 01-253 4355
152/154 Bishopsgate
London EC2M 4LN
Tel: 01-247 7444
14 Eldon Street
London EC2M 7LA
Tel: 01-588 7484
13 Eastcheap
London EC3M 1BU
Tel: 01-929 1758

Bertram Personnel Group
Industries: Media
Placements: Accounts clerks, computer operators, receptionists, secretaries and personal assistants, telephone and telex operators, word processing operators.
Qualifications: Typing 50 wpm for secretaries, 35 wpm for juniors, shorthand 90/100 wpm, O' levels dependant upon the client.
Skills: Computer, shorthand, typing, word processing.
Comments: We are always looking for good temps to fill a variety of positions.
12-14 Devonshire Row
London EC3
Tel: 01-247 0367

Brook Street
Industries: All
Placements: Accounts clerks, receptionists, secretaries and personal assistants,

telephone and telex operators, word processing operators.
Qualifications: Typing 40/50 wpm, shorthand 80/100 wpm, 2 GCSE's including English.
Skills: Shorthand, typing, word processing.
Comments: We are looking for PA's, secretaries, copy typists, clerks, account clerks, switchboard operators, receptionists, catering staff, industrial staff.

Business Efficiency Centre
3-4 Limeharbour
London E14 9TQ
Tel: 01-538 0232

56 Broadway
Stratford
London E15 1NG
Tel: 01-555 8261

238 Hoe Street
Walthamstow
London E17 3AX
Tel: 01-520 7324

172 Bishopsgate
London EC2M 4NQ
Tel: 01-283 7935

108 Fenchurch Street
London EC3M 5JJ
Tel: 01-481 8441

131/133 Cannon Street
London EC4N 5AX
Tel: 01-623 3966

Covent Garden Bureau
Industries: Media, publishing
Placements: Receptionists, secretaries and personal assistants, telephone and telex operators, word processing operators.
Qualifications: None required
Skills: Shorthand, typing, word processing.
Comments: Convent Garden Bureau offers an interesting and wide choice of temporary bookings in the creative fields. All ages are welcome.
Ludgate House
107-110 Fleet Street
London EC4
Tel: 01- 353 7696

Hazell Staton Associates Ltd
Industries: All
Placements: Receptionists, secretaries and personal assistants.
Qualifications: Typing 40 wpm. shorthand 80 wpm, PA speeds shorthand 100 wpm, typing 60 wpm. 5 GCSE's minimum, A'level candidates preferred.
Skills: Computer, shorthand, typing, word processing.
Comments: Specialise in high calibre assignments for high calibre temps.
12 St Michaels Alley
Cornhill
London EC3V 9DS
Tel: 01-621 0686
Fax: 01-621 9907

Jane Wynne Recruitment Ltd
Industries: All
Placements: Accounts clerks, bilingual operators, computer operators, receptionists, secretaries and personal assistants, telephone and telex operators and word processing operators.
Qualifications: None required. Basic GCSE's preferred.
Skills: Computer, shorthand, typing and word processing.
Comments: Jane Wynne seeks intelligent well rounded individuals who will offer an excellent service to our clients.
2nd Floor, Ludgate House
107/111 Fleet Street
London EC4A 2AB
Tel: 01 - 353 9694
Fax: 01 - 583 1784

Jonathan Wren & Co Ltd
Industries: Finance and banking
Placements: Accounts clerks, bilingual operators, computer operators, receptionists, secretaries and personal assistants, telephone and telex operators, word processing operators.
Qualifications: Speeds 50/90 wpm, some clients seek O' and A' level standard of education.
Skills: Computer, shorthand, typing, word processing.

Comments: A financial recruitment consultants, seeking applicants with international banking experience. to work in the City.

1 New Street
London EC2
Tel: 01-623 1266
Fax: 01-626 5258

Kingsway Recruitment Consultants
Industries: All
Placements: Accounts clerks, bilingual operators, computer operators, receptionists, secretaries and personal assistants, telephone and telex operators, word processing operators.
Qualifications: Typing 50 wpm, minimum 6 month's experience for WP operators.
Skills: Shorthand, typing, word processing, computer.
Comments: We are part of the Adia Group and pride ourselves in being honest with both our clients and applicants alike. All applicants including office juniors are welcome to register and we will advise on career choice.

11 Ludgate Circus
London EC4M 7IQ
Tel: 01-489 8032
Fax: 01-329 0210

Kompass Ltd
Industries: All
Placements: Accounts clerks, bilingual operators, receptionists, secretaries and personal assistants, telephone and telex operators, word processing operators.
Qualifications: Typing 50+ wpm, shorthand 50+ wpm, audio 50+ wpm. Good standard of English. Professional qualifications where applicable.
Skills: WP, VDU, shorthand, typing.
Comments: Recruitment consultancy dealing with both permanent and temporary vacancies at all levels.

127 Cheapside
1st Floor
London EC2
Tel: 01-600 8091
Fax: 01-726 4290

Middleton Jeffers Recruitment Ltd
Industries: All, except medical secretaries
Placements: Bilingual operators, computer operators, receptionists, secretaries and personal assistants, telephone and telex operators, word processing operators.
Qualifications: Typing 50 wpm and some experience of word processing an advantage.
Skills: Shorthand, typing, word processing, computer.
Comments: We are a recruitment consultancy with a high calibre profile and a wide and varied client base. We have a small successful team of good reliable temps who take on short, long and temporary to permanent assignments.

15 Devonshire Row
London EC2M 4RQ
Tel: 01-377 6777
Fax: 01-377 5079

Milton Staff
Industries: All
Placements: Accounts clerks, computer operators, receptionists, secretaries and personal assistants, telephone and telex operators, word processing operators.
Qualifications: None required
Skills: Computer, shorthand, typing, word processing.
Comments: We are a small, personal agency with a very good reputation, both with our applicants and with our clients. Temp secretaries are always in demand. We recruit school leavers.

76 Watling Street
London EC4M 9BJ
Tel: 01-248 8141

Mison Recruitment Services Ltd
Industries: All
Placements: Accounts clerks, bilingual operators, computer operators, receptionists, secretaries and personal assistants, telephone and telex operators and word processing operators.
Qualifications: None required. Basic GCSE's preferred.

Skills: Computer, shorthand, typing and word processing.
Comments: Mison seeks intelligent well rounded individuals who will offer an excellent service to our clients.
Ludgate House
107/111 Fleet Street
London EC4A 2AB
Tel: 01 - 583 5441
Fax: 01 - 583 1784

Mistprestige Recruitment Consultants
Industries: All
Placements: Bilingual operators, receptionists, secretaries and personal assistants, telephone and telex operators, word processing operators. Placements also made for Dublin, Ireland.
Qualifications: Every vacancy has a different minimum requirement.
Skills: Shorthand, typing, word processing, audio.
Comments: Predominately have secretarial vacancies for temps and offer long and short term bookings.
5 London Wall Buildings
London EC2M 5NT
Tel: 01-528 7248
Fax: 01-588 8012

Office Angels
Industries: All
Placements: Accounts clerks, computer operators, receptionists, secretaries and personal assistants, telephone and telex operators.
Qualifications: None required
Skills: Computer, shorthand, typing, word processing.
Comments: Medium sized, personalised recruitment consultants dealing in permanent and temporary placements in all categories. Unskilled applicants also catered for.
128 Cheapside
London EC2V 3PD
Tel: 01-606 0011
60 Cornhill
London EC3V 3PD
Tel: 01-621 9363

12 Groveland Court
Bow Lane
London EC4M 9EH
Tel: 01-606 0011

Omegar Personnel Limited
Industries: All
Placements: Receptionists, secretaries and personal assistants, telephone and telex operators, word processing operators.
Qualifications: Typing or word processing 45/50 wpm, shorthand 35/40 wpm. GCSE's in Maths and English.
Skills: Shorthand, typing, word processing.
Comments: We cater for local industry and commerce and seek reliable and well presented temps.
125-129 Middlesex Street
London E1
Tel: 01-929 4133

Personnel Support
Industries: All
Placements: Accounts clerks, bilingual operators, computer operators, receptionists, secretaries and personal assistants, telephone and telex operators, word processing operators.
Qualifications: Qualifications relevant to the position sought.
Skills: Computer, shorthand, typing, word processing.
Comments: We supply a wide range of office staff.
Brushfield House
12 Brushfield Street
London E1 6AN
Tel: 01-528 8877
Fax: 01-375 1045

Portman Recruitment Services Ltd
Industries: Law, banking, computer and general.
Placements: Accounts clerks, computer operators, receptionists, secretaries and personal assistants, telephone and telex operators, word processing operators.
Qualifications: Typing 40 wpm, shorthand 80 wpm, good presentation and speech.

Also relevant requirements for specialist areas of law, computing and banking.
Skills: Computer, shorthand, typing, word processing.
15 Great St Thomas Apostle
London EC4V 2BB
Tel: 01-236 1113
Fax: 01-489 8991

Reed Employment
Industries: All
Placements: Accounts clerks, bilingual operators, computer operators, receptionists, secretaries and personal assistants, telephone and telex operators, word processing operators.
Qualifications: None required. All potential candidates are fully screened and tested.
Skills: Computer, shorthand, typing, word processing.
Comments: Reed Employment recruits permanent and temporary staff in the following areas: secretarial, WP operators and all office skills, accountancy, nursing, industrial, insurance and computing.

76 Broadway
Stratford Centre
London E15 1NG
Tel: 01-555 0313

10 Leather Lane
London EC1N 7RA
Tel: 01-831 7685

192 Bishopsgate
London EC2M 4NR
Tel: 01-283 0066

192 Bishopsgate
London EC2M 4NR
Tel: 01-283 0066

47 Liverpool Street
London EC2M 7PR
Tel: 01-621 0155

34 Wormwood Street
London EC2N 1RE
Tel: 01-638 1666

65 Fenchurch Street
London EC3M 4BE
Tel: 01-481 2661

23 Lime Street
London EC3M 7AE
Tel: 01-623 2213

Cannon Street Station
Cannon Street
London EC4N 6AP
Tel: 01-929 7959

Secretaries Plus
Industries: All
Placements: Receptionists, secretaries and personal assistants, telephone and telex operators, word processing operators.
Qualifications: Typing 50 wpm, shorthand 80 wpm.
Skills: Shorthand, typing, word processing.
Comments: We are valued by companies in the City and West End of London. Our temporary controllers have a Personnel Management background which ensures that the assignments match your skills and requirements as well as meeting the client's needs.
146 Bishopsgate
London EC2M 4JX
Tel: 01-377 8600
Fax: 01-375 1950

The City Word Processing Centre
Industries: All
Placements: Word processing operators.
Qualifications: None required
Skills: None required - WP training available.
Comments: We are a word processing centre, involved in anything related to WP training, temporary and permanent recruitment, bureau facilities and WP consultancy. We look for people who have, or can be trained to have good WP ability.
6 Long Lane
London EC1A 9HA
Tel: 01-600 8391
Fax: 01-600 4207

South London

Atlas Employment Agency Ltd
Industries: All

Placements: Accounts clerks, bilingual operators, computer operators, receptionists, secretaries and personal assistants, telephone and telex operators, word processing operators.
Qualifications: Typing 45 wpm, shorthand 80 wpm, 1 year's WP experience, 1 year's legal secretarial experience.
Skills: None required
Comments: We are a high street employment agency looking for all types of temporaries, both skilled and unskilled. We need hardworking, reliable applicants for a variety of positions.

18 Borough High Street
London SE1 9QG
Tel: 01-406 8311

74 Denmark Hill
Camberwell Green
London SE5 4RZ
Tel: 01-733 6101

14 Streatleigh Parade
Streatham High Road
London SW16
Tel: 01-677 5327

17a Kings Road
London SW3 4RP
Tel: 01-823 5122

84a Rye Lane
Peckham
London SE15 4RZ
Tel: 01-639 6417

64 St John's Road
Clapham Junction
London SW11 1PS
Tel: 01-228 7891

71 Putney High Street
London SW15 1SR
Tel: 01-789 5021

71 Streatham High Road
London SW16 1PH
Tel: 01-677 2641

139 Victoria Street
London SW1E 6RD
Tel: 01-834 5745

Catering Section
139 Victoria Street
London SW1E 6RD
Tel: 01-630 6112

Stockley House
130 Wilton Road
London SW1V 1LQ
Tel: 01-630 1311
Fax: 01-630 1877

167 Earls Court Road
London SW5 9RF
Tel: 01-373 7822

Brook Street
Industries: All
Placements: Accounts clerks, receptionists, secretaries and personal assistants, telephone and telex operators, word processing operators.
Qualifications: Typing 40/50 wpm, shorthand 80/100 wpm, 2 GCSE's including English.
Skills: Shorthand, typing, word processing.
Comments: We are looking for PA's, secretaries, copy typists, clerks, account clerks, switchboard operators, receptionists, catering staff, industrial staff.
52 Lewisham High Street
London SE13 5JH
Tel: 01-852 4454

Catch 22 Employment Agency Limited
Industries: All
Placements: Receptionists, secretaries and personal assistants, telephone and telex operators, word processing operators.
Qualifications: None required. Consider most people at all skill levels.
Skills: Computer, shorthand, typing, word processing.
199 Victoria Street
London SW1E 5NE
Tel: 01-821 1134
Fax: 01-630 6660

Euro Personnel Services
Industries: All
Placements: Computer operators, receptionists, secretaries and personal assistants, telephone and telex operators, word processing operators.

Qualifications: Typing 50 wpm, shorthand 70 wpm.
Skills: Computer shorthand, typing, word processing.

268 The Colonnade
Waterloo Road
London SE1 85F
Tel: 01-620 1121
Fax: 01-401 2545

Hendersons Recruitment
Industries: All
Placements: Accounts clerks, bilingual operators, computer operators, receptionists, secretaries and personal assistants, telephone and telex operators, word processing operators.
Qualifications: None required
Skills: Computer, shorthand, typing, word processing.
Comments: We try to help those with fewer skills where possible.

118 Cromwell Road
London SW7 4EG
Tel: 01-370 5066/7/8
Fax: 01-370 4706

Jane Crosthwaite Recruitment Ltd
Industries: All
Placements: Receptionists, secretaries and personal assistants.
Qualifications: Typing 40 wpm.
Skills: Typing
Comments: JCR is a small and friendly recruitment consultancy.

21 Beauchamp Place
London SW3 1NQ
Tel: 01-581 2977
Fax: 01-581 1766

Kompass Ltd
Industries: All
Placements: Accounts clerks, bilingual operators, receptionists, secretaries and personal assistants, telephone and telex operators, word processing operators.
Qualifications: Typing 50+ wpm, shorthand 50+ wpm, audio 50+ wpm. Good standard of English. Professional qualifications where applicable.

Skills: WP, VDU, shorthand, typing.
Comments: Recruitment consultancy dealing with both permanent and temporary vacancies at all levels.

170 Sloane Street
London
SW1
Tel: 01-245-1267
Fax: 01-235-5003

Mediad
Industries: All
Placements: Receptionists, secretaries and personal assistants.
Qualifications: Typing 50 wpm, shorthand 80 wpm, WP skills preferred. O' and A' level standard education desirable.
Skills: Typing, word processing, shorthand useful.
Comments: Professional, secretarial recruitment consultancy specialising in jobs in media and advertising. We provide quality temp work for people looking to work short or long term.

Finland House
56 Haymarket
London SW1
Tel: 01-925 0139

Meridian Associates Ltd
Industries: All, media, medical, publishing.
Placements: Accounts clerks, bilingual operators, receptionists, secretaries and personal assistants, telephone and telex operators, word processing operators. Occasional overseas placements.
Qualifications: Depends entirely on the assignment.
Skills: Shorthand, typing, word processing.
Comments: Small, privately owned consultancy. Limited temporary department, on avarage 40 temps put out.

1st Floor, 7 Belgrave Road
Victoria
London SW1V 1QB
Tel: 01-828 5757
Fax: 01-828 5569

Mistprestige Recruitment Consultants
Industries: All
Placements: Bilingual operators, receptionists, secretaries and personal assistants, telephone and telex operators, word processing operators. Placements also made for Dublin, Ireland.
Qualifications: Every vacancy has a different minimum requirement.
Skills: Shorthand, typing, word processing, audio.
Comments: Predominately have secretarial vacancies for temps and offer long and short term bookings.
197 Knightsbridge
London SW7 1RB
Tel: 01-581 9799
Fax: 01-581 9411

Office Angels
Industries: All
Placements: Accounts clerks, computer operators, receptionists, secretaries and personal assistants, telephone and telex operators.
Qualifications: None required
Skills: Computer, shorthand, typing, word processing.
Comments: Medium sized, personalised recruitment consultants dealing in permanent and temporary placements in all categories. Unskilled applicants also catered for.
71 The Broadway
London SW19 1QE
Tel: 01-542 6688
189 Victoria Street
London SW1E 5NE
Tel: 01-630 0844

OV Selection
Industries: All
Placements: Accounts clerks, bilingual operators, receptionists, secretaries and personal assistants, telephone and telex operators, word processing operators.
Qualifications: Reasonable presentable people with skills appropriate to the job.
Skills: Shorthand, typing, word processing.
Comments: Single branch recruitment office.
Ashford House
15 Wilton Road
London SW1V 1LT
Tel: 01-828 8345

Reed Employment
Industries: All
Placements: Accounts clerks, bilingual operators, computer operators, receptionists, secretaries and personal assistants, telephone and telex operators, word processing operators.
Qualifications: None required. All potential candidates are fully screened and tested.
Skills: Computer, shorthand, typing, word processing.
Comments: Reed Employment recruits permanent and temporary staff in the following areas: secretarial, WP operators and all office skills, accountancy, nursing, industrial, insurance and computing.
19 Borough High Street
London SE1 9SE
Tel: 01-403 0171
68 Lewisham High Street
London SE13 5JH
Tel: 01-852 7411
112 Powis Street
London SE18 6LU
Tel: 01-317 8591
44 Denmark Hill
London SE5 8RZ
Tel: 01-733 2173
176 Putney High Street
London SW15 1RS
Tel: 01-788 2432
9 Wimbledon Bridge
London SW19 7NW
Tel: 01-947 4473
181 Victoria Street
London SW1E 5NE
Tel: 01-828 2401
143 Victoria Street
London SW1E 5NH
Tel: 01-834 1801

St Stephen's Secretariat Limited, The
Industries: All
Placements: Accounts clerks, receptionists, secretaries and personal assistants, telephone and telex operators, word processing operators.
Qualifications: Typing 45+ wpm.
Skills: Shorthand, typing, word processing.
Comments: A small agency which aims to offer an efficient and friendly service.

316 Vauxhall Bridge Road
London SW1V 1AA
Tel: 01-834 0031
Fax: 01-828 9317

Susan Beck Recruitment
Industries: All
Placements: Accounts clerks, receptionists, secretaries and personal assistants, telephone and telex operators, word processing operators.
Qualifications: Good secretarial skills, smart appearance and flexible manner important.
Skills: Shorthand, typing, word processing.
Comments: We give practical career counselling and advice if needed. Applicants dealt with on a personal basis.

10 Beauchamp Place
Knightsbridge
London SW3 1NQ
Tel: 01-584 6242/3/4
Fax: 01-584 2484

Townselection
Industries: All
Placements: Accounts clerks, bilingual operators, receptionists, secretaries and personal assistants, word processing operators.
Qualifications: None required
Skills: Computer, shorthand, typing, word processing.
Comments: We look for general office staff and marketing staff, including senior managers.

Unity Wharf
Mill Street
London SE1 2BH
Tel: 01-252 0127
Fax: 01-252 0277

Uptown Personnel Services Ltd
Industries: All
Placements: Accounts clerks, bilingual operators, computer operators, receptionists, secretaries and personal assistants, telephone and telex operators, word processing operators.
Qualifications: None required
Skills: Computer, shorthand, typing, word processing.
Comments: We specialise in placing both permanent and temporary staff in the secretarial and administrative sectors. Staff should be multi-skilled and flexible in approach. Word processing is an asset.

1 The Arcade
Victoria Station
London SW1E 8ND
Tel: 01-828 2727
Fax: 01-630 6318

Central London

Ace Foster Beazley Associates
Industries: All, media and bilingual.
Placements: Bilingual operators, receptionists, secretaries and personal assistants, telephone and telex operators, word processing operators.
Qualifications: Typing 45 wpm, shorthand 80 wpm.
Skills: Shorthand, typing, word processing.
Comments: We are a secretarial recruitment agency, placing staff in permanent and temporary assignments, from clerk typist to senior PA level. We also specialise in the world of media and bilingual positions.

23 Red Lion Street
London WC1R 4PS
Tel: 01-242 8844
Fax: 01-404 4212

Acme Appointments
Industries: All
Placements: Accounts clerks, receptionists, secretaries and personal assistants, telephone and telex operators, word processing operators.
Qualifications: Typing 45/60+ wpm, shorthand 100/60 wpm, audio 60+ wpm.
Skills: Shorthand, typing, word processing.
Comments: A privately owned family led group established over 40 years. Always looking for good temporaries for interesting and well-paid bookings.
Head Office
315 Oxford Street
London W1R 2HH
Tel: 01-493 4000
Fax: 01-493 4383

Adair International
Industries: All, specialising in City work, legal, hotel & catering, media.
Placements: Computer operators, bilingual operators, receptionists, secretaries and personalassistants, word processing operators, overseas placements related to hotel and catering.
Qualifications: None required. Skills matched to client requirements.
Skills: Shorthand, word processing.
Comments: Favouritism to Australians and New Zealanders. The company has 5 divisions of recruitment with an office in Sydney.
5 Sherwood Street
London W1V 7RA
Tel: 01-734 9582
Fax: 01-439 1395

Adventure Personnel Ltd
Industries: Media
Placements: Receptionists, secretaries and personal assistants, word processing operators.
Qualifications: None required
Skills: Shorthand, typing, word processing.

12 South Moulton Street
London W1Y 1DF
Tel: 01-629 5747
Fax: 01-499 0841

Advisory Employment Agency
Industries: All
Placements: Accounts clerks, bilingual operators, computer operators, receptionists, secretaries and personal assistants, telephone and telex operators.
Qualifications: None required. All levels of applicants considered.
Skills: Computer, shorthand, typing, word processing.
Comments: Deal with permanent and temporary office staff. Look for WP skills, good typing and if possible, also experienced telephonists.
Third Floor
67-68 New Bond Street
London W1Y 9DF
Tel: 01-408 2313
Fax: 01-495 1111

Albany Appointments Ltd
Industries: Media, publishing
Placements: Accounts clerks, receptionists, secretaries and personal assistants, telephone and telex operators, word processing operators.
Qualifications: Typing 45 wpm, knowledge of WP, minimum o'levels, 6 months work experience.
Skills: Computer, shorthand, typing, word processing.
Comments: A small temporary division of 50-80 Temps, looking for loyalty and flexibility.
5 Dering Street
London W1R 9AB
Tel: 01-493 8611
Fax: 01-493 8216

Alexis Personnel
Industries: All
Placements: Accounts clerks, bilingual operators, computer operators, receptionists, secretaries and personal

assistants, telephone and telex operators, word processing operators.
Qualifications: Typing 25/60 wpm. Accuracy most important.
Skills: Shorthand, typing, word processing.
Comments: Alexis Personnel is a small, professional employment consultancy which specialises in finding the right person with the right skills and personality for their select client base.

Radnov House
93 Regent Street
London W1R 7TF
Tel: 01-439 2777
Fax: 01-437 0470

Alfred Marks Bureau Limited
Industries: All
Placements: Accounts clerks, bilingual operators, computer operators, receptionists, secretaries and personal assistants, telephone and telex operators, word processing operators.
Qualifications: None required
Skills: Shorthand, typing, word processing.
Comments: As one of the major temp agencies, Alfred Marks recruits a variety of staff with a range of qualifications.

ADIA House, PO Box 1AL
84/86 Regent Street
London W1A 1AL
Tel: 01-437 7855
Fax: 01-734 2538

Amanda Barrington Recruitment Cons
Industries: All, media, publishing.
Placements: Bilingual operators, receptionists, secretaries and personal assistants, word processing operators. Overseas placements are made.
Qualifications: Typing 60 wpm, shortand 80/100 wpm.
Skills: Shorthand, typing, word processing.
Comments: Amanda Barrington seeks flexible, efficient, temps with varied WP experience.

13 Upper St Martins Lane
London WC2H 9DL
Tel: 01-379 7007
Fax: 01-379 3267

Angela Mortimer Ltd
Industries: All
Placements: Receptionists, secretaries and personal assistants.
Qualifications: Typing 50 wpm, shorthand 90 wpm. Experience on Monarch/Herald/Plessey. 5 O' levels or more.
Skills: Typing, word processing, shorthand or audio, computer useful.
Comments: Privately owned, quality secretarial recruitment consultancy. We look for committed, reliable secretarial temps who either want a career in temping or a permanent job.

22/23 Princes Street
London W1
Tel: 01-408 1461

Foxglove House
166 Piccadilly
London W1
Tel: 01-629 9686

Atlas Employment Agency Ltd
Industries: All
Placements: Accounts clerks, bilingual operators, computer operators, receptionists, secretaries and personal assistants, telephone and telex operators, word processing operators.
Qualifications: Typing 45 wpm, shorthand 80 wpm, 1 year's WP experience, 1 year's legal secretarial experience.
Skills: None required
Comments: We are a high street employment agency looking for all types of temporaries, both skilled and unskilled. We need hardworking, reliable applicants for a variety of positions.

104 Baker Street
London W1M 2AR
Tel: 01-486 0542

52 James Street
London W1M 5HS
Tel: 01-486 5225

71 Oxford Street
London W1R 1RB
Tel: 01-636 4000

71 Oxford Street
London W1R 1RB
Tel: 01-636 4000

275 Regent Street
London W1R 9BR
Tel: 01-493 2021

7 Harewood Place
London W1R 9HA
Tel: 01-629 1904

31/33 High Holborn
London W1V 6AX
Tel: 01-831 0012

108 High Holborn
London WC1V 9JS
Tel: 01-242 1811

Belle Secretarial Ltd
Industries: All
Placements: Accounts clerks, computer operators, receptionists, secretaries and personal assistants, telephone and telex operators, word processing operators.
Qualifications: Typing, copy and audio 50 wpm, shorthand 90 wpm, general clerical/accounts experience.
Skills: Computer, shorthand, typing, word processing.
Comments: Provides temps to a variety of companies in the West End and the City. Established for 26 years.
24 Chancery Lane
London WC2A 1LS
Tel: 01-404 4655

Brook Street
Industries: All
Placements: Accounts clerks, receptionists, secretaries and personal assistants, telephone and telex operators, word processing operators.
Qualifications: Typing 40/50 wpm, shorthand 80/100 wpm, 2 GCSE's including English.
Skills: Shorthand, typing, word processing.
Comments: We are looking for PA's, secretaries, copy typists, clerks, account clerks, switchboard operators, receptionists, catering staff, industrial staff.

136 Baker Street
London W1M 1FH
Tel: 01-496 6144

63 Oxford Street
London W1R 1FA
Tel: 01-493 8531

230 High Holborn
London WC1V 7DA
Tel: 01-242 6991

32 The Strand
London WC2N 6MA
Tel: 01-930 7399

Catering Section
32 Strand
London WC2N 6MA
Tel: 01-930 9933

Centacom Staff Agency
Industries: All
Placements: Accounts clerks, computer operators, receptionists, secretaries and personal assistants, telephone and telex operators, word processing operators.
Qualifications: None required
Skills: Computer, shorthand, typing, word processing.
Comments: Small agency with branches in Australia and New Zealand.
15 Adam Street
Strand
London WC2
Tel: 01-938 2921

Davis Secretarial Recruitment
Industries: Media, property
Placements: Receptionists, secretaries and personal assistants, telephone and telex operators, word processing operators.
Qualifications: Typing 50 wpm, shorthand for top PA bookings at least 80 wpm, WP experience, Good GCSE education, good speaking voice for reception work.
Skills: Computer, shorthand, typing, word processing.
Comments: Small established consultancy specialising in temporary and permanent appointments with design,

advertising, PR and sales promotion companies. Our clients look for bright, bubbly individuals for long or short term bookings.
13-14 Dean Street
London W1V 5AH
Tel: 01-437 6419

Directors' Temporaries Ltd
Industries: All
Placements: Accounts clerks, bilingual operators, receptionists, secretaries and personal assistants, telephone and telex operators, word processing operators.
Qualifications: Typing 60 wpm and shorthand 85 wpm are the minimum requirements.
Skills: Shorthand, typing, word processing.
Comments: We recruit staff to suit director-level assignments.
Standbrook House, (4th Floor)
2-5 Old Bond Street
London W1X 3TB
Tel: 01-493 2545
Fax: 01-629 4255

Drake International
Industries: All
Placements: Accounts clerks, computer operators, receptionists, secretaries and personal assistants, telephone and telex operators, word processing operators.
Qualifications: Typing 50 wpm, shorthand 80 wpm, 6 -- 12 months office experience required for all temps hired.
Skills: Computer shorthand, typing, word processing.
Comments: An international recruitment consultants, placing permanent and temporary staff in all industries. As well as the obvious office skills, Drake looks for flexibility and loyalty in its recruits.
(Office Overload - Temp Division)
223 Regent Street
London W1
Tel: 01-734 0911
Fax: 01-734 7751

Faithfold Travel Personnel
Industries: Travel
Placements: Retail travel agencies, business travel agencies.
Qualifications: Two years IATA experience, gained in the UK or overseas.
Skills: Experience in the travel industry.
Comments: Faithfold recruit purely for the travel industry. Clients require temps who can fit immediately into a travel consultant position. Previous travel administrative experience is essential.
Suite 220, Linen Hall
162-168 Regent Street
London W1R 5TB
Tel: 01-439 0482
Fax: 01-439 4276

Graduate Appointments Ltd
Industries: All
Placements: Accounts clerks, receptionists, secretaries and personal assistants, word processing operators.
Qualifications: Typing 50 wpm, shorthand 80 wpm; A' levels.
Skills: Computer, shorthand, typing, word processing.
Comments: Look for good secretaries with a flexible approach to temping, for long and short assignments.
7 Princes Street
London W1R 7RB
Tel: 01-629 7262
Fax: 01-434 2055

Hazell Staton Associates Ltd
Industries: All
Placements: Receptionists, secretaries and personal assistants.
Qualifications: Typing 40 wpm. shorthand 80 wpm, PA speeds shorthand 100 wpm, typing 60 wpm. 5 GCSE's minimum, A'level candidates preferred.
Skills: Computer, shorthand, typing, word processing.
Comments: Specialise in high calibre assignments for high calibre temps.
8 Golden Square
London W1R 3AF
Tel: 01-439 6021
Fax: 01-494 0609

Hodge Recruitment
Industries: All
Placements: Accounts clerks, bilingual operators, computer operators, receptionists, secretaries and personal assistants, telephone and telex operators, word processing operators.
Qualifications: Typing 50 wpm minimum. Accuracy as important as speed. A good standard of education.
Skills: Computer, shorthand, typing, word processing.
Comments: A small firm with a client base covering all industries.
Bond House
19/20 Woodstock Street
London W1R 1HF
Tel: 01-629 8863
Fax: 01-408 0961

Jigsaw Limited
Industries: All, medical
Placements: Bilingual operators, receptionists, secretaries and personal assistants, word processing operators.
Qualifications: Typing 50 wpm, shorthand 80 wpm.
Skills: Shorthand, typing, word processing.
Comments: Clients in PR, banking, manufacturing and advertising.
5 Margaret Street
London W1N 7LG
Tel: 01-631 0902
Fax: 01-637 8620

Judy Fisher Associates
Industries: Media
Placements: Receptionists, secretaries and personal assistants.
Qualifications: None required
Skills: Shorthand, typing, word processing.
2 Princes Street
Hanover Square
London W1R 7RA
Tel: 01-493 0238
Fax: 01-499 3649

Kelly Temporary Services
Industries: All
Placements: Accounts clerks, bilingual operators, receptionists, secretaries and personal assistants, telephone and telex operators, word processing operators.
Qualifications: Qualifications relevant to specific assignments required.
Skills: Shorthand, typing, word processing.
Comments: Established in the USA in 1946, 800 branches worldwide, over 30 in the UK. We are always looking for competent, conscientious temporary staff, preferably with work experience.
European Headquarters
87-91 New Bond Street
London W1Y 0HQ
Tel: 01-493 7843
Fax: 01-499 1793

Kingsway Recruitment Consultants
Industries: All
Placements: Accounts clerks, bilingual operators, computer operators, receptionists, secretaries and personal assistants, telephone and telex operators, word processing operators.
Qualifications: Typing 50 wpm, minimum 6 month's experience for WP operators.
Skills: Shorthand, typing, word processing, computer.
Comments: We are part of the Adia Group and pride ourselves in being honest with both our clients and applicants alike. All applicants including office juniors are welcome to register and we will advise on career choice.
145 Oxford Street
London W1R 1TV
Tel: 01-434 9644
Fax: 01-287 0580

1 Kingsway
London WC2B 6XF
Tel: 01-836 9272
Fax: 01-497 9142

Kompass Ltd
Industries: All
Placements: Accounts clerks, bilingual operators, receptionists, secretaries and personal assistants, telephone and telex operators, word processing operators.

Qualifications: Typing 50+ wpm, shorthand 50+ wpm, audio 50+ wpm. Good standard of English. Professional qualifications where applicable.
Skills: WP, VDU, shorthand, typing.
Comments: Recruitment consultancy dealing with both permanent and temporary vacancies at all levels.
10 Hills Place
London W1
Tel: 01-734 2921
Fax: 01-494 2273

La Creme
Industries: All
Placements: Receptionists, secretaries and personal assistants, word processing operators.
Qualifications: Typing 55/60 wpm, shorthand 90 wpm, WP experience an advantage.
Skills: Shorthand, typing, word processing.
Comments: We are a consultancy specialising in the recruitment of all levels of temporary and permanent secretarial and word processing staff. We are looking for temporary staff who have a good educational background and proficient secretarial skills.
4 Princes Street
London W1R 7RA
Tel: 01-491 1868
Fax: 01-495 6171

London Town Staff Bureau
Industries: All, mainly publishing
Placements: Receptionists, secretaries and personal assistants, word processing operators.
Qualifications: Typing 40 wpm, shorthand 70/80 wpm.
Skills: Typing
Comments: We specialise in publishing and non -- commercial companies.
19 Broad Court
London WC2B 5QN
Tel: 01-836 0627
Fax: 01-836 1997

Mackay Personnel
Industries: All
Placements: Receptionists, word processing operators, secretaries and personal assistants.
Qualifications: Typing 40+ wpm, shorthand 80+ wpm.
Skills: Shorthand, typing, word processing.
Comments: We need solid, reliable temps and staff with good WP experience.
70/71 New Bond Street
London W1A 4DY
Tel: 01-491 0383
Fax: 01-409 2555

Medical & General, The
Industries: Medical
Placements: Receptionists, secretaries and personal assistants, word processing.
Qualifications: Minimum typing speed of 40 wpm, shorthand 80wpm.
Skills: Shorthand, typing, word processing.
6 Paddington Street
London W1M 4BE
Tel: 01-935 9426/4061

Meridian Associates Ltd
Industries: All, media, medical, publishing.
Placements: Accounts clerks, bilingual operators, receptionists, secretaries and personal assistants, telephone and telex operators, word processing operators. Occasional overseas placements.
Qualifications: Depends entirely on the assignment.
Skills: Shorthand, typing, word processing.
Comments: Small, privately owned consultancy. Limited temporary department, on avarage 40 temps put out.
Museum House
25 Museum Street
London WC1A 1JT
Tel: 01-255 1555
Fax: 01-487 3018

Merrow Employment Agency Ltd
Industries: All, specialising in linguistics.
Placements: Accounts clerks, bilingual operators, receptionists, secretaries and personal assistants, telephone and telex operators, word processing operators. Overseas placements in Europe only.
Qualifications: Typing 45 wpm minimum, shorthand 90 wpm, audio 45 wpm. A' level standard of education preferred, especially in language subjects.
Skills: Computer, shorthand, typing, word processing.
Comments: We specialise in temps with 2 or more languages.
7 Henrietta Place
London W1M 9AG
Tel: 01-408 1286

Michele Zarak Recruitment
Industries: Advertising, PR and design
Placements: Receptionists, secretaries and personal assistants, word processing operators.
Qualifications: Typing 50 wpm.
Skills: Typing, word processing and switchboard skills.
10a James Street
London WC2E 8BT
Tel: 01-240 5931
Fax: 01-240 5759

Miss Reception
Industries: All
Placements: Receptionists
Qualifications: Minimum of one year's reception and switchboard experience.
Skills: Switchboards
Comments: We only handle reception duties, therefore temps must be very well presented and well spoken with switchboard experience.
2nd Floor, Wells House
79 Wells Street
London W1P 3RE
Tel: 01-580 5522

Mistprestige Recruitment Consultants
Industries: All
Placements: Bilingual operators, receptionists, secretaries and personal assistants, telephone and telex operators, word processing operators. Placements also made for Dublin, Ireland.
Qualifications: Every vacancy has a different minimum requirement.
Skills: Shorthand, typing, word processing, audio.
Comments: Predominately have secretarial vacancies for temps and offer long and short term bookings.
4 Denman Street
London W1V 7RH
Tel: 01-439 2308
Fax: 01-437 1637

25 South Moulton Street
London W1Y 1DB
Tel: 01-408 1117
Fax: 01-629 2031

Multilingual Services
Industries: All
Placements: Bilingual operators, receptionists, secretaries and personal assistants.
Qualifications: Typing 50 wpm and shorthand 90+ wpm and word processing preferrable. For secretary/linguists A' level standard minimum in relevant language.
Skills: Shorthand, typing, WP.
Comments: We look for bilingual secretaries at all levels with good languages and skills. A lesser demand for translators who must also be able to type their work and preferably also use a word processor. We test all languages as well as secretarial skills.
22 Charing Croos Road
London WC2H 0HR
Tel: 01-836 3794
Fax: 01-836 6755

Office Angels
Industries: All
Placements: Accounts clerks, computer operators, receptionists, secretaries and personal assistants, telephone and telex operators.

Qualifications: None required
Skills: Computer, shorthand, typing, word processing.
Comments: Medium sized, personalised recruitment consultants dealing in permanent and temporary placements in all categories. Unskilled applicants also catered for.

111 Baker Street
London W1M 1FE
Tel: 01-935 7248

Wells House
79 Wells Street
London W1P 4AX
Tel: 01-734 1200

12 Swallow Street
London W1R 1RF
Tel: 01-434 0683

25 Oxford Street
London W1R 1RF
Tel: 01-434 9545

311 Regent Street
London W1R 5AJ
Tel: 01-629 0777

115 High Holborn
London WC1V 6JJ
Tel: 01-430 2531

Osborne Richardson Ltd
Industries: All, law, banking
Placements: Receptionists, secretaries and personal assistants, telephone and telex operators, word processing operators.
Qualifications: Typing 50 wpm, shorthand 80 wpm. GCSE or CSE level education.
Skills: Shorthand, typing, word processing.
Comments: Small consultancy specialising in secretarial staff, but covering many different industries.

110 New Bond Street
London W1Y 3AA
Tel: 01-409 2393
Fax: 01-491 3993

Part Time Careers Limited
Industries: All
Placements: Accounts clerks, receptionists, secretaries and personal assistants, telephone and telex operators, word processing operators.
Qualifications: Typing 50 wpm, shorthand 100 wpm, word processing and audio useful. Minimum of 6 O'levels.
Skills: Shorthand, typing, word processing.
Comments: We look for high calibre personnel and specialize in part-time, permanent and temporary office staff.

10 Golden Square
London W1R 3AF
Tel: 01-437 3103
Fax: 01-494 1154

Portman Recruitment Services Ltd
Industries: Law, banking, computer and general.
Placements: Accounts clerks, computer operators, receptionists, secretaries and personal assistants, telephone and telex operators, word processing operators.
Qualifications: Typing 40 wpm, shorthand 80 wpm, good presentation and speech. Also relevant requirements for specialist areas of law, computing and banking.
Skills: Computer, shorthand, typing, word processing.

Ilford House
133-135 Oxford Street
London W1R 1TD
Tel: 01-494 2596
Fax: 01-493 1585

QED (Quest Employment Development Services)
Industries: All
Placements: Accounts clerks, bilingual operators, computer operators, receptionists, secretaries and personal assistants, telephone and telex operators, word processing operators.
Qualifications: Typing 55 wpm, shorthand 80 wpm. 5 O' levels but A' levels preferred.
Skills: Computer, shorthand, typing, word processing.
Comments: Temps must be skilled and reliable.

37 Dover Street
Mayfair
London W1X 3RB
Tel: 01-409 1343
Fax: 01-409 1525

Recruitment Company, The
Industries: All
Placements: Receptionists, secretaries and personal assistants.
Qualifications: None required
Skills: Computer, shorthand, typing, word processing.
Comments: Independent agency with clients in the West End and City. Seeks a wide range of temps in the secretarial field.
5 Garrick Street
London WC2E 9AR
Tel: 01-831 1220
Fax: 01-379 4558

Reed Employment
Industries: All
Placements: Accounts clerks, bilingual operators, computer operators, receptionists, secretaries and personal assistants, telephone and telex operators, word processing operators.
Qualifications: None required. All potential candidates are fully screened and tested.
Skills: Computer, shorthand, typing, word processing.
Comments: Reed Employment recruits permanent and temporary staff in the following areas: secretarial, WP operators and all office skills, accountancy, nursing, industrial, insurance and computing.
197 Regent Street
London W1R 7WA
Tel: 01-439 0303
54 South Molton Street
London W1Y 1HF
Tel: 01-491 4610
5 High Holborn
London WC1V 6DR
Tel: 01-405 6525
80 Kingsway
Holborn
London WC2B 6AE
Tel: 01-404 9542
159 Charing Cross Road
London WC2H 0EN
Tel: 01-734 8694

65 The Strand
London WC2N 5LR
Tel: 01-836 8815

Secretaries Plus
Industries: All
Placements: Receptionists, secretaries and personal assistants, telephone and telex operators, word processing operators.
Qualifications: Typing 50 wpm, shorthand 80 wpm.
Skills: Shorthand, typing, word processing.
Comments: We are valued by companies in the City and West End of London. Our temporary controllers have a Personnel Management background which ensures that the assignments match your skills and requirements as well as meeting the client's needs.
44 Conduit Street
London W1R 9FB
Tel: 01-439 4344
Fax: 01-434 4423

Solution Bureau
Industries: All
Placements: Accounts clerks, computer operators, receptionists, secretaries and personal assistants, telephone and telex operators, word processing operators.
Qualifications: Typing 45 wpm, shorthand 80 wpm, 5 O' levels and a full driving licence.
Skills: Computer, shorthand, typing, word processing.
Comments: Small employment bureau dealing with a wide range of temporary and permanent staff.
29 Maddox Street
London W1R 9LD
Tel: 01-491 3130

Susan Hamilton Personnel Services
Industries: All
Placements: Bilingual operators, receptionists, secretaries and personal assistants, telephone and telex operators, word processing operators.
Qualifications: Typing 50 wpm, shorthand 80 wpm. Education to O'level standard.

Skills: Shorthand, typing, word processing.
Comments: Small, personalised consultancy.
33 St Georges Street
London W1R 9FA
Tel: 01-629 9157
Fax: 01-499 4878

Tate Appointments
Industries: All
Placements: Accounts clerks, receptionists, secretaries and personal assistants, telephone and telex operators.
Qualifications: Typing 50 wpm, shorthand 70 wpm, 5 O' levels or equivalent, friendly and outgoing personality.
Skills: Shorthand, typing, word processing.
Comments: Small independent consultancy that specialises in secretarial, general office and management recruitment both for permanent and temporary vacancies.
70/71 New Bond Street
London W1Y 9DE
Tel: 01-408 0424
Fax: 01-493 8790

Times Computer Services Limited
Industries: All
Placements: Accounts clerks, computer operators, receptionists, secretaries and personal assistants, telephone and telex operators, word processing operators.
Qualifications: Typing 45 wpm. We will consider people with any experience in the office/computer market.
Skills: Computer, shorthand, typing, word processing.
Comments: Place workers into the computer industry. Specialise in computer operators, VDU operators, typists and word processor operators.
95 York Street
London W1H 1DU
Tel: 01-258 1878
Fax: 01-724 5617

Uptown Personnel Services Ltd
Industries: All
Placements: Accounts clerks, bilingual operators, computer operators, receptionists, secretaries and personal assistants, telephone and telex operators, word processing operators.
Qualifications: None required
Skills: Computer, shorthand, typing, word processing.
Comments: We specialise in placing both permanent and temporary staff in the secretarial and administrative sectors. Staff should be multi-skilled and flexible in approach. Word processing is an asset.
61 Oxford Street
London W1R 1RB
Tel: 01-734 6425
Fax: 01-734 8772

West End Staff Bureau (Intl) Ltd
Industries: All
Placements: Accounts clerks, computer operators, receptionists, secretaries and personal assistants, telephone and telex operators, word processing operators.
Qualifications: Typist 50 wpm, shorthand 80 wpm. Attitude and appearance count.
Skills: Computer, shorthand, typing, word processing.
Chesham House
150 Regent Street
London W1R 5FA
Tel: 01-629 0538/439 6288
Fax: 01-434 2469

West London

Atlas Employment Agency Ltd
Industries: All
Placements: Accounts clerks, bilingual operators, computer operators, receptionists, secretaries and personal assistants, telephone and telex operators, word processing operators.
Qualifications: Typing 45 wpm, shorthand 80 wpm, 1 year's WP experience, 1 year's legal secretarial experience.
Skills: None required
Comments: We are a high street employment agency looking for all types

of temporaries, both skilled and unskilled. We need hardworking, reliable applicants for a variety of positions.

84 Uxbridge Road
Shepherds Bush
London W12 8LR
Tel: 01-749 2171

126 The Broadway
West Ealing
London W13 0SY
Tel: 01-579 5451

38 The Broadway
Ealing
London W5 2NP
Tel: 01-579 2971

1st Floor
4 Hammersmith Broadway
London W6 7AL
Tel: 01-748 9434

4 Hammersmith Broadway
London W6 7AL
Tel: 01-741 4771

43 Kensington High Street
London W8 5ED
Tel: 01-938 3011

Brook Street
Industries: All
Placements: Accounts clerks, receptionists, secretaries and personal assistants, telephone and telex operators, word processing operators.
Qualifications: Typing 40/50 wpm, shorthand 80/100 wpm, 2 GCSE's including English.
Skills: Shorthand, typing, word processing.
Comments: We are looking for PA's, secretaries, copy typists, clerks, account clerks, switchboard operators, receptionists, catering staff, industrial staff.

14 Pembridge Road
London W11 3HI
Tel: 01-229 9234

320 Chiswick High Road
London W4 5TA
Tel: 01-995 2311

11 The Broadway
Ealing
London W5 2NH
Tel: 01-567 7799

14 Kensington Church Street
London W8 4EP
Tel: 01-937 5115

Centacom Staff Agency
Industries: All
Placements: Accounts clerks, computer operators, receptionists, secretaries and personal assistants, telephone and telex operators, word processing operators.
Qualifications: None required
Skills: Computer, shorthand, typing, word processing.
Comments: Small agency with branches in Australia and New Zealand.

30 Kensington Church Street
London W8 4EP
Tel: 01-937 6525
Fax: 01-938 2921

Kerr Staff Ltd
Industries: All
Placements: Accounts clerks, bilingual operators, computer operators, receptionists, secretaries and personal assistants, telephone and telex operators, word processing operators.
Qualifications: None required
Skills: Shorthand, typing, word processing.
Comments: We are able to place a range of people from school leavers to executive levels.

41 Haven Green
Ealing
London W5 2NX
Tel: 01-998 4086
Fax: 01-991 5228

Peters & Smyth Staff Bureau Ltd
Industries: All
Placements: Accounts clerks, bilingual operators, computer operators, receptionists, secretaries and personal assistants, telephone and telex operators, word processing operators.

Qualifications: None required
Skills: Computer, shorthand, typing, word processing.
Comments: An employment agency with all grades of temporary workers.

44 The Mall
Ealing
London W5 3TJ
Tel: 01-840 3130

Reed Employment
Industries: All
Placements: Accounts clerks, bilingual operators, computer operators, receptionists, secretaries and personal assistants, telephone and telex operators, word processing operators.
Qualifications: None required. All potential candidates are fully screened and tested.
Skills: Computer, shorthand, typing, word processing.
Comments: Reed Employment recruits permanent and temporary staff in the following areas: secretarial, WP operators and all office skills, accountancy, nursing, industrial, insurance and computing.

62 Nottinghill Gate
London W11 3HT
Tel: 01-229 9452

202 Uxbridge Road
London W12 7JP
Tel: 01-749 2283

116 The Broadway
London W13 0SY
Tel: 01-579 4465

94 High Street
Acton
London W3 9QX
Tel: 01-992 8984

402 Chiswick High Road
London W4 5TF
Tel: 01-994 0106

41 St John's Road
London W4 5TF
Tel: 01-223 8484

26 The Broadway
London W5 2NP
Tel: 01-579 3481

Reed House
65 Westcroft Square
London W6 0TA
Tel: 01-748 3511
Fax: 01-748 2417

Tops Personnel Services
Industries: All
Placements: Accounts clerks, bilingual operators, computer operators, receptionists, secretaries and personal assistants, telephone and telex operators, word processing operators.
Qualifications: None required
Skills: Computer, shorthand, typing, word processing.
Comments: Deal with commercial and industrial vacancies from junior clerks to PA executive secretaries and from an assembler to an HGV 1 Driver.

82a High Street
Acton
London W3
Tel: 01-993 8201
Fax: 01-993 9518

18 the Green
Ealing
London W5 5DA
Tel: 01-840 5888
Fax: 01-579 2970

Types Recruitment
Industries: All
Placements: Secretaries and personal assistants, word processing operators.
Qualifications: Typing 45 wpm.
Skills: Shorthand, typing, word processing.
Comments: We are a small private agency which specializes in WP staff, especially CPT operators. We offer free training on a wide range of systems to candidates who can type at least 45 wpm.

1a The Parade
Haven Green, Ealing
London W5 2PB
Tel: 01-997 5604/991 1734

Bedfordshire

Lewis Recruitment
Industries: All

Placements: Accounts clerks, bilingual operators, computer operators, receptionists, secretaries and personal assistants, telephone and telex operators, word processing operators.
Qualifications: Clerk/typists 40 wpm typing, 2 O'levels. Copy/audio typists 50 wpm, 2 O'levels, including English Language. Shorthand/typists 50 wpm typing, 80+ wpm shorthand, O'levels.
Skills: Shorthand, typing, word processing.
55 High Street South
Dunstable
Bedfordshire LU6 2SF
Tel: 0582 601391
Fax: 0582 661793

Luton Secretarial Staff Bureau
Industries: All
Placements: Accounts clerks, bilingual operators, computer operators, receptionists, secretaries and personal assistants, telephone and telex operators, word processing operators.
Qualifications: No minimum qualification. Personality and attitude are seen as being important.
Skills: Computer, shorthand, typing, word processing.
Comments: Independent bureau which aims to match the requirements of the company with those of the worker.
6 Union Street
Luton
Bedfordshire LU1 3AN
Tel: 0582 451588
Fax: 0582 22069

Reed Employment
Industries: All
Placements: Accounts clerks, bilingual operators, computer operators, receptionists, secretaries and personal assistants, telephone and telex operators, word processing operators.
Qualifications: None required. All potential candidates are fully screened and tested.
Skills: Computer, shorthand, typing, word processing.

Comments: Reed Employment recruits permanent and temporary staff in the following areas: secretarial, WP operators and all office skills, accountancy, nursing, industrial, insurance and computing.
81 George Street
Luton
Bedfordshire LU1 2AT
Tel: 0582 417979

Situations Vacant Ltd
Industries: All
Placements: Accounts clerks, computer operators, receptionists, secretaries and personal assistants, telephone and telex operators, word procesing operators.
Qualifications: None required. Experience preferred.
Skills: Computer, shorthand, typing, word processing.
3/5 George Street West
Luton
Bedfordshire LU1 2BJ
Tel: 0582 405888

Berkshire

Atlas Employment Agency Ltd
Industries: All
Placements: Accounts clerks, bilingual operators, computer operators, receptionists, secretaries and personal assistants, telephone and telex operators, word processing operators.
Qualifications: Typing 45 wpm, shorthand 80 wpm, 1 year's WP experience, 1 year's legal secretarial experience.
Skills: None required
Comments: We are a high street employment agency looking for all types of temporaries, both skilled and unskilled. We need hardworking, reliable applicants for a variety of positions.
6 Windsor Road
Slough
Berkshire SL1 2EJ
Tel: 0753 822424

Brook Street
Industries: All

Placements: Accounts clerks, receptionists, secretaries and personal assistants, telephone and telex operators, word processing operators.
Qualifications: Typing 40/50 wpm, shorthand 80/100 wpm, 2 GCSE's including English.
Skills: Shorthand, typing, word processing.
Comments: We are looking for PA's, secretaries, copy typists, clerks, account clerks, switchboard operators, receptionists, catering staff, industrial staff.

Dudley House
High Street
Bracknell
Berkshire RG12 1[l
Tel: 0344 59118

49/51 High Street
Maidenhead
Berkshire SL6 1JT
Tel: 0628 73327

138 High Street
Slough
Berkshire SL1 1DN
Tel: 0753 34747

Business Back-Up Ltd
Industries: All
Placements: Accounts clerks, bilingual operators, computer operators, receptionists, secretaries and personal assistants, telephone and telex operators, word processing operators, legal, accountancy and catering positions.
Qualifications: None required
Skills: Computer, shorthand, typing, word processing.
Comments: We are a small, privately owned agency and place good quality, well presented, honest and reliable temps at all levels.

1 King Street
Maidenhead
Berkshire SL6 1DZ
Tel: 0628 770124
Fax: 0628 784412

Diamond Staff Bureau
Industries: All
Placements: Receptionists, secretaries and personal assistants, telephone and telex operators, word processing operators.
Qualifications: Minimum qualifications: the ability to read and write, but obviously the more skills and experience one has, the better.
Skills: Computer, shorthand, typing, word processing.
Comments: We provide all categories of office temporaries from junior clerical to senior PAs, as well as accounts and computer staff.

Neville House
High Street
Bracknell
Berkshire RG12 1DE
Tel: 0344 55321
Fax: 0344 51606

Forest Employment Ltd
Industries: All
Placements: Accounts clerks, bilingual operators, computer operators, receptionists, secretaries and personal assistants, telephone and telex operators, word processing operators.
Qualifications: Typing 40 wpm, minimum. Forest look for a positive attitude and good presentation both of which count as qualifications in their book.
Skills: Computer, shorthand, typing, word processing.
Comments: A multi -- disciplined agency with a strong secretarial, commercial division, which always has assignments for good WP operators.

21 York Road
Maidenhead
Berkshire RG1 2JI
Tel: 0628 73242
Fax: 0628 770745

11/12 Gun Street
Reading
Berkshire
Tel: 0734 587272
Fax: 0734 391404

Kemp Recruitment
Industries: All

Placements: Accounts clerks, receptionists, secretaries and personal assistants, telephone and telex operators, word processing operators.
Qualifications: None required
Skills: Shorthand, typing, word processing.
55a Northbrook Street
Newbury
Berkshire RG13 1AN
Tel: 0635 41464
Fax: 0635 521481

L.M.S
Industries: Law, media, medical, clerical/secretarial, publishing.
Placements: Accounts clerks, bilingual operators, computer operators, receptionists, secretaries and personal assistants, telephone and telex operators, word processing operators.
Qualifications: Typing 40/60+ wpm, shorthand 90+ wpm, Less skilled applicants such as school leavers also considered, but must have a good standard of education, be articulate and well groomed.
Skills: Computer, shorthand, typing, word processing.
Comments: We are a small agency giving a very personal service to our candidates and clients. We spend a lot of time with the former and latter alike, establishing the requirments of each party to ensure that our temps are placed correctly.
24 Cheap Street
Newbury
Berkshire RG14 5DB
Tel: 0635 45612
Fax: 0635 43623

Manpower plc
Industries: All
Placements: Accounts clerks, bilingual operators, computer operators, receptionists, secretaries and personal assistants, telephone and telex operators, word processing operators.
Qualifications: We use our own skill measurement tests.
Skills: Shorthand, typing, word processing, computer.
Comments: Market leader in all forms of temporary work, specialising in office automation. We provide free training to our fieldstaff.
Manpower House
272 High Street
Slough
Berkshire SL1 1LJ
Tel: 0753 73111
Fax: 0753 824524

Office Angels
Industries: All
Placements: Accounts clerks, computer operators, receptionists, secretaries and personal assistants, telephone and telex operators.
Qualifications: None required
Skills: Computer, shorthand, typing, word processing.
Comments: Medium sized, personalised recruitment consultants dealing in permanent and temporary placements in all categories. Unskilled applicants also catered for.
Angel House
28 Friar Street
Reading
Berkshire RG1 1DP
Tel: 0734 508001
274 High Street
Slough
Berkshire SL1 1NB
Tel: 0753 691484

Reed Employment
Industries: All
Placements: Accounts clerks, bilingual operators, computer operators, receptionists, secretaries and personal assistants, telephone and telex operators, word processing operators.
Qualifications: None required. All potential candidates are fully screened and tested.
Skills: Computer, shorthand, typing, word processing.
Comments: Reed Employment recruits permanent and temporary staff in the following areas: secretarial, WP operators and all office skills,

accountancy, nursing, industrial, insurance and computing.

19 High Street
Bracknell
Berkshire RG12 1DL
Tel: 0344 486777

19 High Street
Bracknell
Berkshire RG12 1DL
Tel: 0344 486777

103 High Street
Maidenhead
Berkshire SL6 1JX
Tel: 0628 73656

70 Broad Street
Reading
Berkshire RG1 2AF
Tel: 0734 573464

164 High Street
Slough
Berkshire SL1 1JP
Tel: 0753 25062

304 Farnham Road
Slough
Berkshire SL1 4XL
Tel: 0753 34141

114 Peascod Street
Windsor
Berkshire SL4 1DN
Tel: 0753 857624

Buckinghamshire

Aylesbury Staff Bureau
Industries: All, medical
Placements: Accounts clerks, bilingual operators, computer operators, receptionists, secretaries and personal assistants, telephone and telex operators, word processing operators.
Qualifications: Elementary typing, shorthand 80 wpm, 4 GCSE's including English.
Skills: Shorthand, typing, word processing.
Comments: We are a high street employment agency looking for all types of temporaries, both skilled and unskilled. We need hardworking, reliable applicants for a variety of positions.
12 Temple Square
Aylesbury
Buckinghamshire HP20 2QL
Tel: 0296 87371

Crown Personnel Ltd
Industries: All
Placements: Accounts clerks, bilingual operators, computer operators, receptionists, secretaries and personal assistants, telephone and telex operators, word processing operators.
Qualifications: Typing 50 wpm, shorthand 45 wpm, GCSE's in Maths and English preferred.
Skills: Computer, shorthand, typing, word processing.
Comments: We are a successful agency providing temporary staff for a wide range of organisations in and around South Bucks who require skills in all secretarial disciplines.
58 High Street
Aylesbury
Buckinghamshire HP20 1SE
Tel: 0296 436001
Fax: 0296 392938

High Flyers
Industries: All
Placements: Accounts clerks, computer operators, receptionists, secretaries and personal assistants, telephone and telex operators, word processing operators.
Qualifications: None required. Attitude and personal qualities are important.
Skills: Computer, shorthand, typing, word processing.
Comments: A local, friendly, professional agency offering personal service to everyone locally, from filing clerks to senior managers.
2 Dukes Place
Marlow
Buckinghamshire SL7 2QH
Tel: 06284 75703
Fax: 06284 75707

Keynes Personnel Ltd
Industries: All
Placements: Accounts clerks, bilingual operators, computer operators, receptionists, secretaries and personal assistants, telephone and telex operators, word processing operators.
Qualifications: Typing 50 wpm, shorthand 80 wpm.
Skills: Computer, shorthand, typing, word processing.
Comments: We only supply computing staff. Skills, attitude and appearance are important.
356 Silbury Boulevard
Milton Keynes
Buckinghamshire MK9 2LR
Tel: 0908 668385
Fax: 0908 662615

Office Angels
Industries: All
Placements: Accounts clerks, computer operators, receptionists, secretaries and personal assistants, telephone and telex operators.
Qualifications: None required
Skills: Computer, shorthand, typing, word processing.
Comments: Medium sized, personalised recruitment consultants dealing in permanent and temporary placements in all categories. Unskilled applicants also catered for.
Sovereign Court
203 Witan Gate East
Milton Keynes
Buckinghamshire MK9 2HP
Tel: 0908 678600

Reed Employment
Industries: All
Placements: Accounts clerks, bilingual operators, computer operators, receptionists, secretaries and personal assistants, telephone and telex operators, word processing operators.
Qualifications: None required. All potential candidates are fully screened and tested.
Skills: Computer, shorthand, typing, word processing.
Comments: Reed Employment recruits permanent and temporary staff in the following areas: secretarial, WP operators and all office skills, accountancy, nursing, industrial, insurance and computing.
456 Midsummer Boulevard
Milton Keynes
Buckinghamshire MK9 2EA
Tel: 0908 660057

Cambridgeshire

Anglia Recruitment
Industries: All
Placements: Accounts clerks, bilingual operators, computer operators, receptionists, secretaries and personal assistants, telephone and telex operators, word processing operators.
Qualifications: None required
Skills: Computer, shorthand, typing, word processing.
Comments: Anglia Recruitment is a small, independent agency with 2 offices.
31 Hills Road
Cambridge
Cambridgeshire CB2 1NW
Tel: 0223 461526
Fax: 0223 67403

Eastern Staff Services
Industries: All
Placements: Accounts clerks, computer operators, receptionists, secretaries and personal assistants, telephone and telex operators, word processing operators.
Qualifications: None required
Skills: Computer shorthand, typing, word processing.
Comments: Seek reliable, office, secretarial and executive temps for a wide range of vacancies throughout the East Anglian region.
62 Sidney Street
Cambridge
Cambridgeshire CB2 3JW
Tel: 0223 63567
Fax: 0223 63550

Gordon Turner Appointments
Industries: All
Placements: Secretaries, PA's, clerical, receptionists, bilingual operators, WP operators, computer operators, accounts clerks and technical placements.
Qualifications: Secretarial temps need O'levels, typing 45 wpm, shorthand 80 wpm. Typists: 45 wpm and multi-machine knowledge. WP: 6 months experience and ideally a knowledge of a minimum of three packages.
Skills: Computer, shorthand, typing, word processing.
Comments: Deal in high calibre secretarial staff and all kinds of office vacancies. Applicants tested and references taken before employing. Very careful matching procedures.
40-42 Hobson Street
Cambridge
Cambridgeshire CB1 1NL
Tel: 0223 359614

Stilton Staff (ER) Ltd
Industries: All
Placements: Accounts clerks, computer operators, receptionists, secretaries and personal assistants, telephone and telex operators.
Qualifications: None required
Skills: Computer, shorthand, typing, word processing.
32 Long Causeway
Peterborough
Cambridgeshire PE1 1YJ
Tel: 0773 60531/2

Essex

Anglia Recruitment
Industries: All
Placements: Accounts clerks, bilingual operators, computer operators, receptionists, secretaries and personal assistants, telephone and telex operators, word processing operators.
Qualifications: None required
Skills: Computer, shorthand, typing, word processing.
Comments: Anglia Recruitment is a small, independent agency with 2 offices.
24 King Street
Saffron Walden
Essex CB10 1ES
Tel: 0799 21761/25699
Fax: 0799 513473

Atlas Employment Agency Ltd
Industries: All
Placements: Accounts clerks, bilingual operators, computer operators, receptionists, secretaries and personal assistants, telephone and telex operators, word processing operators.
Qualifications: Typing 45 wpm, shorthand 80 wpm, 1 year's WP experience, 1 year's legal secretarial experience.
Skills: None required
Comments: We are a high street employment agency looking for all types of temporaries, both skilled and unskilled. We need hardworking, reliable applicants for a variety of positions.
95 Cranbrook Road
Ilford
Essex IG1 4TG
Tel: 01-514 8600

Brook Street
Industries: All
Placements: Accounts clerks, receptionists, secretaries and personal assistants, telephone and telex operators, word processing operators.
Qualifications: Typing 40/50 wpm, shorthand 80/100 wpm, 2 GCSE's including English.
Skills: Shorthand, typing, word processing.
Comments: We are looking for PA's, secretaries, copy typists, clerks, account clerks, switchboard operators, receptionists, catering staff, industrial staff.
47 Cranbrook Road
Ilford
Essex IG1 4PG
Tel: 01-478 1116

50a South Street
Romford
Essex RM1 1RJ
Tel: 0708 67211

Bryman Personnel
Industries: All
Placements: Accounts clerks, computer operators, receptionists, secretaries and personal assistants, telephone and telex operators, word processing operators. Overseas placements are made.
Qualifications: None required
Skills: Computer, shorthand, typing, word processing.
Comments: A commercial and technical recruitment agency, handling permanent, temporary and contract vacancies in the UK and overseas.
Bryman House
16 Weston Road
Southend-on-Sea
Essex SS1 1AS
Tel: 0702 353990

Carwell Employment Bureau
Industries: All
Placements: Accounts clerks, bilingual operators, computer operators, receptionists, secretaries and personal assistants, telephone and telex operators.
Qualifications: None required
Skills: Computer, shorthand, typing, word processing.
Comments: Established for over 20 years providing all aspects of temporary staff to office, industrial and professional companies.
13 Market House
The High
Harlow
Essex CM20 1BL
Tel: 0279 33033/32727/450220
Fax: 0279 450210

Eastern Staff Services
Industries: All
Placements: Accounts clerks, computer operators, receptionists, secretaries and personal assistants, telephone and telex operators, word processing operators.

Qualifications: None required
Skills: Computer shorthand, typing, word processing.
Comments: Seek reliable, office, secretarial and executive temps for a wide range of vacancies throughout the East Anglian region.
1 Bank Passage
Colchester
Essex CO1 1HZ
Tel: 0206 560460
Fax: 0206 763307

First Personnel
Industries: All
Placements: Accounts clerks, receptionists, secretaries and personal assistants, telephone and telex operators, word processing operators.
Qualifications: Typing 40 wpm, shorthand 75 wpm. Accuracy is more important than speed.
Skills: Computer, shorthand, typing, word processing.
Comments: A privately owned agency providing permanent and temporary staff in the commercial sector. Looking for presentable, reliable staff with accurate skills.
42a Longbridge Road
Barking
Essex IG11 8RT
Tel: 01-594 2666

92c High Street
Billericay
Essex CM12 9BT
Tel: 0277 657000

57a Orsett Road
Grays
Essex RM17 5HJ
Tel: 0375 391111
Fax: 0375 390151

J & M Group
Industries: All, medical
Placements: Accounts clerks, computer operators, receptionists, secretaries and personal assistants, telephone and telex operators, word processing operators.
Qualifications: None required

Skills: Computer, shorthand, typing, word processing.

Comments: A group of companies dealing in industrial, commercial, secretarial, engineering, electronics, mechanical, civil, building and nursing staff.

102 High Street
Southend-on-Sea
Essex SS1 1JN
Tel: 0702 614451
Fax: 0702 460951

Office Angels

Industries: All

Placements: Accounts clerks, computer operators, receptionists, secretaries and personal assistants, telephone and telex operators.

Qualifications: None required

Skills: Computer, shorthand, typing, word processing.

Comments: Medium sized, personalised recruitment consultants dealing in permanent and temporary placements in all categories. Unskilled applicants also catered for.

72 South Street
Romford
Essex RM1 1RX
Tel: 0708 24718

Reed Employment

Industries: All

Placements: Accounts clerks, bilingual operators, computer operators, receptionists, secretaries and personal assistants, telephone and telex operators, word processing operators.

Qualifications: None required. All potential candidates are fully screened and tested.

Skills: Computer, shorthand, typing, word processing.

Comments: Reed Employment recruits permanent and temporary staff in the following areas: secretarial, WP operators and all office skills, accountancy, nursing, industrial, insurance and computing.

19 Station Parade
Barking
Essex IG11 8EA
Tel: 01-591 6900

35 Cranbrook Road
Ilford
Essex IG1 4PA
Tel: 01-514 3777

148 High Street
Southend-on-Sea
Essex SS1 1JX
Tel: 0702 612511

Staffline Employment Agency

Industries: All

Placements: Accounts clerks, computer operators, receptionists, secretaries and personal assistants, telephone and telex operators, word processing operators.

Qualifications: None required

Skills: Computer, shorthand, typing, word processing.

Comments: We also recruit industrial, driving, commercial and technical staff on a temporary or permanent basis.

83-85 Cranbrook Road
Ilford
Essex IG1 4PG
Tel: 01-514 8544
Fax: 01-553 5135

Hampshire

Brook Street

Industries: All

Placements: Accounts clerks, receptionists, secretaries and personal assistants, telephone and telex operators, word processing operators.

Qualifications: Typing 40/50 wpm, shorthand 80/100 wpm, 2 GCSE's including English.

Skills: Shorthand, typing, word processing.

Comments: We are looking for PA's, secretaries, copy typists, clerks, account clerks, switchboard operators, receptionists, catering staff, industrial staff.

6a London Street
Basingstoke
Hampshire RG21 1NU
Tel: 0256 471242

Central Recruitment
Industries: All
Placements: Accounts clerks, computer operators, receptionists, secretaries and personal assistants, telephone and telex operators, word processing operators.
Qualifications: None required
Skills: Computer, shorthand, typing, word processing.
Comments: We have four specialist sections in accountancy, law, insurance and general office vancancies, and consider anyone with office experience.
Hampstead House
New Town Centre
Basingstoke
Hampshire RG21 1LG
Tel: 0256 844228
Fax: 0256 844257

Hall Placements
Industries: All
Placements: Accounts clerks, bilingual operators, computer operators, receptionists, secretaries and personal assistants, telephone and telex operators, word processing operators.
Qualifications: Minimum typing 35 wpm, minimum shorthand 80 wpm, educated to O' level standard.
Skills: Computer, shorthand, typing, word processing.
Comments: We only use temps with proven skills and have built up a reputation of supplying high calibre personnel both in permanent and temporary placements.
Hall Place
South Street
Havant
Hampshire P0G 1DA
Tel: 0705 475541
Fax: 0705 473851

Keynes Personnel Ltd
Industries: All
Placements: Accounts clerks, bilingual operators, computer operators, receptionists, secretaries and personal assistants, telephone and telex operators, word processing operators.
Qualifications: Typing 50 wpm, shorthand 80 wpm.
Skills: Computer, shorthand, typing, word processing.
Comments: We only supply computing staff. Skills, attitude and appearance are important.
Enterprise House Business Centre
Ocean Village
Southampton
Hampshire SO1 1XB
Tel: 0703 331666
Fax: 0703 332050

Office Angels
Industries: All
Placements: Accounts clerks, computer operators, receptionists, secretaries and personal assistants, telephone and telex operators.
Qualifications: None required
Skills: Computer, shorthand, typing, word processing.
Comments: Medium sized, personalised recruitment consultants dealing in permanent and temporary placements in all categories. Unskilled applicants also catered for.
81 Church Street
Basingstoke
Hampshire RG21 1QT
Tel: 0256 464744

Omegar Personnel Limited
Industries: All
Placements: Accounts clerks, computer operators, receptionists, secretaries and personal assistants, telephone and telex operators, word processing operators.
Qualifications: Typing or word processing 45/50 wpm, shorthand 35/40 wpm. GCSE's in Maths and English.
Skills: Computer, shorthand, typing, word processing.
Comments: We cater for local industry and commerce and seek reliable and well

presented temps.
27a High Street
Andover
Hampshire SP10 1LJ
Tel: 0264 57629
Fax: 0264 333350

Paragons Personnel
Industries: All, law, banking
Placements: Accounts clerks, bilingual operators, receptionists, secretaries and personal assistants, telephone and telex operators, word processing operators. Overseas placements.
Qualifications: None required
Skills: Computer, shorthand, typing, word processing.
Comments: Independent agency operating a Commercial and Industrial Division. Looking for temps to cover all aspects of office work.
9 Latimer Street
Romsey
Hampshire SO51 8DF
Tel: 0794 524212

Reed Employment
Industries: All
Placements: Accounts clerks, bilingual operators, computer operators, receptionists, secretaries and personal assistants, telephone and telex operators, word processing operators.
Qualifications: None required. All potential candidates are fully screened and tested.
Skills: Computer, shorthand, typing, word processing.
Comments: Reed Employment recruits permanent and temporary staff in the following areas: secretarial, WP operators and all office skills, accountancy, nursing, industrial, insurance and computing.
22 Wote Street
Basingstoke
Hampshire RG21 1NL
Tel: 0256 463385

TAV Staff Agency Limited
Industries: All
Placements: Accounts clerks, bilingual operators, computer operators, receptionists, secretaries and personal assistants, telephone and telex operators, word processing operators.
Qualifications: None required. All applicants are tested in spelling, filing, arithmetic, shorthand, typing and audio to determine their relevant skill level.
Skills: Shorthand, typing, word processing.
Comments: The secretarial division of our organisation is TAV office team, and is able to place all levels of temporary and permanent applicants in all areas of commerce and industry.
17a Church Street
Basingstoke
Hampshire RG21 1PG
Tel: 0256 471717

67 Leigh Road
Eastleigh
Hampshire SO5 4DF
Tel: 0703 614711

201 West Street
Fareham
Hampshire PO16 OEN
Tel: 0329 282016

12 East Street
Havant
Hampshire PO9 1AQ
Tel: 0705 476731

34a-42a Market Parade
Havant
Hampshire PO9 1QF
Tel: 0705 471711

237 Commercial Road
Portsmouth
Hampshire PO1 4BJ
Tel: 0705 819341

8 Bargate
Southampton
Hampshire SO1 0DP
Tel: 0703 634534

Hertfordshire

Access Personnel Ltd
Industries: All
Placements: Accounts clerks, bilingual

operators, computer operators, receptionists, secretaries and personal assistants, telephone and telex operators.
Qualifications: None required
Skills: Computer, shorthand, typing, word processing.
Comments: Technical and commercial permanent and temporary placements.
103 Victoria Street
St Albans
Hertfordshire AL1 3TJ
Tel: 0727 43255
Fax: 0727 41916

Arena Staff Agency
Industries: All
Placements: Accounts clerks, computer operators, receptionists, secretaries and personal assistants, telephone and telex operators, word processing operators.
Qualifications: Typing 40+ wpm, shorthand 80+ wpm, minimum of 3 O' levels.
Skills: Computer, shorthand, typing, word processing.
Comments: We concentrate on secretarial and general office skills including book-keeping, VDU, as well as good qualified secretaries, WP operators and accounts staff.
54b Leys Avenue
Letchworth
Hertfordshire SG6 3EQ
Tel: 0462 678282
Fax: 0462 672576

Atlas Employment Agency Ltd
Industries: All
Placements: Accounts clerks, bilingual operators, computer operators, receptionists, secretaries and personal assistants, telephone and telex operators, word processing operators.
Qualifications: Typing 45 wpm, shorthand 80 wpm, 1 year's WP experience, 1 year's legal secretarial experience.
Skills: None required
Comments: We are a high street employment agency looking for all types of temporaries, both skilled and unskilled. We need hardworking, reliable applicants for a variety of positions.
11 Holywell Hill
St Albans
Hertfordshire AL1 1EZ
Tel: 0727 40531
12 Market Street
Watford
Hertfordshire WD1 7AD
Tel: 0923 49936

Body Bank, The
Industries: All
Placements: Accounts clerks, bilingual operators, computer operators, receptionists, secretaries and personal assistants, telephone and telex operators, word processing operators.
Qualifications: None required
Skills: Computer, shorthand, typing, word processing.
Comments: The Body Bank employ a variety of temps from secretaries to casual staff. It looks for enthusiastic, flexible personnel with outgoing personalities.
117 High Street
Barnet
Hertfordshire EN5 5UZ
Tel: 01-441 6868
Fax: 01-441 6915

Boxmoor Bureau (Staff Recruitment) Ltd
Industries: All
Placements: Accounts clerks, bilingual operators, computer operators, receptionists, secretaries and personal assistants, telephone and telex operators, word processing operators.
Qualifications: A good level of proficiency in the particular skills offered by each individual.
Skills: Computer, shorthand, typing, word processing.
Comments: We have been established for over 17 years and supply staff to a wide range of local businesses. Our temps receive holiday pay from day one.

5a Marlowes
Hemel Hempstead
Hertfordshire HP1 1LA
Tel: 0442 50437
Fax: 0442 68174
6 Spencer Street
St Albans
Hertfordshire AL3 5EG
Tel: 0727 41102
Fax: 0727 64966

Brook Street
Industries: All
Placements: Accounts clerks, receptionists, secretaries and personal assistants, telephone and telex operators, word processing operators.
Qualifications: Typing 40/50 wpm, shorthand 80/100 wpm, 2 GCSE's including English.
Skills: Shorthand, typing, word processing.
Comments: We are looking for PA's, secretaries, copy typists, clerks, account clerks, switchboard operators, receptionists, catering staff, industrial staff.
76 High Street
Watford
Hertfordshire WD1 2BP
Tel: 0923 42377

Chequers Employment
Industries: All
Placements: Accounts clerks, bilingual operators, computer operators, receptionists, secretaries and personal assistants, telephone and telex operators, word processing operators. Overseas placements are made.
Qualifications: Typing 40 wpm, shorthand 80 wpm.
Skills: Computer, shorthand, typing, word processing.
Comments: Established 1962, specialising in permanent and temporary office staff.
129 St Albans Road
Watford
Hertfordshire WD1 1RA
Tel: 0923 241077/34233
Fax: 0923 818226

Computer Help
Industries: All
Placements: Accounts clerks, bilingual operators, receptionists, secretaries and personal assistants, telephone and telex operators.
Qualifications: Typing 45 wpm, minimum 1 year's work experience, standard education.
Skills: Computer, word processing.
Comments: We specialise in the computer field: VDU, WP operations and programming. Seek high calibre staff.
12a Bushey Hall Road
Bushey
Hertfordshire WD2 2EA
Tel: 0923 817595
Fax: 0923 246447

Femco Employment Agency Ltd
Industries: All
Placements: Accounts clerks, computer operators, receptionists, secretaries and personal assistants, telephone and telex operators, word processing operators.
Qualifications: A range of qualifications is acceptable, from GCSE to degree level; also general clerical, secretarial, accounting, technical and engineering skills.
Skills: Computer, shorthand, typing, word processing.
Comments: Recruitment of permanent and temporary staff in a range of work areas including: secretarial, administration, clerical, accounts, VDU, computers, catering, technical and engineering.
24-25 Stonehills House
Stonehills
Welwyn Garden City
Hertfordshire AL8 6NH
Tel: 0707 323067/329858
Fax: 0707 323067

Head Start Appointments Ltd
Industries: Secretarial, clerical and admin in anything office based.
Placements: Accounts clerks, receptionists, secretaries and personal assistants, telephone and telex operators, word processing operators.

Qualifications: LCC qualification for senior secretarial positions (or equivalent) RSA and Pitman Typing qualifications for non-senior secretarial positions (or equivalent), WP qualification for WP operators (or equivalent).
Skills: Shorthand, typing, word processing.
Comments: We deal broadly with office-based staff. This mainly covers secretarial, clerical and admin vacancies, but we do also deal with accounts bookings.

64 High Street
Harpenden
Hertfordshire AL5 2SP
Tel: 0582 460415
Fax: 05827 62601

20 London Road
St Albans
Hertfordshire AL1 1NG
Tel: 0727 60195
Fax: 0727 45015

83a High Street
Stevenage
Hertfordshire SG1 3HR
Tel: 0438 745555
Fax: 0438 740299

38/40 Stonehills
Welwyn Garden City
Hertfordshire AL8 6PD
Tel: 0707 321196
Tel: 0707 321187

Kingsway Recruitment Consultants
Industries: All
Placements: Accounts clerks, bilingual operators, computer operators, receptionists, secretaries and personal assistants, telephone and telex operators, word processing operators.
Qualifications: Typing 50 wpm, minimum 6 month's experience for WP operators.
Skills: Shorthand, typing, word processing, computer.
Comments: We are part of the Adia Group and pride ourselves in being honest with both our clients and applicants alike. All applicants including office juniors are welcome to register and we will advise on career choice.

5a Town Centre
Hatfield
Hertfordshire AL10 0JZ
Tel: 07072 75411
Fax: 07072 62730

Norton Staff Agency Ltd
Industries: All
Placements: Accounts clerks, computer operators, receptionists, secretaries and personal assistants, telephone and telex operators.
Qualifications: Typing 35+ wpm, shorthand 80 wpm (preferrably not Teeline), RSA I and Audio, Secretarial course (BTEC National, etc), knowledge of at least 1 word processor.
Skills: Computer, shorthand, typing, word processing.
Comments: We are an independent agency, establised for over 25 years. We offer a personalised service to both applicant and client. We are looking for all kinds of temps, from junior secretaries to senior PA's, and warehouse staff.

26 Park Place
Stevenage
Hertfordshire SG1 7BR
Tel: 0438 314501
Fax: 0438 742233

Office Angels
Industries: All
Placements: Accounts clerks, computer operators, receptionists, secretaries and personal assistants, telephone and telex operators.
Qualifications: None required
Skills: Computer, shorthand, typing, word processing.
Comments: Medium sized, personalised recruitment consultants dealing in permanent and temporary placements in all categories. Unskilled applicants also catered for.

112 The Parade
Watford
Hertfordshire WD1 2AU
Tel: 0923 55626

Reed Employment
Industries: All
Placements: Accounts clerks, bilingual operators, computer operators, receptionists, secretaries and personal assistants, telephone and telex operators, word processing operators.
Qualifications: None required. All potential candidates are fully screened and tested.
Skills: Computer, shorthand, typing, word processing.
Comments: Reed Employment recruits permanent and temporary staff in the following areas: secretarial, WP operators and all office skills, accountancy, nursing, industrial, insurance and computing.

2 Newnham Parade
College Road
Cheshunt
Hertfordshire EN8 9NU
Tel: 0992 38121

24 Maidenhead Street
Hertford
Hertfordshire SG14 1DR
Tel: 0992 583251

11 Market Place
St Albans
Hertfordshire AL3 5DR
Tel: 0727 43410

68 High Street
Watford
Hertfordshire WD1 2BS
Tel: 0923 56269

Scan-Tec Employment Service
Industries: All
Placements: Accounts clerks, bilingual operators, computer operators, receptionists, secretaries and personal assistants, telephone and telex operators, word processing operators.
Qualifications: Clerk typist 35 wpm, copy typist 45 wpm, junior shorthand 80 wpm and 40 wpm typing.
Skills: Computer, shorthand, typing, word processing.
Comments: The secretarial/clerical division is one of three divisions in this agency. Looking for workers in all office disciplines but especially secretaries, typists and word processor operators.

Scan-Tec House
19 Church Street
Bishop's Stortford
Hertfordshire CM23 2LY
Tel: 0279 58362

Swift Personnel
Industries: All
Placements: Accounts clerks, computer operators, receptionists, secretaries and personal assistants, telephone and telex operators, word processing operators.
Qualifications: Typing 40 wpm, shorthand 80 wpm, minimum 2 O' levels - English and Maths.
Skills: Computer, shorthand, typing, word processing.
Comments: We are part of Swift Personnel, Swift Technical and Swift Nursing. We look for temporary staff in all office work. Our nursing section look for part-time nurses and our Technical Division look for contract workers in off-shore and building services.

49 High Street
Barnet
Hertfordshire EN5 5UW
Tel: 01-441 5991
Fax: 01-441 7160

Kent

Argosy Employment Group
Industries: All
Placements: Accounts clerks, bilingual operators, computer operators, receptionists, secretaries and personal assistants, telephone and telex operators, word processing operators.
Qualifications: None required
Skills: Computer, shorthand, typing, word processing.
Comments: We recruit a wide range of temps eg., manual labourers, secretarial staff, professionals, etc.

57 High Street
Ashford
Kent TN24 8SG
Tel: 0233 37700

38 High Street
Canterbury
Kent CT1 2RY
Tel: 0227 762170

2a Batchelor Street
Chatham
Kent ME4 4BJ
Tel: 0634 406031

7 Castle Street
Dover
Kent CT16 1PT
Tel: 0304 216432/203946

108 High Street
Edenbridge
Kent TN8 5AR
Tel: 0732 864141

33 Bouverie Square
Folkestone
Kent CT20 1BA
Tel: 0303 850567

11 Pudding Lane
Maidstone
Kent ME14 1PA
Tel: 0622 688488

6/7 Cecil Square
Margate
Kent CT9 1BD
Tel: 0843 297112

The Shambles
Sevenoaks
Kent TN13 1AL
Tel: 0732 451331/2

93/95 High Street
Tonbridge
Kent TN9 1DR
Tel: 0732 770282

Ashton Staff Bureau
Industries: All
Placements: Accounts clerks, bilingual operators, computer operators, receptionists, secretaries and personal assistants, telephone and telex operators, word processing operators.
Qualifications: Typing 50 wpm, shorthand 80 wpm.
Skills: Computer, shorthand, typing, word processing.
Comments: Principally a secretarial agency. It also places drivers, warehouse workers and catering staff.
52 High Street
Orpington
Kent BR6 0JQ
Tel: 0689 78574
Fax: 0689 78574

Atlas Employment Agency Ltd
Industries: All
Placements: Accounts clerks, bilingual operators, computer operators, receptionists, secretaries and personal assistants, telephone and telex operators, word processing operators.
Qualifications: Typing 45 wpm, shorthand 80 wpm, 1 year's WP experience, 1 year's legal secretarial experience.
Skills: None required
Comments: We are a high street employment agency looking for all types of temporaries, both skilled and unskilled. We need hardworking, reliable applicants for a variety of positions.
17a High Street
Bromley
Kent BR1 1LG
Tel: 01-460 2121

Brook Street
Industries: All
Placements: Accounts clerks, receptionists, secretaries and personal assistants, telephone and telex operators, word processing operators.
Qualifications: Typing 40/50 wpm, shorthand 80/100 wpm, 2 GCSE's including English.
Skills: Shorthand, typing, word processing.
Comments: We are looking for PA's, secretaries, copy typists, clerks, account clerks, switchboard operators, receptionists, catering staff, industrial staff.
187 The Broadway
Bexleyheath
Kent DA6 7ER
Tel: 01-303 5651

155 High Street
Bromley
Kent BR1 1JD
Tel: 01-464 1166

1a Grosvener Road
Tunbridge Wells
Kent TN1 2AH
Tel: 0892 44826

Central Recruitment
Industries: All
Placements: Accounts clerks, computer operators, receptionists, secretaries and personal assistants, telephone and telex operators, word processing operators.
Qualifications: None required
Skills: Computer, shorthand, typing, word processing.
Comments: We have four specialist sections in accountancy, law, insurance and general office vancancies, and consider anyone with office experience.

31 Gabriels Hill
Maidstone
Kent ME15 6HX
Tel: 0622 688391
Fax: 0622 688394

Kent Personnel Services Ltd
Industries: All
Placements: Accounts clerks, computer operators, receptionists, secretaries and personal assistants, telephone and telex operators, word processing operators.
Qualifications: Typing 40 wpm, shorthand 80 wpm. 1 year's office experience essential.
Skills: Computer, shorthand, typing, word processing.
Comments: We offer a wide variety of office related work and serve most commercial and industrial companies in Kent.

53 High Street
Maidstone
Kent ME14 1SY
Tel: 0622 673351/2/3/4

Office Angels
Industries: All
Placements: Accounts clerks, computer operators, receptionists, secretaries and personal assistants, telephone and telex operators.
Qualifications: None required
Skills: Computer, shorthand, typing, word processing.
Comments: Medium sized, personalised recruitment consultants dealing in permanent and temporary placements in all categories. Unskilled applicants also catered for.

25 The Mall
Bromley
Kent BR1 1TR
Tel: 01-464 5225

Reed Employment
Industries: All
Placements: Accounts clerks, bilingual operators, computer operators, receptionists, secretaries and personal assistants, telephone and telex operators, word processing operators.
Qualifications: None required. All potential candidates are fully screened and tested.
Skills: Computer, shorthand, typing, word processing.
Comments: Reed Employment recruits permanent and temporary staff in the following areas: secretarial, WP operators and all office skills, accountancy, nursing, industrial, insurance and computing.

104 The Broadway
Bexleyheath
Kent DA6 7DE
Tel: 01-304 8211

20 High Street
Bromley
Kent BR1 1EA
Tel: 01-460 2123

11 High Street
Dartford
Kent DA1 1DT
Tel: 0322 29531

Middlesex

Arron Employment Ageney
Industries: All

Placements: Accounts clerks, bilingual operators, computer operators, receptionists, secretaries and personal assistants, telephone and telex operators, word processing operators.
Qualifications: Junior shorthand 35/70 wpm; shorthand 55/90 wpm; secretary 60/100 wpm, WP 55 wpm, audio 50 wpm. A generally good standard of education, appearance, skills and telephone manner will be taken into account.
Skills: Shorthand, typing, word processing.
Comments: A one office, privately owned company, established over 23 years, concerned with secretarial and office applicants.

223 Imperial Drive
Rayners Lane
Harrow
Middlesex HA2 7HE
Tel: 01-868 0044
Fax: 01-868 0301

Atlas Employment Agency Ltd
Industries: All
Placements: Accounts clerks, bilingual operators, computer operators, receptionists, secretaries and personal assistants, telephone and telex operators, word processing operators.
Qualifications: Typing 45 wpm, shorthand 80 wpm, 1 year's WP experience, 1 year's legal secretarial experience.
Skills: None required
Comments: We are a high street employment agency looking for all types of temporaries, both skilled and unskilled. We need hardworking, reliable applicants for a variety of positions.

202a Station Road
Edgware
Middlesex HA8 7AR
Tel: 01-958 1311

25a Church Street
Enfield
Middlesex EN2 6AF
Tel: 01-367 7367

374 Station Road
Harrow
Middlesex HA1 2DE
Tel: 01-863 6011

20 Station Road
Hayes
Middlesex UB3 4DA
Tel: 01-573 9660

600 High Road
Wembley
Middlesex HA0 2AF
Tel: 01-903 0381

6 Park Lane
Wembley
Middlesex HA9 YRP
Tel: 01-900 2144

Body Bank, The
Industries: All
Placements: Accounts clerks, bilingual operators, computer operators, receptionists, secretaries and personal assistants, telephone and telex operators, word processing operators.
Qualifications: None required
Skills: Computer, shorthand, typing, word processing.
Comments: The Body Bank employ a variety of temps from secretaries to casual staff. It looks for enthusiastic, flexible personnel with outgoing personalities.

485 High Road
Wembley
Middlesex HA9 7AG
Tel: 01-900 2877
Fax: 01-902 6784

Brook Street
Industries: All
Placements: Accounts clerks, receptionists, secretaries and personal assistants, telephone and telex operators, word processing operators.
Qualifications: Typing 40/50 wpm, shorthand 80/100 wpm, 2 GCSE's including English.
Skills: Shorthand, typing, word processing.
Comments: We are looking for PA's, secretaries, copy typists, clerks, account

clerks, switchboard operators, receptionists, catering staff, industrial staff.

97-99 Station Road
Edgware
Middlesex HA8 7JG
Tel: 01-952 8441

17 College Road
Harrow
Middlesex HA1 1BA
Tel: 01-863 1082

45 Station Road
Hayes
Middlesex UB3 4BE
Tel: 01-573 1866

82 High Street
Hounslow
Middlesex TW3 1NH
Tel: 01-570 0111

Industrial Section, Victor House
Norris Road
Staines
Middlesex TW18 4DS
Tel: 0784 56441

Victor House
Norris Road
Staines
Middlesex TW18 4DS
Tel: 0784 62381

425 High Road
Wembley
Middlesex HA9 7AB
Tel: 01-902 3636

Computer Help
Industries: Media, publishing
Placements: Accounts clerks, bilingual operators, receptionists, secretaries and personal assistants, telephone and telex operators.
Qualifications: Typing 45 wpm, minimum 1 year's work experience, standard education.
Skills: Computer, word processing.
Comments: We specialise in the computer field: VDU, WP operations and programming. Seek high calibre staff.

1a Elmside Rod
Wembley Park
Middlesex HA9 8JA
Tel: 01- 903 9344
Fax: 01- 903 6803

Crest Employment Bureau
Industries: All
Placements: Receptionists, secretaries and personal assistants, telephone and telex operators, word processing operators.
Qualifications: Typing 45 wpm, Shorthand 80 wpm.
Skills: Computer, shorthand, typing, word processing.
Comments: Mainly secretarial and clerical, but also seek packers, porters and manual workers.

14 Market Parade
Hampton Road West
Hanworth
Middlesex TW7 4BX
Tel: 01-898 4051

461 London Road
Isleworth
Middlesex TW13 6AL
Tel: 01-568 9611
Fax: 01-569 7861

Drayton Secretarial
Industries: All
Placements: Accounts clerks, computer operators, receptionists, secretaries and personal assistants, telephone and telex operators, word processing operators.
Qualifications: Typing 50/90 wpm, shorthand 50/90 wpm.
Skills: Computer shorthand, typing, word processing.
Comments: Covers all office, warehouse and industrial temps.

2-6 Horton Road
West Drayton
Middlesex UB7 8ED
Tel: 0895 448141
Fax: 0895 444639

Gregorys Staff Agency Ltd
Industries: All
Placements: Accounts clerks, computer

operators, receptionists, secretaries and personal assistants, telephone and telex operators, word processing operators.
Qualifications: Typing 45 wpm, shorthand 80 wpm, GCSE Maths and English preferred, common sense.
Skills: Computer, shorthand, typing, word processing.
Comments: Seeks temps for commercial, technical and secretarial placements.
20 Station Road
West Drayton
Middlesex UB7 7BY
Tel: 0895 443181
Fax: 0895 422565

Office Angels
Industries: All
Placements: Accounts clerks, computer operators, receptionists, secretaries and personal assistants, telephone and telex operators.
Qualifications: None required
Skills: Computer, shorthand, typing, word processing.
Comments: Medium sized, personalised recruitment consultants dealing in permanent and temporary placements in all categories. Unskilled applicants also catered for.
76 College Road
Harrow
Middlesex HA1 1BQ
Tel: 01-861 2949
251 High Street
Hounslow
Middlesex TW3 1EA
Tel: 01-572 8787

Peters & Smyth Staff Bureau Ltd
Industries: All
Placements: Accounts clerks, bilingual operators, computer operators, receptionists, secretaries and personal assistants, telephone and telex operators, word processing operators.
Qualifications: None required
Skills: Computer, shorthand, typing, word processing.
Comments: An employment agency with all grades of temporary workers.

1 The Bridge
Wealdstone
Harrow
Middlesex HA3 5AB
Tel: 01-861 1311
Head Office, Pharmacia House
Prince Regent Street
Hounslow
Middlesex TW3 1NE
Tel: 01-569 4242
2a Kingsley Road
Hounslow
Middlesex TW3 1NP
Tel: 01-577 3434
53a Church Street
Staines
Middlesex TW18 4EN
Tel: 0784 65575

Reed Employment
Industries: All
Placements: Accounts clerks, bilingual operators, computer operators, receptionists, secretaries and personal assistants, telephone and telex operators, word processing operators.
Qualifications: None required. All potential candidates are fully screened and tested.
Skills: Computer, shorthand, typing, word processing.
Comments: Reed Employment recruits permanent and temporary staff in the following areas: secretarial, WP operators and all office skills, accountancy, nursing, industrial, insurance and computing.
7 The Town
Church Street
Enfield
Middlesex EN2 6LE
Tel: 01-367 6699
22 The Centre
Feltham
Middlesex TW13 4UA
Tel: 01-890 7156
52 The Broadway
Greenford
Middlesex UB6 9QA
Tel: 01-578 6853

310 Station Road
Harrow
Middlesex HA1 2DX
Tel: 01-863 0244

267 Station Road
Harrow
Middlesex HA1 2TB
Tel: 01-863 9211

42 Station Road
Hayes
Middlesex UB3 4DD
Tel: 01-573 6272

178 High Street
Hounslow
Middlesex
TW3 1HL

352 Bath Road
Hounslow
Middlesex TW4 7HW
Tel: 01-572 1821

91 High Street
Staines
Middlesex TW18 4PQ
Tel: 0784 58526

12 King Street
Twickenham
Middlesex TW1 3SN
Tel: 01-892 9107

20 High Street
Uxbridge
Middlesex UB8 1JN
Tel: 0895 51665

4 Ealing Road
Wembley
Middlesex HA0 4TL
Tel: 01-903 0151

451 High Road
Wembley
Middlesex HA9 7AF
Tel: 01-902 6111

RNW Recruitment Ltd
Industries: Law, media, medical, publishing, office, secretarial, catering.
Placements: Accounts clerks, receptionists, secretaries and personal assistants, telephone and telex operators, word processing operators.
Qualifications: Typing 40 wpm+, for secretarial bookings. Shorthand and WP skills an advantage, but not essential. Good level of education and work experience preferred.
Skills: Shorthand, typing and word processing.
Comments: RNW Recruitment is part of the RNW group -others cover contract engineering, recruitment, executive search and selection, accounting services and debt collection. Looking for temps in these fields - secretarial, WP, admin, accounts and catering.

7 Church Street
Staines
Middlesex TW18 4EN
Tel: 0784 57513/5

Norfolk

Central Recruitment
Industries: All
Placements: Accounts clerks, computer operators, receptionists, secretaries and personal assistants, telephone and telex operators, word processing operators.
Qualifications: None required
Skills: Computer, shorthand, typing, word processing.
Comments: We have four specialist sections in accountancy, law, insurance and general office vancancies, and consider anyone with office experience.

9 Bank Plain
Norwich
Norfolk NR2 4SF
Tel: 0603 620203
Fax: 0603 619965

Team-Sel
Industries: All
Placements: Accounts clerks, computer operators, receptionists, secretaries and personal assistants, telephone and telex operators, word processing operators.
Qualifications: None required
Skills: Computer, shorthand, typing, word processing.
Comments: We have four specialist divisions: Offshore, Overseas, Computer and Secretarialdministrative.

Team-Sel House
148 King Street
Great Yarmouth
Norfolk
Tel: 0493 851611
Fax: 0493 854833

Oxfordshire

Armstrong Staff Bureau
Industries: All, law, media, medical, publishing.
Placements: Accounts clerks, bilingual operators, computer operators, receptionists, secretaries and personal assistants, telephone and telex operators, word processing operators.
Qualifications: Typing 50 wpm, shorthand 100 wpm.
Skills: Computer, shorthand, typing, word processing.
Comments: A privately owned employment agency which aims to match the right skills to the right job.
221a Banbury Road
Summertown
Oxford
Oxfordshire OX2 7HQ
Tel: 0865 310416
Fax: 0865 310652

8a Market Square
Witney
Oxfordshire OX8 7BB
Tel: 0993 778541
Fax: 0993 702012

Brook Street
Industries: All
Placements: Accounts clerks, receptionists, secretaries and personal assistants, telephone and telex operators, word processing operators.
Qualifications: Typing 40/50 wpm, shorthand 80/100 wpm, 2 GCSE's including English.
Skills: Shorthand, typing, word processing.
Comments: We are looking for PA's, secretaries, copy typists, clerks, account clerks, switchboard operators, receptionists, catering staff, industrial staff.
16 High Street
Oxford
Oxfordshire OX1 4AG
Tel: 0865 722571

Downtown Burea, The
Industries: All
Placements: Accounts clerks, computer operators, receptionists, secretaries and personal assistants, telephone and telex operators, word processing operators.
Qualifications: None required
Skills: Computer shorthand, typing, word processing.
Comments: Independent bureau looking for reliable temps with good skills, keen to recruit those returning to work.
11 Friday Court
24 North Street
Thame
Oxfordshire OX9 3GA
Tel: 0864 421 6976/7459

Info-Tech Employment Agency
Industries: All
Placements: Receptionists, secretaries and personal assistants, telephone and telex operators, word processing operators.
Qualifications: None required
Skills: Shorthand, typing, word processing.
Comments: A flexible agency looking for reliable staff.
9 Park End Street
Oxford
Oxfordshire OX1 1HH
Tel: 0865 791558

Teamwork Recruitment
Industries: All
Placements: Accounts clerks, computer operators, receptionists, secretaries and personal assistants, telephone and telex operators, word processing operators.
Qualifications: Typing 45 wpm.
Skills: Shorthand, typing, word processing.
Comments: Local to Banbury and its ten mile radius.

Tintern House
37 High Street
Banbury
Oxfordshire OX16 8EQ
Tel: 0295 53440
Fax: 0295 69188

Suffolk

Eastern Staff Services
Industries: All
Placements: Accounts clerks, computer operators, receptionists, secretaries and personal assistants, telephone and telex operators, word processing operators.
Qualifications: None required
Skills: Computer shorthand, typing, word processing.
Comments: Seek reliable, office, secretarial and executive temps for a wide range of vacancies throughout the East Anglian region.

49 Abbeygate Street
Bury St Edmunds
Suffolk IP33 1LB
Tel: 0284 67561
Fax: 0284 750031

157 Hamilton Road
Felixstowe
Suffolk IP11 7DR
Tel: 0394 279111
Fax: 0394 670181

10 Northgate Street
Ipswich
Suffolk IP1 3BZ
Tel: 0473 219755
Fax: 0473 231217

Find-A-Job (East Anglia) Ltd
Industries: All
Placements: Accounts clerks, bilingual operators, computer operators, receptionists, secretaries and personal assistants, telephone and telex operators, word processing operators.
Qualifications: None required
Skills: Computer, shorthand, typing, word processing.

8a Queen Street
Ipswich
Suffolk IP1 1SS
Tel: 0473 58277

Surrey

Atlas Employment Agency Ltd
Industries: All
Placements: Accounts clerks, bilingual operators, computer operators, receptionists, secretaries and personal assistants, telephone and telex operators, word processing operators.
Qualifications: Typing 45 wpm, shorthand 80 wpm, 1 year's WP experience, 1 year's legal secretarial experience.
Skills: None required
Comments: We are a high street employment agency looking for all types of temporaries, both skilled and unskilled. We need hardworking, reliable applicants for a variety of positions.

22/26 George Street
Croydon
Surrey CR0 1PB
Tel: 01-686 8314

28 London Road
Croydon
Surrey CR0 2TA
Tel: 01-686 4631

64 Fife Road
Kingston
Surrey KT1 1SP
Tel: 01-541 5511

164 High Street
Sutton
Surrey SM1 1LX
Tel: 01-642 0640

Bridge Street Bureau Ltd, The
Industries: All
Placements: Accounts clerks, computer operators, receptionists, secretaries and personal assistants, telephone and telex operators, word processing operators.
Qualifications: Typing 50 wpm, shorthand 80 wpm.
Skills: Computer, shorthand, typing, word processing.
Comments: Deals with office staff and serves local businesses within a 10 mile radius. Provides WP and computer training.

34 Bridge Street
Walton on Thames
Surrey KT12 1AJ
Tel: 0932 228420
Fax: 0932 232141

Brook Street
Industries: All
Placements: Accounts clerks, receptionists, secretaries and personal assistants, telephone and telex operators, word processing operators.
Qualifications: Typing 40/50 wpm, shorthand 80/100 wpm, 2 GCSE's including English.
Skills: Shorthand, typing, word processing.
Comments: We are looking for PA's, secretaries, copy typists, clerks, account clerks, switchboard operators, receptionists, catering staff, industrial staff.

47a High Street
Camberley
Surrey GU15 3RB
Tel: 0276 66451

6 George Street
Croydon
Surrey CR0 1PA
Tel: 01-686 7312

96 High Street
Guildford
Surrey GU1 3HU
Tel: 0483 302979

9 Eden Street
Kingston-upon-Thames
Surrey KT1 1BQ
Tel: 01-546 4586

51a George Street
Richmond on Thames
Surrey TW9 1HJ
Tel: 01-948 1481

99 High Street
Sutton
Surrey SM1 1JF
Tel: 01-642 4493

4a Commercial Way
Woking
Surrey GU21 1ET
Tel: 04862 26167

Catherine Johnstone Recruitment
Industries: All
Placements: Accounts clerks, bilingual operators, computer operators, receptionists, secretaries and personal assistants, telephone and telex operators, word processing operators.
Qualifications: None required. Those offering qualifications bring certificates. References will be undertaken.
Skills: Computer, shorthand, typing, word processing.
Comments: Small privately owned Croydon based company serving most aspects of commercial recruitment.

Saffron House
15 Park Street
Croydon
Surrey CR0 1YD
Tel: 01-680 5777

Futures Recruitment Advisors
Industries: All
Placements: Bilingual operators, receptionists, secretaries and personal assistants, word processing operators.
Qualifications: Typing 40+ wpm, shorthand 90 wpm, GCSE English or equivalent, a knowledge of commerce preferred.
Skills: Shorthand, typing, word processing.
Comments: Futures specialises in office staff. It is attached to a private secretarial college and can arrange training for candidates.

28 Commercial Road
Guildford
Surrey GU1 4SX
Tel: 0483 302201
Fax: 0483 34777

Kingsway Recruitment Consultants
Industries: All
Placements: Accounts clerks, bilingual operators, computer operators, receptionists, secretaries and personal assistants, telephone and telex operators, word processing operators.
Qualifications: Typing 50 wpm, minimum 6 month's experience for WP operators.

Skills: Shorthand, typing, word processing, computer.

Comments: We are part of the Adia Group and pride ourselves in being honest with both our clients and applicants alike. All applicants including office juniors are welcome to register and we will advise on career choice.

2 High Street
Kingston-upon-Thames
Surrey KT1 1EY
Tel: 01-549 5501
Fax: 01-547 1918

Office Angels

Industries: All

Placements: Accounts clerks, computer operators, receptionists, secretaries and personal assistants, telephone and telex operators.

Qualifications: None required

Skills: Computer, shorthand, typing, word processing.

Comments: Medium sized, personalised recruitment consultants dealing in permanent and temporary placements in all categories. Unskilled applicants also catered for.

12 Suffolk House
College Road
Croydon
Surrey CR0 1PF
Tel: 01-681 3039

18 Jeffries Passage
Guildford
Surrey GU1 4AP
Tel: 0483 578989

89/91 Clarence Street
Kingston-upon-Thames
Surrey KT1 1QY
Tel: 01-541 0544

Peters & Smyth Staff Bureau Ltd

Industries: All

Placements: Executive secretarial appointments only.

Qualifications: None required

Skills: Computer, shorthand, typing, word processing.

Comments: An employment agency with all grades of temporary workers.

Senior Executive Secretaries Div
4 The Green
Richmond
Surrey TW9 1PL
Tel: 01-332 2999

Reed Employment

Industries: All

Placements: Accounts clerks, bilingual operators, computer operators, receptionists, secretaries and personal assistants, telephone and telex operators, word processing operators.

Qualifications: None required. All potential candidates are fully screened and tested.

Skills: Computer, shorthand, typing, word processing.

Comments: Reed Employment recruits permanent and temporary staff in the following areas: secretarial, WP operators and all office skills, accountancy, nursing, industrial, insurance and computing.

1 Cambridge Walk
Camberley
Surrey GU15 3SW
Tel: 0276 691547

36 George Street
Croydon
Surrey CR0 1PB
Tel: 01-688 3498

115 North End Road
Croydon
Surrey CR0 1TG
Tel: 01-686 7803

23 high Street
Epsom
Surrey KT19 8DD
Tel: 03737 43522

51 High Street
Guildford
Surrey GU1 3DY
Tel: 0483 300428

68 Clarence Street
Kingston-upon-Thames
Surrey KT1 1NN
Tel: 01-549 9381

64 London Road
Morden
Surrey SJ4 5BE
Tel: 01-640 5426
74 High Street
New Malden
Surrey KT3 4ET
Tel: 01-949 1935
21 George Street
Richmond on Thames
Surrey TW9 1HY
Tel: 01-948 2151
24 Victoria Road
Surbiton
Surrey KT6 4JZ
Tel: 01-399 5367
101 High Street
Sutton
Surrey SM1 1JF
Tel: 01-643 6331
20 High Street
Walton-on-Thames
Surrey KT12 1DA
Tel: 0932 231414
3 Harland House
44 Commerical Way
Woking
Surrey GU21 1HW
Tel: 04862 24184

Ridgeway Employment Agency Limited
Industries: All
Placements: Accounts clerks, bilingual operators, computer operators, receptionists, secretaries and personal assistants, telephone and telex operators, word processing operators.
Qualifications: None required. All potential candidates are fully screened and tested.
Skills: Computer, shorthand, typing, word processing.
C I Tower - St George's Square
High Street
New Malden
Surrey KT3 4HH
Tel: 01-336 2666
Fax: 01-336 1981

Stirling Recruitment
Industries: All
Placements: Accounts clerks, bilingual operators, computer operators, receptionists, secretaries and personal assistants, telephone and telex operators.
Qualifications: None required
Skills: Computer, shorthand, typing, word processing.
Comments: Mainly concerned with secretarial/office recruitment area, with a specialist temporary division.
36 Station Road
Redhill
Surrey RH1 1PH
Tel: 0737 768847
Fax: 0737 766938

Swift Employment
Industries: All
Placements: Accounts clerks, bilingual operators, computer operators, receptionists, secretaries and personal assistants, telephone and telex operators, word processing operators.
Qualifications: The ability to liaise with the client.
Skills: Computer, shorthand, typing, word processing.
Comments: We are a single branch high street agency operating on high principles and personal relationships, established almost 9 years. We are fully computerised.
3 Homesdale Road
Reigate
Surrey RH2 0BA
Tel: 0737 22531
Fax: 0737 249253

TAV Staff Agency Limited
Industries: All
Placements: Accounts clerks, bilingual operators, computer operators, receptionists, secretaries and personal assistants, telephone and telex operators, word processing operators.
Qualifications: None required. All applicants are tested in spelling, filing, arithmetic, shorthand, typing and audio to determine their relevant skill level.
Skills: Shorthand, typing, word processing.

Comments: The secretarial division of our organisation is TAV office team, and is able to place all levels of temporary and permanent applicants in all areas of commerce and industry.

56 High Street
Camberley
Surrey GU15 3RS
Tel: 0276 691930

Whitehead Recruitment Ltd
Industries: Law, media, medical, publishing.
Placements: Accounts clerks, computer operators, receptionists, secretaries and personal assistants, telephone and telex operators, word processing operators.
Qualifications: Typing 40 wpm, shorthand 80 wpm, 3 O' levels.
Skills: Computer, shorthand, typing, word processing.
Comments: Our aim is to offer local companies a professional recruitment service with an understanding of local business needs. We cover all personnel requirements but concentrate primarily on administrative, secretarial and accounts staff.
Still House
29 East Street
Farnham
Surrey GU9 7SW
Tel: 0252 725934
Fax: 0252 713691

Sussex

Baileys Employment Bureau
Industries: All
Placements: Accounts clerks, computer operators, receptionists, secretaries and personal assistants, telephone and telex operators, word processing operators.
Qualifications: Typing 45 wpm, shorthand 80/90 wpm.
Skills: Computer, shorthand, typing, word processing.
Comments: We recruit for both long term and short term bookings in all categories.
36a White Rock
Hastings
Sussex TN34 1JL
Tel: 0424 444555

Brook Street
Industries: All
Placements: Accounts clerks, receptionists, secretaries and personal assistants, telephone and telex operators, word processing operators.
Qualifications: Typing 40/50 wpm, shorthand 80/100 wpm, 2 GCSE's including English.
Skills: Shorthand, typing, word processing.
Comments: We are looking for PA's, secretaries, copy typists, clerks, account clerks, switchboard operators, receptionists, catering staff, industrial staff.
77/78 North Street
Brighton
Sussex BN1 1ZE
Tel: 0273 202991

Reed Employment
Industries: All
Placements: Accounts clerks, bilingual operators, computer operators, receptionists, secretaries and personal assistants, telephone and telex operators, word processing operators.
Qualifications: None required. All potential candidates are fully screened and tested.
Skills: Computer, shorthand, typing, word processing.
Comments: Reed Employment recruits permanent and temporary staff in the following areas: secretarial, WP operators and all office skills, accountancy, nursing, industrial, insurance and computing.
18 The Martlets
Crawley
Sussex RH10 1ES
Tel: 0293 547455

TAV Staff Agency Limited
Industries: All

Placements: Accounts clerks, bilingual operators, computer operators, receptionists, secretaries and personal assistants, telephone and telex operators, word processing operators.
Qualifications: None required. All applicants are tested in spelling, filing, arithmetic, shorthand, typing and audio to determine their relevant skill level.
Skills: Shorthand, typing, word processing.
Comments: The secretarial division of our organisation is TAV office team, and is able to place all levels of temporary and permanent applicants in all areas of commerce and industry.
62 Chapel Road
Worthing
Sussex BN11 1BN
Tel: 0903 820911

East Sussex

Argosy Employment Group
Industries: All
Placements: Accounts clerks, bilingual operators, computer operators, receptionists, secretaries and personal assistants, telephone and telex operators, word processing operators.
Qualifications: None required
Skills: Computer, shorthand, typing, word processing.
Comments: We recruit a wide range of temps eg., manual labourers, secretarial staff, professionals, etc.
14 Dyke Road
Brighton
East Sussex BN1 3FE
Tel: 0273 24883/24282
30 Terminus Road
Eastbourne
East Sussex BN21 3LP
Tel: 0323 643417/8/9
7 Havelock Road
Hastings
East Sussex TN34 1BP
Tel: 0424 720117

West Sussex

Argosy Employment Group

8 The Broadway
1st Floor
Crawley
West Sussex RH10 1DS
Tel: 0293 27131

Constructive Services Division
6 The Broadway (1st Floor)
Crawley
West Sussex RH10 1DS
Tel: 0293 21896

Management Recruitment Division
6 The Broadway (First Floor)
Crawley
West Sussex RH10 1DS
Tel: 0293 29014

Knight Benton
Industries: All
Placements: Accounts clerks, bilingual operators, computer operators, receptionists, secretaries and personal assistants, telephone and telex operators, word processing operators.
Qualifications: Typing 40 wpm, shorthand 70/90/100 wpm, audio stages 2 and 3. We look for good grammar and numeracy skills. Tests given at interview.
Skills: Computer, shorthand, typing, word processing.
Conwell House
42 East Street
Chichester
West Sussex PO19 1HX
Tel: 0243 776036

Link Recruitment Services
Industries: All
Placements: Accounts clerks, bilingual operators, computer operators, receptionists, secretaries and personal assistants, telephone and telex operators, word processing operators.
Qualifications: Typing 30 wpm, minimum. Shorthand 60 wpm.
Skills: Shorthand, typing, word processing.
Comments: We look for temps who enjoy a varied work environment.

71 London Road
East Grinstead
West Sussex RH19 1EQ
Tel: 0342 313234 (5 lines)

LRS Ltd
Industries: All, law
Placements: Accounts clerks, bilingual operators, computer operators, receptionists, secretaries and personal assistants, telephone and telex operators, word processing operators.
Qualifications: Minimum O' level standard. Typing and shorthand speeds depends upon demands of temporary positions.
Skills: Computer, shorthand, typing, word processing.
Comments: We are an independent agency dealing with a variety of temporary and permanent vacancies, including legal secretaries, audio typists, general clerks and VDU and WP operators.

31 Beach Road
Littlehampton
West Sussex BN17 5JA
Tel: 0903 716782
Fax: 0903 726318

Office People Recruitment Consultants
Industries: All
Placements: Accounts clerks, computer operators, receptionists, secretaries and personal assistants, telephone and telex operators.
Qualifications: Equivalent RSA I Typing for clerk typists (35 wpm), equivalent RSA II for anything secretarial (typing 45 wpm, shorthand 80 wpm). GCSE or good CSE in English and Mathematics useful.
Skills: Computer, shorthand, typing, word processing.

3-5 North Street
Chichester
West Sussex PO19 1LB
Tel: 0243 778021

Valentine Staff Services Ltd
Industries: All
Placements: Accounts clerks, computer operators, receptionists, secretaries and personal assistants, telephone and telex operators, word processing operators.
Qualifications: None required
Skills: Computer, shorthand, typing, word processing.
Comments: Mainly secretarial/office vacancies, plus a small number of accounting, drawing office, surveying vacancies. Their two other divisions are permanent office employment and managerial and technical personnel.

30a East Street
Horsham
West Sussex RH12 1HL
Tel: 0403 64811/2

Woolwich Staff Agency Limited
Industries: All
Placements: Accounts clerks, receptionists, secretaries and personal assistants, telephone and telex operators, word processing operators.
Qualifications: None required
Skills: Shorthand, typing, word processing.
Comments: Family owned agency specialising in office recruitment. Looking for experienced office workers with energy and enthusiasm.

2 Green's End
Woolwich
Horsham
West Sussex SE18 6HX
Tel: 01-854 7651

Private Secretarial Colleges

Private Secretarial Colleges

College	Course Title	Minimum Entry Requirements	Duration	Mode of Study	Fee
Adanac Commercial College 189 South Street Romford Essex IG1 1QA Tel: (0708) 42868	Shorthand, typing audio, letter layout and office practice course, from scratch through to guaranteed speeds of 80 wpm shorthand and 40 wpm typing.	Entrance examination to be taken.	16 weeks	Full-time	£833.75
	Typing and/or shorthand.	None Required.	Variable - according to subjects taken.		£45.00
	Intensive typing, shorthand, audio and word processing courses.	Entrance examination to be taken.	Variable - according to subjects taken.		£74.75 to £161.00
	Refresher classes in typing or shorthand.	Proficiency in the subject.	25 hours per subject.		£95.45
Beckenham Secretarial College 43 Beckenham Road Beckenham Kent BR3 4PR Tel: 01-650 3321	Pitmans Shorthand (New Era)	GCSE English standard and interview, for all courses.	22/23 weeks	Full-time	£550.00
	Speedwriting		11/22 weeks	Full-time	£550.00
	Typing		4 weeks	Full-time	£3.50 per hour
	Word Processing		Variable	Full-time	£3.50 per hour
	Office practice		Part of other courses	Full-time	£3.50 per hour

Private Secretarial Colleges 207

College	Course Title	Minimum Entry Requirements	Duration	Mode of Study	Fee
Belair Education Centre 10 Denmark Street London WC2H 8LS Tel: 01-836 1316/7	Word Processing Certificate WORDSTAR system.	None required, designed for absolute beginners.	2 weeks, beginning every month throughout the year.	A choice of: mornings 10 - 1 afternoons 2 - 5 evenings 6 - 8 Saturdays 10 - 1	From £95.00
Broadway Secretarial Training Centre Central Chambers Suites 15 to 19 2nd Floor The Broadway Ealing London W5 2NR Tel: 01-840 2762	Basic Touch Typing (course no. 01)	None required	16, 2 hour lessons	Once a day or twice a week	£145.00
	Typing (extension II)	Basic typing skills	12, 2 hour lessons	As above	£130.00
	Typing (extension III)	RSA Stage 1 standard	12, 2+ hour lessons	As Above	£130.00
	Typing (extension IV)	RSA Stage 2 standard	12, 2+ hour lessons	As above	£130.00
	Typing refresher course	Some experience	18, 2+ hour lessons	As above	£150.00
	Audio Typing	Typing speed of 30 wpm	12, 2 hour lessons	As above	£130.00
	Audio Typing (extension 1)	Some experience	12, 2 hour lessons	As above	£130.00
	Typing Speed Development	Basic touch typing	10, 2 hour lessons	As above	£85.00
	Keyboard training	None required	8, 2 hour lessons	As above	£100.00
	Word Processing (Wang system)	Some typing skills	5 day course, 6 hours per day	5 day intensive course	£275.00

College	Course Title	Minimum Entry Requirements	Duration	Mode of Study	Fee
Broadway Secretarial Training Centre Cont.	Teeline shorthand	None required	30, 2 hour lessons	Once a day or twice a week	£225.00
	Pitman 2000 shorthand	None required	30, 2 hour lessons	Once a day or twice a week	£225.00
Crown College of Further Education 5 - 13 Leeke Street Kings Cross London WC1X 9HZ Tel: 01-837 5184	Secretarial Diploma and Extension Courses Shorthand Typewriting English Business Communication Secretarial and Office Skills	No requirement other than an ability to write and speak good English.	Secretarial Diploma Course - 1 year	Full and part-time courses	£900.00 full course £300.00 extension course
	Information Technology Word Processing Database Spreadsheet Graphics	No requirement other than an ability to write and speak good English.	Course - 1 year Extension courses 1 term (12 weeks)	Full and part-time courses	£900.00 full course £300.00 extension course
	Computer Studies	Good command of the English language and GCSE maths.	1 year	Full and part-time courses	£1,250.00 full course, £450 one term

Private Secretarial Colleges

College	Course Title	Minimum Entry Requirements	Duration	Mode of Study	Fee
Crown College of Cont.	Programming basic/ COBOL Business systems Accounting method Machine code System analysis				
David Game Tutorial College 86 Old Brompton Road South Kensington London SW7 3LQ Tel: 01-584 2599	Integrated Secretarial Course Core subjects: Typing and Shorthand, plus 2 or 3 options, eg. WP, book keeping, office practice, French Intensive typing	None required	3 months, 6 months or 1 academic year	Full-time 15 hours per week secretarial training (typing and shorthand, plus options)	1 term £630.00 (shorthand and typing only) options extra 2 terms £1,260.00 3 terms £1,680.00
		None required	30 hours, students may join anytime	Part-time 10 - 1 mornings or 2 - 4 afternoons	£120.00 (30 hours block)
	Refreshers shorthand classes - theory/ speed	None required	10 hours, students may join anytime	Part-time 10 - 1 mornings Tuesday and Thursday only	£50.00 (10 hours block) £120.00 (30 hours block)

College	Course Title	Minimum Entry Requirements	Duration	Mode of Study	Fee
Dean College of London 97/101 Seven Sisters Road Holloway London N7 7QP **Tel: 01-281 4461/2**	Secretarial Course (Beginners' course)	Minimum age 16 Aptitute test in Mathematics and English	Nine months (Sept - June)	Full-time	£1,375.00
	Advanced Secretarial course	Successful completion of beginners, secretarial course. Typewriting 45 wpm, shorthand 70/80 wpm	Nine months (Sept - June)	Full-time	£1,375.00
	Individual subject course: typewriting, shorthand	Aptitute test in Mathematics and English	From one month to nine months	Full and part time	£100.00 per subject per month
Guildford Secretarial College Friary Mews 28 Commercial Road Guildford Surrey GU1 4SX **Tel: (0582) 64885**	Executive Personal Assistant Diploma Course		1 year	Full-time	£3,300.00
	Personal Assistant/Secretarial Diploma Course		9 months	Full-time	£830.00
	Intensive Personal Assistant Secretarial Diploma Course		24 weeks	Full-time	£1,700.00
	Intensive Secretarial Course		15 weeks	Full-time	£1,070.00
	Audio Typewriting Course		6 weeks	Full-time	£650.00

Private Secretarial Colleges 211

College	Course Title	Minimum Entry Requirements	Duration	Mode of Study	Fee
Guildford Secretarial Cont.	Typewriting Course		4 weeks	Full-time	£450.00
	Day Release Secretarial Course		1 day/week for 12 weeks	Part-time	£275.00
	Refresher Course		One month	Full-time	£450.00
	Refresher Course		One week	Full-time	£115.00
	Word processing		Per day	Full-time	£90.00
	European Language option				£390.00 per term
Hampstead Secretarial College 9 Regency Parade Finchley Road Swiss Cottage NW3 5EG Tel: 01-483 2121	Intensive Secretarial Course (basic typing, word processing, typing speed development)	None required	Full-time 4 weeks Part-time 8 weeks	Part-time day or evening	£400.00
	Full Secretarial Course	None required	Full-time 8 weeks Part-time 16 weeks	Part-time day or evening	£750.00
	(typing, audio, shorthand, word processing) One Year College Course (typing, audio shorthand, word processing, book-keeping - all to advanced level)	None required	Part-time for one year	Part-time day or evening	£1,500.00

College	Course Title	Minimum Entry Requirements	Duration	Mode of Study	Fee
Hendon Secretarial College 15 Watford Way London NW4 3JL Tel: 01-202 4188	Intensive Secretarial Course (typing, word processing, typing speed development)	None required	Full-time Part-time 8 weeks	Full or part-time 4 weeks	£400.00 day or evening
	Full Secretarial Course (typing, audio, shorthand, word processing)	None required	Full-time Part-time 16 weeks	Full or part-time 8 weeks	£750.00 day or evening
	One Year College Course (typing, audio, shorthand, word processing, book-keeping)	None required	Part-time	Part-time day or 1 year	£1,500.00 evening
London Chamber of Commerce Enterprise Training Impress House Vale Grove Action London W3 7QP Tel: 01-749 9651	Computer Applications: Introductions to PCs SMART, LOTUS, DBASE, etc	None required Intro to PCs recommended	4 hours 12 hours (2 days)	Part-time day Full-time	£36.00 £120.00
	Intro to Word-Pro Word Processing Typewriting, (PEI/RSA/	Keyboard skills Typewriting skills Beginners to	6 hours 2 - 4 days 30 - 60 hours	Part-time day Full-time Full and Part-time	£54.00 £120.00 £60.00 -

College	Course Title	Minimum Entry Requirements	Duration	Mode of Study	Fee
London Chamber Cont.	LCC) Audio Typing	advanced Typewriting skills	60 hours	Full and Part-time	£120.00
	Book-keeping	None	6 - 12 days	Full and Part-time	£120.00
	Language English (second language	Basic English	6 - 10 weeks	Full and Part-time	£120.00 - £140.00 £400.00 - £670.00
	Telephone Technique	None required	2 days	Full-time	£80.00
	Business Administration	None required	4 weeks	Full and part-time	£270.00
	Business Calcs or English	None required	Open	Full and part-time	£54.00
Office Skills Centre 4th Floor 20 Bedford Street Covent Garden London WC2 Tel: 01-836 3901	Intensive Commercial Typing (includes introduction to RSA II syllabus audio typing)	None required	4 weeks	Part-time 9 - 1 or 1 - 5 Monday - Friday	£270.00
	Shorthand (Teeline), typing	Good general standard of education	8 weeks	Part-time	£670.00
	Word Processing	Typing at 35 wpm plus knowledge about layout of document	1 week or 2 days	Monday - Friday plus homework Part-time	£140.00
	Refresher Speed Development Courses	Basic skills	Various lengths	2 hours per day or 2 days Part-time	

College	Course Title	Minimum Entry Requirements	Duration	Mode of Study	Fee
St Anthony's Secretarial College 19 South End Kensington Square London W8 Tel: 01-938 3755	College Diploma	'O' level English/ RSA II English First Certificate	9 months	Full and part-time	£2,875.00
	College Certificate	'O' level English/ RSA First Certificate	6 months	Full and part-time	£2,070.00
	3-month Secretarial	'O' level English RSA I/II English	3 months	Full-time	£1,207.50
	4-month Typewriting		4 weeks	Full and part time	£391.00
	Private Tuition	None required	Hourly, weekly, daily		£12.00 per hour
St Godric's College 2 Arkwright Road Hampstead London NW3 6AD Tel: 01-435 9831	Liberal Studies and Secretarial Course (shorthand, typing, lectures and visits, personal development, business practice	Minimum age, 16 years	Two years (six terms)	Full-time	£1,425.00 per term
	Executive Secretarial (shorthand, typing and business studies)	'A levels studied	One year	Full-time (three terms)	£1,425.00 per term
	Private Secretaries' Course (shorthand, typing, office practice and business English)		One year (three terms)	Full-time	£1,425.00 per term
	Private Secretaries' Course for Overseas Students	Cambridge First Certificate or GCE 'O' level English	One year (three terms)	Full-time	£1,645.00 per term

Private Secretarial Colleges 215

College	Course Title	Minimum Entry Requirements	Duration	Mode of Study	Fee
St Godric's College Cont.	(shorthand, typing, office practice, business English) Intensive Secretarial Course	'A' levels, University Degree or mature students (shorthand, typing, office practice, business English)	Six months (two terms)	Full-time	£1,425.00 per term
	Advanced French Secretarial French shorthand, translation, correspondence and geography	Secretarial Diploma 'O' level French	Three months (one term)	Full-time	£1,425.00 per term
	Business Studies law, economics, statistics, personnel management, IT, marketing, management	'A' levels studied Cambridge Proficiency	One year (three terms)	Full-time	£1,645.00 per term
Modules Legal secretaries, Medical secretaries					
St James's Secretarial College 4 Wetherby Gardens London	Executive Secretarial Diploma Course	GCSE level in 4 subjects	3 terms (1 year)	Full-time	£3,285.00
	Executive Secretarial	A level or above	2 terms (6 months)	Full-time	£2,190.00

College	Course Title	Minimum Entry Requirements	Duration	Mode of Study	Fee
St James's Secretarial Cont. SW5 0JN	Certificate Course				
Tel: 01-373 3852/2190/5389	Intensive Course for Graduates	Degree	1 term (3 months)	Full-time	£1,095.00
	Short Office Training Courses	None	From 1/2 week to 4 days	Full or part-time	From £100.00

The Principal may select a student who has the aptitute and desire to train well, over and above the entry requirements

N.B. Check if prices are inclusive or exclusive of VAT

Glossary of terms

The following lists represent a selection of terms commonly used in a wide range of business activities.

Word Processing and Information Technology

application software Software which instructs a computer to perform a specific function.

closed user group Where only certain users have access to certain frames of Viewdata system.

compatibility The ability of one system to handle something designed for another.

computer graphics Graphical representations on screen, produced by computer.

cursor The flashing signal on a VDU identifying the position of the next character to be typed.

daisy wheel A type of print element where the characters are positioned at the end of spokes round the hub of a wheel like petals on a flower. Widely used in high-speed, letter-quality printing.

database A computerised information store.

dot matrix A type of printing head where characters are formed from a pattern of dots. Often used in high-speed draft-quality printers.

electronic filing The storing of information on machines for computerised access rather than paper stored in conventional filing cabinets.

electronic mail Communication between two or more parties using electronic technology to send computerised information, via satellites, cables or telephone wires. Information is displayed visually and need not be translated into hard copy.

electronic mailbox A computer-based message system. Messages may be left at any time and remain there until the user makes an enquiry.

fibreoptics Smooth, glass-like, hair-thin tubes which send out a light source generated from electric power and are capable of carrying information at very high speed.

font A particular style of typeface design and print size; sometimes used as an alternative name for a typing or phototypesetting element.

gateway An interfacing device by which information may be passed from one network to another.

global search and replace A word processing term used to describe the process whereby a search is made through a document for a word or 'string' with the intention of substituting an alternative.

headers and footers Terminology used in word processing given to specified information which would go to the top and/or bottom of each page in a multipage document.

housekeeping The term given in word processing whereby documents can be deleted or rearranged on the storage media.

information processing The integration of data processing and word processing.

integrated software Packages which combine functions such as word processing, electronic spreadsheets and graphics into a single, easy-to-use programme.

interactive The mode of operation by which a computer-based system can stop and start in reaction to each input from the user, eg. interactive video.

interface Used as a noun or a verb and refers to the connecting of devices.

justify The process of ensuring an even right-handed margin.

light pen A graphical input device used directly on the display screen to create or modify graphics.

Local Area Network (LAN) A means of linking electronic devices within a restricted area via a special cable.

microfiche A sheet of film that may contain several hundred exposures in a grid pattern.

network A series of points connected by communications channels.

off-line An operation performed without the piece of equipment being connected to the CPU.

on-line The opposite of off-line, ie. dependent upon the CPU for its operation.

pagination The control of page usage and the allocation of sequential numbers to pages in a multipage document.

password A confidential security device made up on a unique string of characters in the form of a code. Access will be denied to anyone who cannot produce the password.

peripherals Pieces of equipment designed to work with, but not connected to a word processor or computer, eg. an OCR machine.

pitch The number of characters or spaces horizontally to the inch.

Prestel British Telecom's viewdata service.

program The detailed set of instructions necessary to carry out specific tasks.

reverse video The facility whereby normal screen presentation is thrown into reverse display, ie. light on dark becomes dark on light or vice versa.

scrolling The movement of a document vertically or horizontally within the window represented by the screen, so that other areas of the document may be seen.

shared logic Where more than one device shares the same central processing capability.

shared resource Where other facilities, not necessarily the processing power, are shared by more than one workstation, eg. a shared printer.

software The generic name for program.

stand alone A system which is complete in itself, ie. it has its own CPU, VDU, keyboard and printer.

status information Details at the top of a VDU relevant to the work being carried out, eg. page length, characters per line, margins, tab stops.

systems software The programs which start up the computer, ensure that it is operational and that it can perform a series of utility functions.

teleconference A meeting held in various locations using the telephone to connect the participants.

text editing The revision of typewritten material via a word processor or software package designed to perform edit functions.

thimble An alternative print element to a daisy wheel, used on high-quality printers.

upgradeable The term used where new features can be added to existing equipment, so enhancing its present power and eliminating the need to replace.

utility functions Functions performed by the operating system, many of which are concerned with file management.

videoconferencing Two or multi-way audio and television link ups between individuals or groups. Often referred to as electronic meetings, links may be made within the UK or internationally.

viewdata The generic term for computer-based information systems like Prestel.

Meetings Terminology

abstention Where someone refrains from casting a vote either for or against a motion.

action minutes In addition to providing an account of events these minutes specify the action to be taken, and by whom, following any recommendation made, course of action demanded or decision reached, at a meeting.

addendum An amendment which adds words to a motion.

ad hoc From the Latin, meaning 'for the purpose of'. For example as in ad hoc committee or 'special' committee.

agenda Schedule of items drawn up for discussion at a meeting.

Articles of Association The rules required by law which govern a company's internal organisation and activities.

consensus Agreement by general consent without a formal vote being taken.

Constitution Document describing the objects of an association or voluntary body and setting out the rules which govern its activities and limit its powers.

convene To call a meeting.

co-opt To invite an individual to serve on a committee, usually because of some specialist knowledge or expertise he can provide.

ex officio One invited to attend a meeting 'by virtue of his office' but with no voting rights.

in camera In private.

motion A formal proposal moved that a certain topic be discussed at a meeting and certain action be taken upon it.

nem con No one contradicting, ie. no votes against the motion, but some members may have abstained.

out of order The chairman can rule a member 'out of order' where the member is not keeping to the point under discussion or is speaking improperly.

point of order A query raised in respect of procedure or a possible infringement of the standing orders or constitution.

proposer The person putting forward a motion for discussion.

proxy Someone appointed to vote on behalf of someone else, eg. a member who is unable to attend a meeting.

quorum The minimum number of persons who must be present at a meeting to make it valid.

resolution Once passed, a motion becomes a resolution.

rider This is an addition to a resolution after it has been passed. It adds to a resolution rather than altering it and must be proposed, seconded and put to the meeting in the usual way.

Standing Orders The rules compiled by an organisation in respect of the way in which businesses must be transacted.

status quo As things stand at present.

Statutory Meeting One which must be held in order to comply with the law.

Sub-committee A group of members from the main/parent committee, appointed to deal with a specific aspect of the main committe's work.

tabled The description applied to a document to be presented to a committee and which has not been included with the agenda and supporting papers.

terms of reference A statement of the work to be carried out by a group or committee, providing guidelines as to how it should be done and expressing any limitations in respect of methods to be adopted.

unanimous All being in favour.

verbatim Word for word.

General business and finance

active file Those currently in use.

annuity Retirement pension.

archival storage High-volume, long term storage of information.

assets All property, both tangible and intangible, belonging to a company or business.

assurance A form of insurance to cover an inevitable event, the timing of which is unknown, hence life assurance to cover death.

Blue Chip Share One regarded as a safe investment, ie. in a well known and highly respected company.

budget A statement indicating the allocation and use of resources.

budgetary control A system of financial control based on forecasts.

cash flow Cash needed to finance operating expenses.

Dow Jones Index The index of share prices on the Wall Street Stock Exchange in New York.

Eurobonds Bonds which are negotiable within the member states of the EEC.

ex works Where the buyer is required to meet all expenses from the moment the goods leave the works, eg. the buyer pays any carriage.

face value Nominal value as opposed to market value of a share.

franchise The licence to manufacture, market or distribute goods or services, often under a trade name.

free on board (fob) Where the seller is responsible for all costs incurred, eg. delivery charges and insurance, up to the point where the goods are on board ship.

gilt-edged securities The term used for those stocks and shares — often Government securities — where there is little risk of loss in the investment.

gross profit The margin by which sales exceed the cost price of goods or services.

index linked Adjusted in line with changing policies particularly in times of inflation.

inflation An economist's term to describe a situation in which there is a general increase of prices and a fall in the purchasing power of money.

Inland Revenue The UK government agency responsible for assessing and collecting income tax.

insider dealing Using inside knowledge of a company, its plans and financial state to personal advantage by using the information to make a profit before such information becomes public knowledge.

insolvency Inability to settle debts.

invisible exports/imports Receipts/payments made for services of some kind, eg. banking and insurance services or shipping and tourism, featuring in the current account of a country's Balance of Payments.

liability Extent of debt owed to others.

limited liability The restriction of liability, in the event of a company's going into liquidation, ie. the amount which can be lost or claimed is restricted to the amount that has been invested in capital terms.

liquidated damages Damages estimated to have been incurred by a breach of contract.

liquidation Legal proceedings causing a company to cease trading.

monopoly A situation where at least a third of a market is controlled by one company, so leading to exclusive trading privilege.

Monopolies (and Mergers) Commission A UK body appointed by the Department of Trade and Industry which maybe called upon to investigate any apparent monopoly in the production or supply of goods and services, perhaps brought about following a merger.

Nikkei Dow Index The index of share prices on the Tokyo Stock Exchange.

open cover The insurance of goods for a general sum where precise volume is unknown.

par value Nominal value of shares.

rights issue A new issue of shares, on advantageous terms, to existing shareholders in proportion to their present holdings.

subsidiary company A company controlled by another company which holds more than 50 per cent of the issued share capital.

visible exports/imports Physical goods exported/imported and appearing as receipts/payments in the current account of a country's Balance of Payments.

Abbreviations and acronyms

AGM	Annual General Meeting
APR	Annual Percentage Rate of charge
ATM	Automated Teller Machine
BACS	Bank Automated Clearing System
BSI	British Standards Institution
CAD	Computer Aided Design
CAM	Computer Aided Manufacture
CHAPS	Clearing House Automated Payments System
CIM	Computer Input Microfilm
COM	Computer Output Microfilm
CPS	Characters Per Second
CPU	Central Processing Unit
cif	cost, insurance and freight
DBMS	Data Base Management System
ECU	European Currency Unit
EFTPOS	Electronic Funds Transfer at Point of Sale
EMS	European Monetary System
E&OE	Errors and Omissions Excepted
FAX	Facsimile Transmission
FIFO	First In First Out
fob	free on board
IDD	International Direct Dialling
IMF	International Monetary Fund
ISBN	International Standard Book Number
K	Kilo (a thousand)
LAN	Local Area Network
LCD	Liquid Crystal Display
LED	Light Emitting Diode
LIFO	Last In First Out

M	Mega (a million)
MLR	Minimum Lending Rate
NCC	National Computing Centre
NCR	No Carbon Required
NEC	National Exhibition Centre (at Birmingham)
OCR	Optical Character Recognition
PBX	Private Branch Exchange (also referred to as PABX Private Automatic Branch Exchange)
PIN	Personal Identification Number
PROM	Programmable Read Only Memory
PSS	Packet Switch Stream
PSTN	Public Switched Telephone Network
RAM	Random Access Memory
ROM	Read Only Memory
RPI	Retail Price Index
SAD	Single Administrative Document
SEAQ	Stock Exchange Automated Quotations System
SSP	Statutory Sick Pay
SYSTEMX	Telephone Switching System
VDU	Visual Display Unit
WIMPS	Windows, Icons, Mouse and Pull-down menus
WYSIWYG	What you see is what you get

The Federation of Recruitment and Employment Services Limited Code of Good Recruitment Practice

Introduction

The FRES Code of Good Recruitment Practice is binding on all members of the Federation of Recruitment and Employment Services and their staff. The Code is intended to ensure that members conduct their business ethically to help to promote good recruitment practice.

General

1. Members shall state their terms of business to clients without ambiguity.

2. Members shall satisfy themselves that candidates are suitable for the positions for which they are being submitted.

3. Members shall not deliberately attempt to induce any candidates to leave his or her employment where the member has previously received a fee for placing him or her in that employment, with a view to placing him or her elsewhere, unless the present employer agrees to such an approach.

4. Members shall make themselves and their staff fully aware of the provisions of the Employment Act, 1980, and its Regulations and any other relevant legislation.
   Such legislation must be complied with both in spirit and to the letter of the law. Breach of the law shall be deemed to be a breach of this Code.

5. Members shall seek to develop a positive policy towards, and take necessary steps to promote equal opportunities in employment.

6. The Federation will act as arbitrator where a dispute arises between members, and its decision will be binding and final. In the case of a dispute between members and third parties, the Federation will act as arbitrators if the third party so requests, and the Federation's decision will be binding and final.

7. Members shall ensure that they reach a clear understanding with candidates and clients on the members' procedure for submitting CVs to clients.

8. Members must take all reasonable steps to protect the security of information provided by both clients and candidates.

9. Members' terms of business are subject to approval by the Director of the FRES.

Employment businesses

10. Wherever practicable, members shall take up references for temporary workers before supplying them to clients.

11. Members shall ensure that they comply fully with the law relating to deduction of Tax and National Insurance from temporary and contract workers.

12. Members shall ensure that temporary or contract workers are suitable for the assignments for which they are supplied.

Advertising

13. Members are required to abide by the Code of Advertising Practice as implemented by the Advertising Standards Authority.

14 Members' advertisements shall not be misleading in any way. All descriptions, claims and comparisons must be capable of substantiation.

15 All specific vacancies advertised must be genuinely open at the time of going to press, and be removed from advertising displays once filled.

16 For the purpose of this Code, the words 'advertising' or 'advertisement' apply to advertising or promotion material of any description.

Overseas placements

17 Members and their staff must make themselves aware of, and comply with any legislation on private employment services in the country in which they operate.

18 Members shall ensure that all candidates, temporary or contract workers are provided with full written information relating to the work they will undertake.
Such information must include statements on: —

   a) Who is responsible for obtaining work permits and other papers, and for making and paying for travel arrangements.
   b) Pay, accommodation, leave, payment intervals and method, taxation.
   c) The whereabouts of the nearest British Consul or Vice Consul.
   d) The need to hold adequate personal and medical insurance cover.

19 Breach of any part of this Code of Practice shall be dealt with as a disciplinary matter under FRES rules.

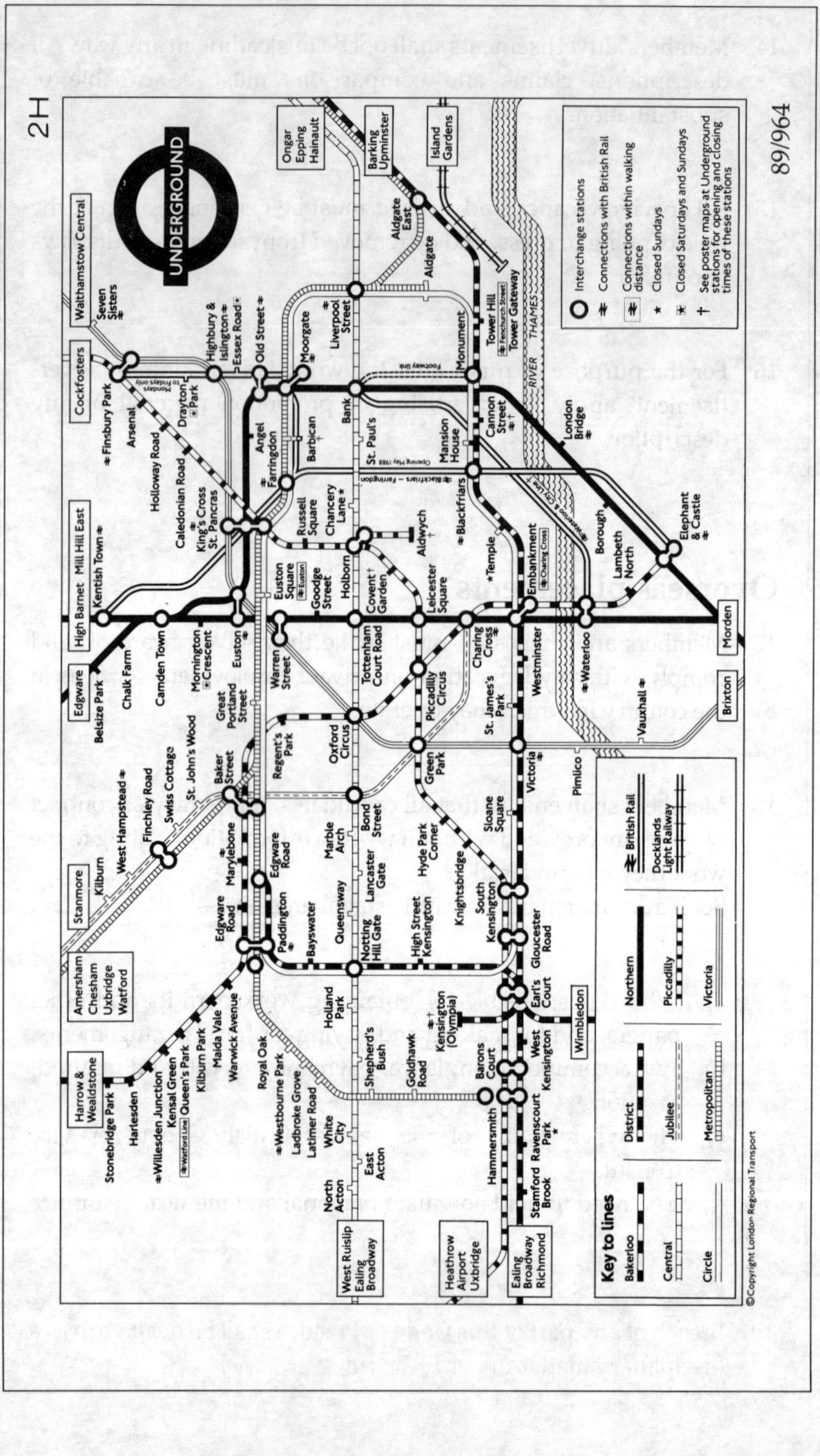

230 *The London Temp's Handbook*